SEE YOU IN COURT

SEE YOU IN COURT

JEFF HICKEN

Lutsen Shores Publishing Co.

CONTENTS

Wherever law ends, tyranny begins.

- John Locke (1689)

CHAPTER 1

Breath of the Law

"Breaking Up is Hard to Do", the song goes. Divorce is easy for some people, I admit. They do it with a text message – even on Facebook. Others sit down at the kitchen table and draw a line down the middle of a notebook. His and hers. We lawyers, with our gallows humor, call that "splittin' up the silverware." But just spend a day in divorce court and you'll see where dreams die – sometimes more than dreams. After forty-five years in the biz I should know.

Marge was my first client of the new year. Short and squat, with a head of improbably dyed black hair, she trundled into the office carrying a shopping bag full of papers and documents.

If I hadn't known better, I'd have thought she was a homeless bag lady off the street. She wore a tattered coat. Her nose was red from the winter cold, and she clutched a shredded Kleenex. It was hard to ignore the devastation of fat and wrinkles, and her face, which was clotted with anger. Had she ever been attractive?

"Two other lawyers already turned me down," she said. "They wanted their money up front, but I don't have it yet. Our son's an invalid. Between helping him and working, I can't get ahead."

She claimed to have a $20,000 pension refund coming in soon, and promised to sign it over. Her sad story had moved me, and I broke my own rule of requiring a cash retainer fee.

I asked my assistant, Jeannie, to prepare a representation contract for our new client. I feared that Jeannie, a Pentecostal Texan with a head for business, would chastise me for taking a case without a retainer. It was a bone of contention with her. As she walked in with the agreement, she shot me a look, as if to say – You really want to do this?

From the moment the papers were signed and I was committed to her case, a transformation occurred with Marge. All bounds of civility disappeared.

No longer the helpless bag lady, she exclaimed, "I want you to get that fucking asshole! I've got all the emails between him and his chippie girlfriend. Just give 'em to the judge. He'll string him up by the balls."

I'm sorry if you're offended, but profanity is the *lingua franca* of my practice.

She dumped her bag on my desk and I paged through her trove of evidence. It was the usual back-and-forth of infidelity, both banal and obscene.

"One thing's clear," I said, "he loves her and he doesn't love you. The problem is that we've had no-fault divorce for years. Marital misconduct isn't relevant. This stuff doesn't get us anywhere."

She rolled her eyes up to the ceiling, as if imploring God. "This is what I pay him $375 an hour for?"

You'll get plenty for your money, I thought. And, don't forget, you haven't paid me anything yet.

"Well, how about our son, Steven – he's done with high school but he's disabled. Can't we use that for some financial leverage?"

"That's something we can work with," I said. Child support can continue indefinitely for an unemancipated, dependent adult.

"Tell me about Steven."

"He's always been sickly. Small for his age. I'm sort of angry with him, though. When I told him about his loser father and that slut of a girlfriend he has, Steven said he wasn't going to take sides."

Two months later, it was time for the trial. My relationship with Marge – which had never been that good — had reached an abysmal level. This happens a lot in family law. The waiting, the lawyer's bills, and the antics of her soon-to-be ex-husband had taken their toll.

I asked about the $20,000 refund she was supposed to sign over to us. After dodging the question a couple of times, she announced that she'd cashed it in. "Had some other bills to pay," was the excuse. Why didn't I drop her then? To abandon a client right before the trial was unethical. Marge would call the Board of Professional Responsibility, which would be on us like a ton of bricks. I was stuck. I should have followed the rule about getting paid first.

"Meet me here tomorrow," I told Marge, "in the courtroom." That morning she'd camped out at my office, bitching at me, her unpaid mouthpiece, while I was trying to prepare the case. I wasn't going to let that happen again.

The next problem was the judge. He was a Mensa guy. You know -- the high IQ society. If you weren't already aware of this, you'd find out quick enough -- from him. He claimed to model himself after the great jurist and writer, Felix Frankfurter.

This begged the question. If you're the great Frankfurter, what are you doing herding cats in divorce court?

As we walked into the courtroom on the day of trial, we encountered Marge's husband. What was he like, you ask? He had a receding chin and protruding belly, which his loose shirt failed to completely conceal, and reeked of unwashed clothes and tobacco. Looking at him and Marge, the adage we divorce lawyers use seemed appropriate – "Twos don't marry tens." It was hard to imagine what sort of woman would choose to be his girlfriend.

Of course, he hated me. I was his wife's lawyer. More importantly, I'd gotten a court order confiscating his prized duck decoy collection, which was safely ensconced in my office closet.

We went first. The husband had to continue to pay for Steven, his disabled son. The doctor's report concluded that Steven was too frail to work full-time. Marge testified about her dreary financial situation and her need for help. It seemed things were going our way until it was the other side's turn.

"We're calling the young man, Steven, as a witness," said the lawyer. "We'll show that he's an adult who can support himself."

"No, your Honor, we object! To force a child to testify in his parent's divorce trial is highly improper, and even emotionally damaging."

My objection was a loser and I knew it from the start.

"Overruled – he's over eighteen," the exalted erstwhile Frankfurter said.

I was outraged, and persisted, "But , but. . . "

The great jurist rapped his gavel.

"Bailiff, bring in the witness," he said.

There he was. Steven. Exhibit A in the right honorable case of *Mom v. Dad.*

As Steven entered the courtroom, I realized with horror that I'd seen him before! It was at my son's high school graduation the previous spring. He'd crossed the stage a few minutes after my son.

Steven was wearing a winter coat. He was short and stooped, with a concave chest. He carried a breathing apparatus over his shoulder.

He timidly approached the clerk's desk holding the subpoena.

"What do I do with this, your Honor?"

Not deeming the question worthy of a response, and without an ounce of humanity, his eminence pointed to him and said, "Raise your hand and take the oath."

The clerk pointed Steven toward the witness stand and directed him to raise his right hand. He placed his respirator on a ledge. His eyes nervously darted between his parents, then the lawyers, as if searching for a savior.

His father's lawyer, red-faced and agitated, approached him.

"You scored 1200 on the SAT and you say you can't find a job?" he asked.

Steven took a hit from his inhaler. "I'm sorry."

"How many job applications have you sent out?" the lawyer demanded.

Another blast of oxygen.

As time crept on, Steven's left eye started twitching and the color drained from his face. I continued objecting to the lawyer's questions, and even though I was continually overruled, it slowed down the relentless badgering.

Finally, the afternoon drew to a close and the judge called a halt to the proceedings. He pointed at Steven, and barked, "Be back at 9:00 tomorrow morning."

Steven hoisted his breathing machine over his shoulder and maneuvered his way out of the courtroom, while his parents glared at each other.

As I left the courthouse, I thought. What an atrocity of a trial. How could I rid myself of the stink of it? Sweat it out at the gym? Drown it with whiskey?

But there was no escape.

When I got to the courtroom the next morning Marge was waiting, breathing fire.

"Great job, asshole," she said. "Steven died an hour after court last night."

My jaw dropped. "What happened?"

"He just couldn't catch his breath," she said.

I was struck to the core. I stammered through some clichés, all the while surprised at how much I cared for this young man whom I'd met for the first time only yesterday. I was angry with myself for letting it all happen, at the would-be Frankfurter and the nasty opposing lawyer. This should be on their consciences, I thought, and I vowed to let them know my feelings.

Marge seemed to have recovered, though. Her face lightened up, and she looked at her notes. "Do you think we'll finish today?"

Out to the Porce-leen

From a cultural standpoint, my hometown, Macomb, Illinois, would have straddled the Mason-Dixon line, had it extended westward beyond Pennsylvania. It was populated in the early nineteenth century by settlers from western Virginia and Kentucky. Some were given free land as veterans of the War of 1812. Others followed throughout the century, the most prominent being Kentucky-born-woodsman-turned-small-town lawyer in nearby Springfield – Abraham Lincoln. It was a stopping point of the Underground Railroad, and fertile ground for hunters of escaped slaves from nearby Missouri.

The folks who settled in Macomb and its environs, with their countrified ways and speech, were the bedrock of the community. The father of our country? George Warshington! In the neighborhood? Then you were "prett-n-neer." Surprised by something? You might say – "Well, dog my cats!" And, speaking of cats, you'd want to sample the local delicacy – a "cat-feesh" dinner. It would be advertised on the windows of the town-square taverns as "Fried Cat - $2.50." Once inside the establishment, you could choose between the supposedly pure farm-raised "pond cat" or the less expensive, but dubious, "river cat." The true budget diner could go for the cheap, but dreadful "Boned Carp Special."

Interested in some musical entertainment? You could drive out to Gin Ridge and take in the Possum Hollar Opry, starring Toby Dick Ellis, accompanied by his portly girlfriend, Flossy Frizzle, who would arrive in the bed of a pickup truck.

Our little corner of western Illinois is known for its agriculture. Sometimes in August you can "almost hear the corn growing," as they say. That's because of the six or more inches of fertile black topsoil, but equally valuable is what lies below -- abundant deposits of pure clay. This resource led to the development of some unique industries in our town – a brick factory, a sewer pipe factory, porcelain products, and the largest art pottery facility in the world.

Illinois Electric Porcelain was where I worked. To save up for law school tuition, I needed the money. You could earn twice as much as you could flipping burgers, my old job that paid ninety cents per hour. I spent three summers "out to the Porce-leen."

I'm sure you've seen electric insulators before, but you may not have paid them any attention. Just glance up at the power poles. The insulators are there -- protecting against dangerous conductivity between the charged lines and the fixtures, like the wooden poles. Some of them look like inverted cups, usually brown or gray in color, or they're like oblong hockey pucks, with the guy wires running through them. Others resemble overgrown mushrooms on vertical stalks. Take it from one who knows. Those cups? They're RX270's. The mushrooms? They're PS110's. Even after all these years, I can rattle off the model numbers.

Here's how things worked at the Porce-leen. The dump trucks would arrive from the clay mines, dropping huge loads into the giant hoppers. The guys working the presses would liquefy the clay and squeeze it into fifty-pound disks. The two-man pug mill crews threw the disks into their smaller hopper, producing tubes of wet clay. The racks full of tubes were transported by fork lifts into the giant white-hot kiln to be baked, then the hardened tubes went to the molders, who would fashion them into the hockey pucks, mushrooms and other familiar shapes. Then it was on to the glazers, and finally back to the kiln one more time for the finished product.

I worked in the ware-dusting room, assigned to the graveyard shift, starting at 11:00 p.m. and finishing at 7:00 a.m. It took me all of fifteen minutes to learn the job. I stood in a stiflingly hot room, just feet from the kiln. Armed with a rubber hose, my job was to blow the dust off the still hot ware, which had just arrived on pallets, so there wouldn't be any bubbles formed when it was glazed. Giant fans sucked up the dust (or some of it) that we created with our high-pressure air hoses. I wore steel-toed boots to protect my feet from dropped insulators. Foam ear plugs for the noise. Safety glasses to protect the eyes from the little chips of porcelain that flew up in the blowing process and, finally, a respirator mask that covered the face.

The respirator mask, earplugs and safety glasses, created a parallel universe in the ware-dusting room, allowing the monotony of the job to be alleviated by daydreams and fantasy. The mind of the twenty-year-old male is normally consumed with sexual ideations, but the ugly industrial environment didn't suggest romance. Instead, I consumed the hours by creating a perfect hypothetical murder.

This is no easy undertaking. Certainly, it would be satisfying to do in that dumb jock who came up behind you and smashed your face into the locker while calling you a "little pussy," but it would be too obvious. The sure bet would be to perpetrate a motiveless crime.

Drive to another city to buy a gun, using false identification. A few weeks later, drive to another city, carefully selecting a random victim. Do the deed and promptly leave, driving home carefully. There are hundreds of permutations of it.

The entire Porce-leen, but especially our work area, was permeated with dust. Despite the safety measures, my ears rang day long, and after a few weeks I found myself coughing up muddy phlegm. It was common for veterans at the plant to suffer from silicosis – sometimes referred to as "potter's rot." It didn't seem like the company cared about it, either.

On my first day on the job, the foreman introduced me to a couple of old hands – Si and Walt. They'd both been ware-dusters for years, although Si had moved on to a nearby molding unit.

Even though they didn't have to be, Si and Walt were friendly to me. Si was a slight, bald fellow with a fringe of white hair. Although he was missing a few teeth, he had a ready smile. Walt was a heavy-set, avuncular fellow.

"So, you're the new ware duster?" Si said. "Shittiest job in the whole damn place." I was informed by the foreman that the Porce-leen was an "open shop." That meant that union membership was non-mandatory, and short-timers like me could avoid joining up. This allowed the company to dominate the workers. If the union got too "uppity" the company could divide and conquer by firing the old hands and hiring more entry-level types like myself.

Thanks to the company's poor treatment of the workers, spirits remained low. Instead of cheering things up with some art or posters, a blackboard hung on the wall, announcing "89 days since an accident." I even detected some industrial sabotage – graffiti depicting the personnel director in demeaning sexual acts and pallets of insulators mysteriously upended.

There were no employee facilities save the dirty latrines. Not even a break room. For lunch at 3:00 a.m., you had the choice of sitting next to your machine or going outside. We younger guys preferred congregating on the concrete blocks in the parking lot along the tracks. Entertainment was provided by the nocturnally active colony of rats, at whom we would launch missiles of broken ware. We usually missed, just scattering the ugly vermin, but occasionally one could get a clean kill.

Sometimes Walt and Si would join us. They'd bring along their old-fashioned covered wagon-style lunch boxes. Si had the yellow, tobacco-stained fingers of a confirmed smoker, and he'd always offer us one of his Camels. Walt enjoyed eating peaches right out of the can, finishing them off by guzzling the thick, sweet syrup. One day, I noticed that Walt had a paperback book in his pocket. I asked him what he was reading.

"Take a look – it might do you some good," he said.

It was a thin volume – more pictures than print – describing religious miracles that had been conferred on people. There were the expected cures for terminal cancer, but also tales of sudden riches bestowed on deserving believers.

"Could happen to any of us," Walt said. "You love the Lord, don't you?"

"Um, sure," I responded, although I think he could detect the insincerity of one who had given up on the concept long ago.

You might think that Si and Walt would resent me for shuttling in and out of the job for the school year, while their futures were set within the dreary walls of the Porce-leen. They couldn't have been nicer, though. They seemed proud that someone from their ranks was headed to a professional career.

One evening in my third summer I arrived for the 11:00 p.m. punch-in at the time clock. Si was walking in the opposite direction. His right arm was wrapped in gauze, and there were blood stains seeping through. He was in obvious distress. Still, he managed a friendly, though strained, smile as he passed.

Arriving at my station, I noticed two gentlemen from the front office standing next to Si's machine. You could tell they were management by their cheap, short-sleeved dress shirts and clip-on ties. One was training a camera on the machine. I quietly moved behind him to sneak a glance at the scene. What did I see? Lying on the metal table, next to the lathe were two tobacco-stained fingers, perfectly severed. Ironically, the "89 days without an accident" blackboard loomed behind the machine.

I started back to the dressing room. Si would probably be back on the job in a few days, I thought. What choice did he have? As I rigged myself up with my respirator, safety glasses, and the rest, I decided I did have a choice. I'd miss Si and Walt. I might even miss killing the rats. But this would be my last day "out to the Porce-leen."

CHAPTER 3

Guilty as Charged?

I'm chatting with my doctor friend at a cocktail party. I thoroughly enjoy these events -- the buzz of the alcohol, the saltiness of the hors d'oeuvres, the sociality of it all. A heavily made-up woman in a business suit appears out of nowhere, inserting herself into our conversation.

"Hello," she says, offering her hand. We exchange niceties and indulge in some more Chardonnay.

Then it starts.

"My sister says you're a lawyer and I was just wondering how you lawyers can represent someone when you know they're guilty." The once pleasant expression on her face has taken on an edge, and hive-like blotches appear on her neck and chest.

I never know what to think of when I am asked this question. Had she been a victim of a crime? What experience had she had with lawyers?

I respond carefully that every person, guilty or not, is entitled to legal counsel by the Sixth Amendment. Even for the guilty, sometimes the charges don't fit the crime, or the prosecutor is seeking an over-zealous sentence. If you were charged with something, wouldn't you want a lawyer?

Lawyers are confronted with this question all the time, even if we've never had a criminal case. Frankly, it's annoying. And, our new friend seems unconvinced by my answer.

I wonder to myself why no one ever asks my doctor friend why he still gets paid when his patient dies?

The conversation brings me a memory from years past.

It was 1972 and I, a newly minted lawyer, had recently snagged a job. The State of Illinois would pay me $150 a week to review cases of convicted and incarcerated felons and, where possible, write up their appeals. It wasn't much money, but after three years of working my way through school at the porcelain factory, I was thrilled to be paid anything for using my mind.

Our clients were slumdog criminals, ranging from minor offenders to murderers. Most of them had confessed to their crimes or even pled guilty, and were rotting in prison. Some hoped against hope that we could pull a rabbit out of a hat and get them out. Others sought us simply because we provided free legal assistance and they got a "field trip" from prison to attend their hearing. What was our win-loss ratio? That's easy -- we almost never won.

One day a hefty parcel labeled *People v. J.T. Darling* appeared on my desk. It contained a trial transcript, documents, and reports about the burglary conviction of Mr. Darling, or "JT" as I will call him, who was in the midst of a lengthy sentence at the state penitentiary in Menard. JT was from Goofy Ridge, Illinois, where the crime took place. You heard me right – he was from the "Ridge," a hamlet on the Illinois River, near Havana. It's not unusual in our little corner of the state -- originally populated by hill folk from Tennessee and Kentucky -- to find places like this. My own hometown is nestled between "Gin Ridge" and "Possum Holler." Western Illinois is sometimes referred to as "Forgottonia" due to the propensity of the state legislature to ignore our pleas for roads and services.

It was pretty much an open-and-shut case. Oh, he did it. JT broke into a bait and concession store and made off with over ninety pounds of frozen catfish and turtle meat. That night, he visited a neighborhood establishment and confided his exploits to a drinking buddy. Unfortunately, his trust was misplaced, as his friend stopped by the local cop shop to reveal the deed. Within 24 hours, the deputies showed up at

JT's house with a search warrant, opened his freezer, and JT Darling was toast. Being a three-time loser, he was dispatched to the "Big House" at the conclusion of the trial.

Part of my job as an appellate intern was to go to the prison and consult with the client. Being fresh out of law school, I was excited to do this. But, while riding the Illinois Central down to the prison, I paged through the transcript of JT's trial. It seemed that the appeal would be a futile gesture.

Should I tell him this? Would he hold it against me or even act out?

The State Penitentiary in Menard was a classic gray stone fortress-like building. I was escorted through a series of iron gates, searched each time, and finally ensconced in a claustrophobic gray room, awaiting the arrival of my client. What would he be like? I had visions of a burly, hardened criminal.

At last, a guard entered with JT, whom he cuffed to the metal table where I was sitting. I was shocked. There he was, the "three times and you're out" felon. But he was just a wisp of a man. Slight, balding, and shy, with a kindly smile -- a minnow among sharks in that wretched place.

In my naivete, I pictured myself as Atticus Finch, the hero of *To Kill a Mockingbird*, and the inspiration for many young men who sought to become lawyers. Without looking at JT, I launched into a scholarly disquisition about the issues of his case. On finishing, I was ready for his questions or perhaps to learn from him some new, dramatic evidence that would help him out of that hellhole.

After a while, though, I realized that he wasn't responding to a thing I said.

Finally, I looked up from the thick file.

"What do you think of our theory of the case?" I asked.

For the first time, he spoke. "Sure do appreciate y'all coming down here," he said. This humble man hadn't understood a word I'd said, but he was thanking me nonetheless.

I realized that further discussion of his case was a fruitless endeavor, and began to stuff the file in my briefcase. JT seemed disappointed to see me leaving.

"You gonna come visit again?"

"Maybe after the court's decision," I lied.

Returning on the train, I decided to read the Presentence Report -- a social evaluation provided to the court after the guilty verdict but before the sentencing. It was a revelation. Why hadn't I looked at it before visiting him? Sure, JT had three felonies, but they all involved the theft of food! His IQ was 85. He was the head of a family of four, surviving on a welfare grant of $385 per month. In return for this generous concession from the taxpayers, the county required that he mow cemetery lots forty hours a week. How could he get by with these rules?

Of course, none of this affected the merits of his case, so I forged ahead with the writing of his appellate brief, hopeless as it seemed. Six to twelve years for stealing food? It was an outrage.

Before concluding, I reminded myself of my criminal law professor's admonition: "No matter how simple or complex it is, start with the basics." So, I took a final look at the case filings, especially the indictment, or charging document.

There it was - - staring me in the face! Through carelessness or neglect, someone had failed to specify that the concession stand, or the catfish and turtle meat that was stolen from it, was owned by somebody else. In technical legal terms, it meant that JT wasn't really charged with a crime.

I was embarrassed not to have seen this error in the first place, but JT never would have understood it anyway, so I didn't bother telling him about our new defense. Instead, I did some research, finding pertinent case law, and finished the brief. Sometime thereafter, the case was taken under advisement by the Court of Appeals.

Three months later, I'd moved on to greener pastures. I was now employed by a prosperous law firm that actually paid a living wage. Meanwhile, JT's case was presented to the Court of Appeals by my former boss.

One day an official delivery arrived regarding JT's case. The burglary conviction was reversed and JT was discharged on the accompanying theft charge. People v. Darling, 7 Ill. App.3d 687, 286 N.E.2d 502 (1972). As our brief had argued, the court found that the "proof did not conform to an essential element of the information charging burglary." I never learned if things turned around for JT after that, or if he just got caught stealing food again.

The bigger question remained. Whose crime was this in the first place – JT's or ours?

A few years ago, I did a Google search, and found a one-sentence obituary, stating that JT passed away in Pekin, Illinois, at age eighty-three. At least he died a free man.

Back at the cocktail party, our friend has refreshed her Chardonnay. "It seems like only the bad guys have rights. What about us?" I nod my head, hoping she's done, but she isn't.

"What really bugs me is when these criminals get off on technicalities. Is that justice?"

"You're so right," I say.

(This story was originally published in the Illinois Bar Journal, March, 2022.)

CHAPTER 4

The Fault Line

Her name was Jackie Peterson. She came with her sister. Like a lot of clients, she needed the support of a friend or relative, just to meet with a lawyer.

I was new in my profession. Although I'd passed the bar exam and was endowed with lots of classroom knowledge from law school, I had little practical experience. I'd been assigned to the library my first two years at the law firm doing research. Then, without prior consultation, my employers designated me as "the divorce lawyer." They provided no guidance, except that I was expected to turn a profit for them.

Jackie was in her late thirties, pleasant-looking but fragile, like a glass vase that could shatter in an instant. She reached into her purse and clutched her rosary beads. I, too, was nervous and didn't notice at first that she was wearing large, dark sunglasses.

"Okay dear," her sister said, "take off your glasses so he can see."

There was an ugly, incipient bruise on her cheek, and her left eye was already bright scarlet.

"She didn't want to come, but my husband and I told her that this is the last time Maurice can get away with this."

"Your husband did this?" I asked.

"He humiliates me, he hits me and then . . ." she hesitated. "He forces himself on me. If I don't give in, this is what happens. He hits our sons. He drinks, too." She stopped again, adding tentatively, "I have to divorce him, but I don't have to say all of this in court, do I?"

"Unfortunately, you do," I said.

"No-fault divorce" was still a few years away. To get a divorce, you had to prove your grounds, and "divorce denied" would sometimes be the verdict of the judge.

The grounds could be adultery, intoxication, insanity, physical or mental cruelty – to name some of the most common. Even in uncontested cases, corroborating witnesses were required. If your marriage didn't work out because of incompatibility, you'd still have to round up a couple of friends to testify – often falsely – that your spouse had committed one of the above-named "sins."

"The judge will want to know that you've tried marriage counseling," I added. "Oh, we did that. We went to the priest. Maurice denied everything. He said I was crazy. The priest told me to pray. He assigned me some psalms. My husband said that he'd never give me a divorce."

After she left, I drew up a Summons and Complaint, alleging physical cruelty. I also asked my secretary to call the police department for a check on the criminal records of both Jackie and Maurice.

A month later we were in court. Jackie's bruises were healed by then, but her sister had brought some photos of her injuries.

The judge called the lawyers into chambers for a pretrial briefing. He was a nice man – a staunch Baptist with a reticent personality. "What can we do to stop this divorce?" he asked.

Maurice's lawyer, Tony Antonelli, jumped in. "Your Honor, I've saved a lot of marriages. I always counsel with my clients against divorce, unless it's the last resort. We're going to fight this with everything we can."

The judge smiled and nodded his head. He was soaking it up.

I'd heard of Antonelli and his game. He was big in the local Catholic church, and known for talking up his "Save the Marriage" line, which was great for business. When he'd get a case, he'd contest it to the hilt, and charge his clients three times the going rate. "Counselor," the judge said to me, "go out and talk to your client – I'm thinking we can reconvene the case in a couple of months. They can stay together and do some more counseling at the church. Then your client can decide if she really wants this."

"No, your Honor," I protested, "She's in danger – this is an abuse case."

"Well, then, we'll start the trial, but I can't assure you that you'll succeed." He paused for a moment, giving me a skeptical look. "So you take a lot of these cases? "

"It's my job," I said.

"You know what they called divorce law in my old firm?" he said. "Ditch work."

We assembled in the courtroom. Maurice was seated to my right. He was a pipefitter, and looked it – muscular body, florid face, and meaty hands. I got the impression that he'd used his fists a few times to defend taunts about his less-than-masculine name. A rancid, unwashed odor wafted from his direction.

Jackie, on the other hand, was conservatively dressed, looking pale but determined. I'd worked hard with Jackie preparing her for the ordeal of testifying. "State your name, please," I asked.

"Objection," Antonelli interrupted. "Leading question, your Honor."

"It's not even a question," I responded to the judge. "This is standard procedure." His response astounded me. "I'm sure you can get this information without leading the witness, counsel. Proceed."

I had no choice but to comply with this ridiculous ruling. "Do you have a name?"

"Yes," Jackie said, her eyes darting between the judge and I.

"And what is your name?" I asked.

"Jacqueline Peterson."

"Do you reside in Hennepin County, Minnesota?"

"Objection to the leading question, your Honor," Antonelli said.

"Sustained," the judge said.

"What is your home address, Ms. Peterson?"

"Objection, your Honor. Leading."

Again, Antonelli was sustained.

"Do you have a home, Ms. Peterson?" I asked.

"Yes."

"Does it have an address?"

"Yes."

"And what is the address?"

It continued this way for an hour. Eventually the judge tired of the charade. "I'm going to allow counsel to lead on a limited basis."

Things began to move along. I was proud of Jackie for persevering as she soldiered through her testimony, describing the sordid details of Maurice's abuse. She even held together during Antonelli's insulting cross-examination.

We rested our case. It was time for Maurice's defense.

Antonelli rose. "Your Honor, we have a witness who will prove that Plaintiff is mentally ill. With the Court's permission, we call Anders Peterson.

"I saw his name on the witness list," the judge said. "I'm hoping he isn't a relative. I hate it when families fight among themselves."

"Actually, he's the nineteen-year-old son of the parties. I would rather not have had to do this, but he's legally an adult, so he's entitled to tell his story. Remember, the sanctity of this marriage is at stake."

I was furious and should have strenuously objected, but my lack of experience and self-confidence got the better of me.

"It's highly irregular," the judge said. "I'll allow it, but I'm not giving you much leeway. Stick to the facts."

A teenager entered the courtroom, was administered the oath and took the stand. He was a younger, slimmed-down version of his father.

"My name is Anders Peterson, and I agreed to come here because I hope my parents will stay together. I just wish they'd stop fighting." It sounded completely rehearsed.

"Your mother is the one who wants this divorce. You know that, right?" Antonelli asked.

"Yup, I do," Anders said.

"Do you agree with her?"

"No."

"Why?"

"Because she's crazy," Anders said, averting his eyes from Jackie.

"Objection, your Honor," I said. "This witness has no foundation to make such an opinion."

"That's right, counsel," the judge said. "Mr. Antonelli, you're going to have to do better than that."

"Okay," Antonelli responded. "Anders, please give us an example of your mother's behavior."

"Mom's part Indian. Our grandad still lives up at White Earth Reservation. We all went up there last year for a visit and midway through, she just plain lost it. We were at the community center, and she started talking in tongues. Then she fainted. When we woke her up, it was like she had amnesia. She was in the hospital for three days. That wasn't the only time she's done something like that."

"What's your message to the judge, Anders?" Antonelli asked.

"I want her to stop this divorce, and I want my dad to have custody of my two younger brothers if she gets it."

Jackie grasped my wrist. "I need to talk to you about this!"

I requested a brief recess, and we found a conference room."

"It's true what Anders said about me fainting. I am a mystic. It's in my blood. When I stand on the grounds of my ancestors, I feel the earth vibrating beneath me. Sometimes I hear their voices, in their ancient tongues. Do you think I should tell the judge about this?"

I cringed at the thought, but broke it gently to Jackie. "Maybe later, if we really need to," I said. It was like being stuck in quicksand. Ander's testimony hurt us, but Jackie's explanation would dig the hole deeper.

When we resumed, Antonelli rose to address the court. "Your Honor, at the outset I said that we would fight to save this marriage, and to do so we will be using the defense of condonation."

My stomach sank. I'd never heard of this. I'd gone to school in a different state, where no-fault divorce was already the law, and no one had taught me about "condonation."

Even the judge seemed unfamiliar with the concept. "Please define condonation for the record, counsel."

"When marital misconduct has been alleged, your Honor, if there are subsequent sexual relations, then the conduct is excused, or condoned. The grounds fail and the case must be dismissed. That's what we're about to prove."

"I remember now," the judge said. "Go ahead, counsel."

Maurice lumbered up to the witness stand, carrying a grocery bag.

His lawyer said, "Open up the bag and have the exhibit marked."

It was a blue sofa cushion, and as the clerk tagged it and handed it back to Maurice, I saw the color drain from Jackie's face.

"Why did you bring this, Maurice?" the lawyer asked.

"Jackie made up this story about me hitting her and said she was filing for divorce. I begged her to stop it. One thing led to another and, well, we had sex." Maurice held up the pillow. "She used this to prop up her butt because we were on the floor."

Suddenly, Jackie let out a shriek. "You raped me!" She bolted from her seat, racing toward the courtroom door. She didn't make it, though, losing control of her bodily functions, from both ends.

Even the judge was shocked. "We'll return this afternoon. The court is adjourned." Fortunately, Jackie's sister was in the courtroom and gave her a coat to cover up and leave with.

Two hours later, we began again. The janitor had cleaned up the mess and Jackie had gone home to change clothes. The unpleasant odor remained, and I tried not to look at the affected area. Jackie looked even more shaky than she had been in the morning. Antonelli rose. "Your Honor, my client denies the outrageous allegation made by his wife, but, even so, I'd like to point out that there is no such thing as marital rape."

He was right, as the law stood at that time. Since then, legislation has gotten rid of this anomaly. Still, it was an unwelcome interruption on the part of Maurice's lawyer. "Mr. Peterson," the judge said, "pass the pillow over to your wife's counsel." I walked up to Maurice, holding out my hand, but he quickly rose in a fighter's stance – fists at the ready.

"Come and get it, chicken," he challenged me. I raised my hands in mock surrender. After a far too lengthy interval, Antonelli said with a smirk, "Back off, Maurice."

I was happy it had happened. Any judge would put Maurice in jail for such an egregious act, I thought.

I was astonished again, though.

"The court observed the defendant possibly taking aggressive action toward counsel," the judge said. "Another act like this, sir, and I'll find you in contempt of court." Why did this abusive, ignorant bully get the kid-glove treatment?

"Take the stand, Mr. Peterson. Go ahead, counsel," the judge said.

"She didn't consent to it, did she?" I asked Maurice, pointing to the pillow that had been set on the counsel table, which I avoided touching.

"Never hurt a woman." Maurice shot a hateful look toward Jackie's sister, who was sitting behind us. "It's her family that put her up to this, especially that one."

I opened the file prepared for me by my secretary, marked "Criminal History Report – Maurice Peterson." It showed a prior conviction for criminal sexual assault by strangulation, as well as two misdemeanor assaults. I approached Maurice with a copy. "Happened twenty years ago," Maurice responded. "Didn't even know Jackie then. Plus, my lawyer screwed me. Pled me out. I would've beat it with a jury."

I addressed the judge. "Your Honor, this clearly impeaches Mr. Peterson's allegations. I move for a directed verdict and a dismissal of his case."

We rested, and the next morning the judge was back with his decision. "Folks, I'm going to grant this divorce. I have my doubts about both of you. Mr. Peterson, your actions belie the Christian values you claim to espouse. Mrs. Peterson, I am concerned with your mental stability. I'm sorry to say, though, that if I do nothing, I'll just find you folks back here again."

"I find that the husband should have custody of the two minor boys. Wife will vacate the house, and husband will pay her fifty-thousand dollars for her share of the equity."

I was happy that Jackie got her divorce, but chagrined that she lost her home and her boys, especially based on the questionable testimony of her own son.

A few weeks later, I was informed that Jackie was waiting at the front desk to see me, and I walked out to greet her.

"I got my money," she said with a smile. "I settled up with your bookkeeper on the bill, and I gave my tithe to the church."

"And this is for you," she said. She handed me a check for five thousand dollars. "It's for sticking through this with me, and don't try to talk me out of it." I was flabbergasted. The first 'tip' I'd ever received.

The timing was fortuitous. I was planning to strike out on my own. The fees clearly belonged to the law firm, but the 'tip' was for me. Still, I wondered whether I could ethically keep it. After a prolonged phone conversation with a starched-shirt fellow at the Board of Professional Responsibility, I got the go-ahead. As a result, Jackie funded my new and successful venture as a family law practitioner.

Twenty years later, I saw the name, Anders Peterson, on my appointment calendar. I now had gray hairs and a corner office on the top floor of a new office building, which I owned.

Anders had grown a few inches and widened by many more. He looked very much like his father, but instead of an angry scowl, he flashed a friendly grin.

"Thanks for seeing me," he said. "I'm here because in my AA group, we have a series of steps to accomplish, and the final one is to make amends to those you've hurt. It was wrong for me to testify against my mother. My dad bribed me by giving me a new car. I'm not denying my own responsibility for the mess I've made of my life, but doing what I did in that courtroom is a big reason for it. I just want you to know my brothers and I have made up with my mom. "

"How are you doing with your dad?"

"We haven't seen him for years."

CHAPTER 5

Which Kind of Lawyer Are You?

What are your most vivid memories? Are they from the first moments of a new stage of your life, such as your wedding, or the birth of a child? As for me, I'll never forget the first day of law school.

Hundreds of us, mostly young and male, shuffled into the auditorium as the dean took the podium to welcome us. After the usual salutations, he said, "Look to the person to your left and your right, by the end of the year one of the three of you will be gone." Why did he say this? Was he trying to scare us? We were already plenty scared. Since then, lots of my colleagues have told me of hearing the same platitude at their law schools.

He went on. "I'd like to think we produce two kinds of lawyers. The first kind are the plumbers. They clean up people's problems and they're well paid for it. And they're certainly important in our world." His voice took on an air of condescension. It was as if he'd said, "They shovel the shit and clean out the pipes."

"Then there are the visionaries -- those who make a difference. Those who strive to improve the lives of others."

He continued on, but from my perspective he could have stopped right there, since I'd already chosen my path. I would be a crusader for justice. Another Atticus Finch – protector of the downtrodden – a hero to the underprivileged.

My idealism took a blow when, in a down economy, I entered the job market. I scrambled to find a job -- any job. I got one as an associate lawyer with a mid-size suburban law firm.

"Glad you're here," the senior partner said when we met on the first day. "We had to part company with our divorce lawyer, so we need you to get right into his caseload." I found out later that my predecessor had been stealing money from the firm.

My new boss took my arm and guided me to a small office at the end of the hall. It wasn't what I had in mind that first day of law school, but as it happened, I started to like the job, was good at it and eventually developed a successful and surprisingly lucrative family law practice. As the dean said, plumbers are paid well.

A few years later I opened my own law firm. One day I had a new client named Barbara. She looked like the then-popular model and actress Farah Fawcett, perky in a beige jumpsuit and permed blond hair.

She was a legal secretary in a small real estate firm. Her estranged husband was a high-earning trader at the Grain Exchange.

"He's a great father," she said. "The kids love him, and he should always have equal time with them. But he's been cheating on me." The tears welled up. "I can't take it anymore."

I nudged over the fancy embossed leather box – befitting of a successful divorce lawyer – holding the Kleenex.

Barbara had sleuthed out her husband's infidelities, and presented me with proof of shared business trips with a young lady – even a secret apartment downtown. "Have you thought about your long-term goals?" I asked. "It would help us map out a strategy."

"We'd always planned for me to go to law school so I could be a real estate lawyer like my boss," she responded, "and I want him to pay me alimony so I can."

"That's a smart plan," I said. But, I wondered, you want to be a real estate lawyer? I couldn't imagine anything more sterile and boring.

We had a real estate lawyer in our firm. I'd walk by his office half a dozen times a day. While I was chatting it up with my clients or fellow lawyers, this guy would be sitting at his desk with a stack of property abstracts in front of him, staring out the window. The only worse thing would be probate law, which consists of representing dead people.

* * * * * * * *

Barbara's case dragged on for months -- her husband wouldn't budge on the alimony. I set up a conference about a week ahead of the trial to do our final preparation. Shortly before the meeting, Barbara called ahead to ask if she could bring her boss, just to introduce him to me. I was reluctant to do it, since we didn't have time to spare, but it seemed important to her, so I agreed.

Perry was a preppy type, sporting a dark blue suit and one of those narrow yellow, "power ties." He sat very close to Barbara. It took my trained eye about fifteen seconds to figure out what was going on between them. Glancing down at Perry's wedding ring, I was reminded of what happened to a lawyer friend of mine.

Marty, my friend, was one of the courthouse regulars, and a good guy. One day, Marty, always one to bare his soul, had a confession to make. He'd been having a long-term affair with his secretary, and after sneaking around for months, they decided to come clean to their spouses about it. A dinner was arranged so that confessions would be made.

I asked him how it went.

"It was terrible. The next morning my wife told me to clear out by the end of the day. When I got to the office there was a note on the desk asking me to call my secretary at home. She told me that she and her husband had stayed up all night talking and decided to patch things up and make a go of it. She'd promised him to quit her job immediately." I feigned sympathy, but I couldn't believe he'd come up with such a bone-headed plan. I shared the story with my law partners and we laughed about how in one day Marty lost his wife, his mistress and his secretary.

It crossed my mind to pull Perry aside and relate this cautionary tale.

Our pretrial meeting proceeded, but Perry was becoming a pain in the ass. He pulled out a list of questions for me about Barbara's case. It was like he'd seen a TV show about divorce and, based on this, had some crackpot ideas about how the case should go. I think he perceived himself as the valiant knight to his helpless maiden girlfriend. When he started to question my trial strategy, I'd had enough.

"Say, Perry," I said, "I'd like your reflections on Justice Coyne's opinion in the *Nardini* case." It was a landmark case in our state and any competent divorce lawyer would know it by heart, but, of course, Perry was stumped.

"Look pal," I said, raising my voice, "for all I know you may be an international expert on incorporeal hereditaments, but you don't know jack-shit about family law." I looked over to Barbara, who shot me a surreptitious smile.

"Another thing. Stay away from here, stay away from our case and, for Chrissakes, stay away from the courtroom." The latter admonition was necessary because, more than once, I'd had paramours show up unexpectedly at a trial to offer their "moral support."

* * * * * * * *

We had a bifurcated case, meaning that we would have a trial on the financial issues first, and then deal with the kids in a second trial. The judge was a hale fellow well-met, as they say. He enjoyed staying late after bar association meetings, swapping war stories over Manhattans and, I must admit, I liked to do that too. We'd forged a nice bond, so I was happy we drew him for our trial. The judge was close to retirement and, knowing that he wouldn't have to run for election again, he'd become quite uninhibited in his courtroom conduct.

The successful grain trader husband was asserting the so-called "SIDS" strategy. No, not Sudden Infant Death Syndrome, but what we divorce lawyers cynically call "Sudden Income Deficiency Syndrome." This happens when the husband, having bragged all his life about being a captain of industry, suddenly shows up in divorce court claiming that he doesn't have two quarters to rub together.

The economy had hit him hard, he claimed. Much as he'd love to be able to help Barbara go to law school, it just wasn't in the cards.

This was bullshit, and I had the goods on him for the upcoming cross-examination. As the moment arrived, I caught the judge's eye with a wink and a nod, just to let him know that the fun part was starting.

Approaching the husband on the witness stand, I handed him a stack of numbered exhibits that Barbara had helped prepare for me. They included receipts for adjoining hotel rooms, expensive dinners for two and cancelled checks for the heretofore undisclosed love nest.

"So, sir," I said, "You say you're broke, but I ask you what these documents show, and I ask you who Ms. Carlson is."

He paged through the exhibits. His hands shook and the color drained from his face. He opened his mouth but no sound was forthcoming. Finally, his lawyer jumped to his defense. "Your Honor, I object! I don't know what counsel has, but we have No-Fault divorce here. The Court cannot consider marital misconduct in making its decision."

He had a point, but I had the winning rebuttal. "He's right about the No-Fault divorce, your Honor, but the Court is entitled to know if a party has diminished the marital estate by diverting money to a third party, and it's painfully clear that he's keeping a mistress and taking money off the family table to pay for his indulgences."

The judge looked at the husband's lawyer, and said, "Counselor, it's obvious that your client's contracted a case of *penis erectus*, and he wants his family to take the fall for it. Objection overruled." Turning to me, he added, "Continue with your questions." My cross-examination was long and brutal, but, for me, rather enjoyable. The judge's decision was a slam-dunk victory – a rare thing in a divorce case. Barbara was awarded enough alimony for law school and then some. Before the judge could finish, the husband loudly exclaimed to his lawyer, "No – he can't do this!"

The judge gave him a quick look and shot back, "It's the screwing you get for the screwing you got!"

I noticed that the court reporter had turned her machine off. There would be no record of his statement in the event of an appeal.

Barbara and I retired to a nearby conference room. "You were great," she gushed. "I just loved your cross-examination." I basked in the flattery from this smart, pretty young woman.

"I wonder," she said, "now that the next part of our case is coming up, can I ask for full custody of the kids?"

"But you told me he was a great dad," I said. "You didn't want to ever keep him from the kids."

"I'd get more money if I had custody, wouldn't I? You can get that for me, can't you?"

I was speechless for a few moments. She must have been a little worried that I wouldn't do it, because she was giving me a doe-eyed, pleading look.

I remembered again the dean's speech. I was no crusader for justice. I was, and always would be, a plumber.

CHAPTER 6

The Prized Child

After four years of toiling away for a suburban law firm, it was time to hang up my own shingle.

My first case as a solo practitioner came not from a billboard or a boisterous television commercial, but from a friendly assistant from the assignment office who convinced a judge to refer a case to me. The pay was low, but it beat sitting around waiting for the phone to ring.

It was a termination of parental rights proceeding, or TPR for short. My client was Gloria Grantham, the mother, who was facing serious charges by the county.

My new office was in a strip shopping center, which afforded me a rather unattractive view of a parking lot. There wasn't much going on the afternoon of my meeting with Gloria, so I sat at my desk reading some recent appellate court cases, keeping an eye out for my new client. About thirty minutes after our meeting was scheduled to begin, a rusty Plymouth Duster pulled up. It was orange, but with a green-colored hood from another vehicle strapped onto it with bungee chords. A man and a woman emerged – both of them wearing sweatshirts and tattered jeans. The man wore a black felt hat, and his long, stringy brown hair hung below his shoulders. He had a FuManchu mustache and goatee. The woman – surely my client Gloria – was short and a little overweight. Her blond hair had an unwashed look, but she had a friendly face, smiling at me as I opened the front door.

"I'm Gloria and this is Black," she said, as we exchanged handshakes. They were handshakes that made me long for warm water and soap. Black fired up a cigarette. He could have asked, I thought, as I dug an ashtray out of my desk.

"How long you been a lawyer?" He asked.

"About four years," I said.

Looking over to Gloria, he said, "See, that's what I told you. They give you some rookie. That PD I had last year didn't know his ass from a hole in the ground either!"

"Oh, you had a public defender?" I asked. "How come?"

"None of your business. This ain't about me, asshole," he said.

I'd had enough of this guy. I told him he had to sit in the lobby, for confidentiality purposes. It was a thin excuse, but he bought it.

As I closed the door, Gloria said, "I'm really sorry about that. He's my old boyfriend. We're split up, and that, but he's still after me. He was the only ride I could get."

The petition says your daughter is two years old. Is he the dad?"

"Oh, no. Gina's real dad? I didn't know him for long. He just wanted one thing from me, then when I came up pregnant he was outta' here. They tried serving him with the petition, but they can't find him."

"So, this guy 'Black'" – what's his real name? He's white. How'd he end up being called "Black?'"

"Well, his real name's Vernon, but everyone calls him 'Black' because he got arrested for selling black tar heroin. I guess that doesn't sound so good."

"That's for sure." I said, "We've got two problems here. First, the judge is Black, so it's gonna be awkward as hell if you call him 'Black', and, second, we don't want the judge to ask about how he got his name. So, from now on, his name's 'Vernon.' Okay? "

"His name is Vernon," she said it deliberately, with a smile.

I reviewed the petition. It stated that Gloria had been stopped by the police six months earlier for erratic driving. Although she passed the breathalyzer test, she had been drinking while her daughter, Gina, was a passenger. This required a child welfare investigation, and the social worker had determined that Gloria had numerous deficiencies as a parent. This included the drinking and driving incident and her association with Vernon Gunderson – or "Black" - a convicted drug offender. Gloria lived in sub-standard housing and had failed to comply with the corrective goals set by the social worker.

"Gloria," I said, "this is very serious. Do you understand that Gina could be permanently taken from you and put up for adoption? That's why it's called a termination of your parental rights."

"Really? I didn't understand it that way." She said, "Jackie Swenson – the social worker – said she was just trying to help me be a better mother, and that. I told her I hadn't had a drink since I got stopped, and that was six months ago. She knows I'm done with Black. She even had the cops stop by and give me surprise breathalyzer tests. I thought I was doing okay, but then she came up with all these other requirements, like I'm supposed to go to Alcoholics Anonymous, which I don't even need. I'm sorry but it's hard when you're trying to keep your job and take care of your baby and you don't even have a car, and that."

On my way home that afternoon I stopped at Gloria's so-called sub-standard home. Neither the neighborhood nor her double-wide trailer were remotely attractive.

When I knocked on the door a woman's voice said, "It's open, come right in." She turned out to be Gloria's mother. "Gloria's over at the park with Gina. She'll be right back. Sit here with me for a while. I want to tell you something."

The mother was obese – maybe sixty years old. Her hair was thinning and she had the gray, wrinkled face of a veteran smoker. She was rigged up to an oxygen pack, with little plastic breathing tubes extended to each nostril. Next to her on the table was a full ashtray.

"Gloria's had a hard life and I know she's made some mistakes, but she's really a good person and she's a great mom. Her poppa died when she was just three. She's got this older sister, Betty, who's got spina bifida. Betty lives in a rehab house now, but Gloria always treated her so kind-like. She changed her diapers and everything. I couldn't have handled that without her."

She hesitated, as if challenged by what was to come next.

"Sorry, I'm going to turn this thing off so I don't start a fire," she said, referring to the oxygen unit. She reached into her purse and found her cigarettes, promptly lighting one up.

"I married this guy who lived with us for ten years or so. When Gloria was about twelve she started having a lot of trouble. Finally, she told me that her stepfather was messing with her. He fessed up and now he's in prison. I hope he rots!"

She took a deep drag in her cigarette. "Gloria got really depressed cuz she thought it was her fault, and she was sorta' a wild child in high school. But she graduated and got a job. Now she's got Gina and she's really growing up."

"Do you think she has a drinking problem?" I asked.

"Oh, she likes to party sometimes, but she's only twenty-four. You know that time she got stopped for drinking and driving? That was Black's fault. He was drugged up and passed out, and she wasn't going to let him stay here, so she got his keys and drove him back to his place – that's when she got stopped. She didn't mean to be driving that day."

As she was talking, I took a look around the house. It was filled with second-hand furniture, aged appliances, and a worn carpet. But it was clean, and someone had pinned cheerful pictures of Gloria and Gina on the wall. I had brought along a disposable camera and was shooting some pictures when Gloria and her daughter walked in the front door.

I was astonished to see Gina – she was a stunning child. Bright red hair, green eyes and freckles. She sprinted over to her grandmother and hugged her. But she also smiled at me. She was about the opposite of what I expected, after my first encounter with Gloria, Black, and the trailer park scene. I snapped several more photos. I sensed a strong family bond.

We'd been given only a small budget for the case and had to prepare for the trial on limited time. The court had appointed a separate lawyer to represent Gina. Maybe he'd pitch in to help us, I hoped.

"Ms. Swenson and her team's done their usual good job on this one," he said when I called. "I'm going with the county's recommendation for termination. It's the best thing for the child."

This turned out to be the longest utterance I ever heard from this guy. From then on, all he said was "No" each time the Judge asked him if he had any questions. It seemed like he wanted his money with the smallest effort possible. I wondered if the county used him because he was such a pushover.

Soon enough it was the day of the trial. I'd asked Gloria to wear a dress or a suit, or even nice slacks to court. All I'd ever seen her in were the dirty jeans, but she showed up in the same pair --although clean --along with yet another sweatshirt. I was furious, knowing how much of a difference a first impression can make – but I suppressed my anger. Gloria's mother arrived, complete with an oxygen tank and walker, to lend her support.

As we were waiting outside the courtroom, a clerk approached.

"The judge wants the attorneys and the social workers to meet first. Maybe you can come up with an agreement."

The county already had their conference room established. It was populated by the county attorney, Gina's court-appointed lawyer, and Jackie Swenson, the social worker. After introductions, the county attorney opened his file.

"Counsel," he said to me, "I don't envy you. Your gal's had her chances. Why doesn't she save everybody's time and just consent to the petition?"

"Wait a minute!" I said. "We're here to work on an agreement and you're telling us to roll over. It's only been six months since the traffic stop. What's the big rush? My client, Gloria . . ."

I was interrupted by Jackie Swenson. "You mean Gloria gonorrhea," she said with a giggle. The other two chuckled at this, apparently sharing an inside joke.

"Off the record," the attorney for the county said with a smile. "If we didn't have a little humor in these cases, we'd all go crazy."

He was right about the humor. Family court, with its non-stop *sturm und drang*, is enough to test the sanity of anyone. But he was wrong about this comment.

"That isn't funny," I said. "It's cruel. The hell with an agreement. We're going to trial. I expect you to treat my client with respect. Period."

Jackie Swenson was the first witness. As she walked up to the stand, I took a good look at her. She was tall and slender, dressed in black slacks, a bright yellow silk blouse, and the then stylish platform shoes. She was poised, professional, and, I have to admit, sexy – everything that Gloria was not.

She testified that she'd received the case after the traffic stop. She had met with Gloria at the trailer park a few times. She conducted a criminal record test, which showed that Gloria had no adverse history. Still, she felt that Gina was a dependent child, a legal term justifying the intervention of governmental supervision. She'd tried to provide guidance to Gloria by giving her a list of goals, which, if fulfilled, would have forstalled the proceedings. The list included:

No further contact with Vernon Gunderson.

Attendance and completion of a ten-week parent education program.

No consumption of drugs or alcohol.

Twice weekly attendance at AA and establish progress on a 12-step program.

A viable plan to move out of the trailer park.

She'd given Gloria several months to comply, but Gloria had only partially completed the goals. Yes, she acknowledged that termination was a severe penalty, but the welfare of the child was superior to the wishes of the parent.

The judge asked if I had any cross-examination.

"Ms. Swenson," I said, "my client has been sober for six months. She's been spot-checked four times with a breathalyzer and passed each time. Correct?"

"She's been lucky, I guess. We can't test her every day. But she'll never stay sober if she doesn't get rid of her friends and do the AA program. She's been to exactly two meetings and she hasn't gone to a single parenting class."

"You really expect 100% compliance with all of your goals?" I said. "I submit to you that my client has been set up for failure."

"How so?" she said. Her face colored, and her eyes darted between the county attorney and the judge.

"Let's just go down the list," I said. "She told you Mr. Gunderson was out of the picture, but you don't believe anything she says. You give her no credit for passing the spot checks on drinking. Then she's supposed to go to parenting classes and AA meetings, both of which involve half-day cross-town bus trips, and at the same time she's supposed to be taking care of her daughter and holding down a job. Finally, you expect her to find a new home when you know that she's living on a minimum wage. How in the world is she supposed to succeed?"

"If she wanted to keep her child, she'd find a way," Ms. Swenson said.

"Ms. Swenson," I said as I approached the witness stand, "haven't you referred to my client as 'Gloria gonorrhea?'"

"Objection!" The county attorney sprang to his feet. "Our settlement discussions are not admissible! Counsel well knows this – he should be held in contempt of court for even mentioning it!"

The lawyer appointed to represent Gina, who was sitting to my right, seemed to shrink in his chair, and actually turned his face to the back of the room, as if he could make himself invisible.

"This had nothing to do with an offer or proposal," I responded. "It was a gratuitous insult and it goes to the witness' credibility and bias."

The judge cast a stern look at Ms. Swenson. "Is this what you said?"

"Yes, your Honor."

"I'm allowing it," he said.

The next witness was a chemical dependency counselor for the county. He'd been sitting in the empty jury box. He was a middle-aged, dour guy -- dressed a little informally for court. As he ascended to the witness stand, he tripped on the step and spilled the contents of his file on the floor. He nervously glanced at the lawyers and Gloria.

He testified that he was trained on the subject of chemical dependency, having received a certificate, and he had testified many times as an expert witness on the subject.

He had interviewed Gloria and determined that she was addicted to alcohol.

"You know, sir, that Ms. Grantham is professing sobriety," the county attorney said, "does that change your opinion?"

"Not a bit," he said, "even if she's been sober, that doesn't address the problem. She's what we call a 'dry drunk.' In my professional opinion, she has no chance of staying sober until she completes alcohol treatment, or, at a minimum, a lengthy twelve-step program."

That sounded pretty damning for Gloria, but I'd done a little research on this guy and was ready as the judge nodded to me to begin the cross-examination.

"Since you are giving us your expert opinion, sir," I said, "what scientific evidence do you base it on? Did you administer the MMPI to my client?" I was referring to the Minnesota Multi-Phasic Personality Inventory, a nationally recognized psychological evaluation often used to determine personality disorders.

"No, I did not," the so-called expert said.

"Specifically, the McAndrew scale of the MMPI is especially informative as to the existence of a chemically-dependent personality, isn't it?"

"Correct, but again, she wasn't given this test," he said.

"Why didn't you test her?" I asked, already knowing the answer.

"I wasn't authorized to give her the test."

"You would have to be a licensed psychologist or have a graduate degree in chemical dependency to give and interpret the MMPI, right."

"Yes," he answered softly.

"Exactly how much training have you had?"

"I attended a two-week conference, and passed the exam at the end of it."

"And," he said solemnly, "I am an alcoholic myself."

It was as if it should end the conversation. Only he – an admitted alcoholic - could truly diagnose Gloria's problem and know how to solve it.

I would have no part of this.

"Your Honor, I object the entirety of this witness' testimony. The fact that he's an alcoholic and went to a two-week class doesn't entitle him to render an opinion in this case, especially when the most fundamental right – that of a parent – is at stake."

The judge leaned back in his chair, closed his eyes and stroked his chin, then looked at me and said, "I have great concern about this, but I can separate the wheat from the chaff. I'll allow it for what it's worth."

The county's case ended shortly thereafter and it was our turn. I called Gloria to the stand. I spread out the photos I had taken of her home as well as those of she and Gina, and she went through them one by one for the Judge.

"Now, Ms. Grantham, describe what you've done to remedy the problems Ms. Swenson addressed."

"Everything I could," Gloria said. "I stopped drinking – I'll never do it again. I got rid of Black, and that."

I quickly looked up to the judge, cringing at the mention of Black's name, but before anything else happened, Gloria turned to the judge.

"I'll do anything they want, your Honor. Don't let them do this to us!"

The tears began to fill her face, but she continued.

"I've made a lot of mistakes, but I knew God loved me when Gina was born. She's my life. Please don't take her!"

The judge took a long pause, then said, "The court is dismissing this case. The county has failed to meet its burden, and the court has grave concerns about its methods and motives."

He then turned to Gloria.

"Young lady, I am giving you a tremendous opportunity here. Don't blow it. If this case ever comes up again, it will be assigned to me, and I'll remember it. I want you to succeed. Love your child."

With that, the judge quickly left the courtroom. I looked over at the county's table, and the attorney, Ms. Swenson and the chemical dependency witness appeared to be in a state of shock. They must not have been used to losing, because they began to raise their voices, gesticulating to each other and to where the judge had been sitting. I hustled Gloria out to the hallway. But, within a minute, Jackie Swenson approached me.

"We need to talk," she said, pointing to a conference room. As we entered, she confronted me with fury in her face. "All you lawyers care about is winning," she said. "This is about a beautiful child, and you just ruined her life. How do you like that?" I looked at her in blank astonishment. How could she say such a thing?

"My sister and her husband were ready to adopt Gina. They already signed the application. It was all set up. They're successful people and want to be parents. This little girl could have had a great life with them, but thanks to you she'll grow up with that – that loser out there!"

That was it for the case. I quickly moved on to the next project. But, every once in a while, I wondered. Did Gloria stay out of trouble? What happened with Gina?

* * * * * * * *

Twenty-five years later a new client was scheduled to see me about her divorce. It was Gloria. She'd filled out a bit, but she was bright and clean and wearing a sharp business suit. She gave me a big smile and a hug.

"My husband and me are getting divorced," she said. "It's no big deal. We've grown apart but we're still friends, and that.

"I got my GED, then I went to the community college for a year." She was working as an administrative assistant for the chamber of commerce in her small exurban community.

"This time, I can pay you out of my own pocket," she said.

"Let me tell you about Gina. She got her associate degree in law enforcement at Metro State and she's working as a 911 dispatcher until she can afford to finish college. And, guess what? I'm a grandmother!"

Gloria showed me the baby pictures, and then she said, "I really want to thank you for everything you did for me, but there are two things you should know. Remember when you got so mad at me for wearing my jeans to Court?" I did, of course.

"Well, that's all I had to wear - I knew you'd be disappointed but I couldn't help it. And the second thing is that after the case was over I started drinking again. Remember that guy from Court about the AA program? I thought he was sort of a dud, but it turned out he was right. I started going to meetings and I've stayed sober ever since."

She reached into her purse and pulled out her twenty-year AA pin to show me.

"But, most important, I'm happy, and that."

CHAPTER 7

Rats Aweigh!

When you start a business, you'll take anyone who walks in the door. My partner and I, freshly departed from our old firm, had hung up our shingle in eager anticipation of new clients.

They trickled in. Drunk drivers, shoplifters, hopeless bankrupts and low-paying referrals from the legal aid committee. It was depressing.

One day, I got a call from our accountant.

"I recommended you to a business owner we represent. Morey's done well with his pest-control company, but now he's in a fix with the government over some regulations. He's sort of a hot-head. When they sent him a cease-and-desist notice, he told them to go to hell. Now, they've pressed criminal charges against him. "

"Thanks, Roland. It'll be nice to get someone who can pay his bill."

"Oh, I should thank you," he said. "Just a heads-up, though. He's not fond of lawyers. He'll probably try to chisel you on the fees."

The next day, I got a call from Morey Frankman, who set up an appointment later in the week. I was careful to set a time when none of our regular lowlife clients would be around and made sure the waiting area was spruced up for the occasion.

When the day arrived, I walked out to greet Morey. He was in the company of a woman. As we stood and exchanged handshakes, I looked them over.

Morey was not an attractive gentleman. His face was dominated by an expansive forehead, made even more so due to a receding hairline. His eyes were exceptionally wide-set. His nose was long and narrow, and he had pointy ears.

He wore a nameplate that read, "Morey's Exterminating." Although he smiled as he shook hands, it did not look like a natural expression for him.

"I hear you're our local version of *Petrocelli*," he said. He was referring to a then-popular television series depicting a young lawyer who constantly extricated his clients from legal jeopardy.

"I brought my wife Jenny with me. Since the government's trying to destroy our business, she oughtta be in on the conversation."

Jenny was a stunning contrast to Morey. Probably in her late twenties, she was easily a decade younger than he. She had long hazel hair, cerulean-blue eyes, and a killer figure.

It wasn't just how she looked, though. It was how she looked at me. Her gaze went from top to bottom, then back up. She flashed an inviting smile.

"You're so young for a lawyer," she said. "I bet you're just full of energy."

I was momentarily at a loss for words, but quickly recovered, and invited them down the hall to the office.

"What's the government doing to you?"

"You know, they really enjoy picking on us little guys. We've only been around for ten years or so, and we're just getting off the ground. Now their spies are out watching our every move."

I asked about his company.

Morey handed me a brochure. The company logo depicted a muscular sailor – Popeye-like – wielding a sword that has impaled a rat. "Rats aweigh!" it said.

"We started with residential pest control, but the big money is in commercial work. The warehouses and shopping centers have constant issues with bugs and rodents. Our biggest projects have been the hotels. For example, the Radisson South has a serious problem with bats. We've been working with them, but that's where the trouble with the EPA started."

He was referring to the major hotel in the I-494 corridor, just south of the central cities. The Radisson was a twenty-story behemoth of two towers and a giant connecting atrium.

"It never occurred to me that that would be a perfect environment for bats," I said.

"It's not just the bats, either. They've got problems with insects and mice in the rooms, and rats in the kitchen and loading bays. We were knocking them dead until we got hit with these FIFRA violations."

FIFRA? I had no idea what he was talking about. Instead of pretending otherwise, I asked Morey.

"It's the Federal Insecticide, Fungicide, and Rodenticide Act. After the DDT fiasco of the fifties, Congress went crazy and created this list of prohibited substances. Then they set up the EPA. Just like every other governmental agency, the EPA's gone way overboard. They keep adding more illegal pesticides all the time."

He pulled a packet of papers from his briefcase and handed it to me. It was correspondence from the EPA to Morey – mostly warnings to stop the use of diazinon, a prohibited poison. The last document was a criminal complaint, venued in Hennepin County District Court, charging Morey with several violations of FIFRA, each count carrying a maximum sentence of one year in jail and a fine of $1,000.

There also was a government-printed pamphlet that contained the text of the law. The print was tiny. There was an appendix that contained molecular diagrams of chemical substances. I realized that I'd need to learn all of it before we got to court.

While I was going through the paperwork, Morey suddenly rose.

"Excuse me!" He made a quick exit. I assumed it was an urgent bathroom issue. As the door closed, I sensed Jenny's eyes on me.

"So, are you married?"

"Um, yes," I stammered.

"Kids?"

"Yes, three young ones."

"Well, how about that? Wish we had kids."

"I'm sure this legal stuff can be aggravating."

"Morey's just consumed by it. He hardly notices me anymore. I pretty much have to take my clothes off to get his attention."

I was trying to figure out how to respond to this when, fortunately, Morey walked back in.

"How much is this gonna cost me?" he said as he sat.

"My standard retainer fee is $2,500, then I'll bill you when we go over," I said. Actually, I didn't have a standard fee. I'd just picked a number out of the air. It was a step up from what I'd been getting from our normal clients, but probably only a fraction of what an established lawyer would quote.

Morey hesitated before responding. "Okay. Let's settle on $1,500." His nose twitched, a habit of his that I would become used to.

I was glad Roland had prepared me for this. "Sorry, but it's $2,500."

"Sure enough," Morey said, pulling out his checkbook. "You know, I like a man who sticks with his guns."

We discussed the upcoming court hearing.

"Can I come?" Jenny asked.

"Sure. It's open to anyone," I said.

As is typical for such proceedings, the courtroom was packed with lawyers, defendants, police officers, and family members. We were told to wait our turn out in the hallway until the prosecutor was ready for us.

Jenny seemed to be getting bored. "I'm going to take a walk," she said. Meanwhile, Morey and I found some seats and talked about the case.

After a half-hour or so, I noticed that Jenny was back. Instead of returning to us, though, she was chatting it up with three or four young male lawyers. They were clearly enthralled by Jenny, and she was obviously enjoying it.

Morey caught my stare. "That's Jenny for you," he said. "Her very favorite thing in life is to be the center of attention among men, sort of like Scarlett O'Hara at the plantation ball."

"She seems to be devoted to you, though, Morey. She's stuck with you through this."

"She should. When I met her, she was a dancer at a strip bar over in Hudson. I scraped her up off the floor, and now she's living in a nice house. She's got everything she could want. Yeah, she's a flirt, but it's all harmless."

Morey was referring to Hudson, Wisconsin, located just across the St. Croix River from the Twin Cities. In days past, Wisconsin had a lower drinking age than Minnesota, and Hudson was a magnet for young guys looking for action.

A bailiff called Morey's name and escorted us into a small, sterile conference room to meet with the prosecutor, who was a middle-aged, conservatively dressed gentleman. He had an officious air. He pulled Morey's case file out of a large stack.

"I've been looking forward to meeting your client face-to-face, counsel," he said.

He turned to Morey.

"If it wasn't for your big mouth, Mr. Frankman, you probably wouldn't be here." Before I could respond, Morey stood up and announced, "I've gotta step out. Be back in a few minutes."

The prosecutor gave me a puzzled look. "What's with him? Got the scary shits?" He opened his file. "You know how we found out about your client? It was because of a confidential informant."

"Someone who worked for Mr. Frankman?"

"I'm not at liberty to say, but we have photos of his warehouse showing boxes of the diazinon. He even has DDT, believe it or not, but we can't prove he's used it. "

"He bought the diazinon when it was still legal," I said. "He's just been using it until the supply runs out. All his competitors have been doing the same thing."

"I don't know about the competitors, but the rest of that's bullshit," the prosecutor said. "We've got proof that he bought a huge supply of it on the cheap after it had been outlawed. Do you know why the EPA is so serious about this stuff?"

"No, not really."

"Because it causes serious respiratory disease in humans, and that's exactly what's happened to two of your client's former employees. Still, he could've signed a consent decree and settled this civilly. Instead, he called my boss a cocksucker."

After fifteen minutes, Morey returned. I could smell alcohol on him. I couldn't tell if the prosecutor did as well, but he was non-plussed by his absence.

"Thank you for the privilege of your time, Mr. Frankman," he said, sarcastically. "Go to hell!" Morey said. "I suppose you've been having fun, sitting around here making jokes about me."

Morey looked terrible. His face was flushed -- his eyes bloodshot. His attitude, previously docile, was now belligerent. He reminded me of something, but I couldn't put my finger on it.

"You should consider yourself fortunate, Mr. Frankman." the prosecutor said. "If you'd been charged in federal court, there would have been a fifty thousand dollar fine for each count against you. Plead guilty now so you don't end up there."

"Never," Morey snapped back. "You and your pointy-head bureaucrat friends can suck it." He stood up and left again.

The prosecutor responded with a rueful chuckle. "I hope your bill is paid because we're going to trial."

I hadn't even thought about Morey's account. It occurred to me that we'd already burned through the $2,500 retainer fee. I decided to take up the matter when I got back with Morey, but when I found him outside the courtroom, he was with Jenny amid a throng of people.

"How'd it go in there?" Jenny asked. Looking at her next to Morey, I continued to be astounded by the contrast.

"Okay," I answered, noncommittally.

"I'm sorry about Morey," she said. "He's upset, but I told him you're the best." That night, I couldn't sleep. Every time I started to doze off, Morey's face kept appearing. After a few fitful moments of semi-consciousness, I awoke, with a start. I'd seen an apparition. It was a large rat, but Morey, his broad forehead, wide-set eyes, narrow nose and pointed ears was imposed on its face. It looked at me, then twitched its nose. From that moment on, I thought of it whenever I looked at Morey.

* * * * * * *

A month later, we were back at the Government Center for the trial. We really didn't have a defense. Morey wanted to tell the jury that he didn't intend to violate the law because he'd bought the diazinon when it was legal.

It was a lie, of course. I assumed the prosecution would have the confidential informant on hand to prove that. Even if it had been legally purchased, it's use was still illegal. Ignorance of the law was no defense.

The only strategy I could think of was to have his lovely wife sit behind us. Maybe just one juror would hate the government enough to vote not guilty.

It didn't help that Morey wore the same red-faced, angry expression that he'd had when I last saw him in court. He'd been drinking again.

Jenny, however, was a sight for sore eyes. She wore a short, black pencil skirt, with a clingy lavender silk blouse, and matching purple heels.

I stuck my head into the courtroom. One side was filled with potential jurors. The prosecutor was at counsel table, alone. He saw me, and gestured for me to join him.

"Let's grab a room," he said. The arrogant demeanor that I'd observed at our last hearing was missing.

"I'm going to get a continuance," he said, after closing the door.

"Says who?" I responded, with false confidence. "We're ready for trial. What's the deal?"

"It's the EPA. They're using our informant to infiltrate a national pest-control outfit. They don't want his cover blown on our case, so they're asking me to get the judge to continue this for six months."

"You can try, but we're objecting. The jury's already here. You think the judge is going to feel sorry for you?"

"Between you and me, my job is to put drunk drivers and wife beaters in jail. If the EPA really cared about this case, it would be in federal court. Instead, they've got me doing their dirty work, going after small fry like your client. Then they leave me hanging like this. Fuck 'em."

I was getting a warm feeling.

"Tell you what. Plead your guy guilty, and we'll hold off imposing sentence for a year, then we'll dismiss it with prejudice if there's no same or similar."

I couldn't believe our luck. "I'll be right back."

I went out to the hallway to brief Morey about what happened but found Jenny alone. She was sitting with her legs crossed, and greeted me with a nice smile.

"Morey stepped away for a few minutes. So, what's new with you?"

As enjoyable as it might seem, I had too much on my mind to engage in small talk with her. Morey was back in a minute, anyway. The specter of his rat-like face struck me again.

I explained the plea bargain that had been proposed.

"I'm paying you to get me off. Why should I plead guilty?"

"If the judge grants a continuance, which he probably will, you'll be found guilty. With this deal, you can end up with a clean record."

After a half hour of imploring Morey to exercise some common sense, he finally knuckled under. Jenny took my side every time he fought me.

The bailiff informed the judge of the plea deal and the jurors were excused. Morey and I stood before the judge as the prosecutor set out the details of the agreement. While he was doing so, I felt Morey's hand on my arm. He was trembling.

After going through his rights, the judge addressed Morey directly. "Mr. Frankman, will you plead guilty to the use of a controlled substance in violation of federal and state law?"

"Yes, I will," Morey responded softly.

The judge proceeded to describe in detail the terms of the sentence that Morey would receive if he violated the agreement, including incarceration of up to a year. As he did so, Morey's grip on my arm strengthened. Was my big-talking client going to pass out?

"What is your plea?"

"Guilty, your honor."

The judge stood, ready to go. But then he looked at Morey. "Are you all right, sir?

"Yes," Morey said meekly.

I was perplexed. What was that all about?

Then I smelled something pungent. As the judge left, I turned to Morey. The entire left leg of his slacks was drenching wet, and there was a puddle around his shoe.

* * * * * * *

I never saw Morey again. We got paid, but only after threatening to turn his bill over to a collection agency.

I heard from Jenny, though. About six months after our last court appearance, she called me.

"Can you be my divorce lawyer?"

"Sorry, I can't. What happened?"

"It's his drinking. It's his temper. And, to tell you the truth, I've met someone else."

How many "someone else's" there had been? I wondered.

"How's his company doing?" I asked.

"Oh, that. They caught him using that stuff again, but this time it's the feds. They're serious."

CHAPTER 8

Afternoon Justice

Thanks to some good fortune and the fact that my father knew the local military commander, the Army decided to let me enlist in the Reserves instead of shipping me off to Vietnam. The only requirement was that I stay in school continuously. To take a break meant getting drafted. The consequence of this was that I finished law school and got admitted to practice at the age of twenty-four.

My first boss was friends with Monsignor Riesling, who commanded the largest congregation in the county. His parishioners, or their children, often needed legal assistance, so he was a pipeline of business for the firm. The downside of the deal was that the we had to take every case he sent over, which meant someone got the dregs -- usually, me.

Ed was a scruffy fellow who smelled like he needed a shower. He had unruly hair and crazy eyes. When he walked into the office, he was wearing a cap that looked like it was glued to his head, and sporting a dirty T-shirt which read, "Drink till she's cute."

It was Ed's third DUI. This time he'd be headed to the county jail for a lengthy stretch. He was scared to death at the prospect.

"I watch the news. It's easy to beat the rap on these cases. You can get me out of this, right? My grandma's gonna' pay you."

Getting the bill paid outweighed my common sense. Not thinking of the consequences, I responded, "We'll fight this all the way. Take it to the jury, if they don't throw it out."

My bravado was ill-considered. To date, I had had exactly one jury trial. Which I had lost.

With modern technology, drunk driving cases like Ed's are usually signed, sealed and delivered by the time a client hires a defense lawyer. Years ago, criminal cases were tried primarily on the testimony of the policeman. A good defense lawyer could sway a jury, convincing them that the evidence consisted only of the opinion of the officer, without objective proof.

Nowadays, probable cause for the traffic stop has been recorded by dashboard video. There's often a certified breathalyzer analysis and another video of the defendant flunking the roadside coordination exercises, or making a fool of himself back at the police station.

I tried in vain to get the prosecutor in Ed's case to reduce the charges.

"Three-time offender? No way," was all he'd say. He'd declared his candidacy for the district attorney's job, so being a hard-ass was a winning political strategy.

Our case was scheduled to be tried in front of the Honorable Joseph Warfield. The judge was popular in established circles for his financial support of local charities. Whitehaired and rotund, he looked the part of the learned judge, but he was actually a crude bully. Lawyers knew not to schedule their hearings with him in the afternoon. He took long, liquid lunches with his business associates, and when he got back, he was mean. On the morning of the trial Ed showed up on time. He was wearing presentable -- if not stylish -- khaki pants, but his shaky hands and nervous demeanor belied a long night of drinking.

John, Judge Warfield's court reporter, entered the room. He pointed to the prosecutor and me. "Come back to chambers to meet with the judge."

I should explain about court reporters. They're actually stenographers, and each judge has his or her own. They also act as unofficial liaisons between the judge and the lawyers. It's smart to stay on good terms with these people. Some lawyers send them an annual Christmas gift. A court reporter will often return the favor with inside information. What is the judge thinking about your client? What annoys the judge, or what does he like? John was both a friend and a reliable source for me.

Judge Warfield liked to do business in his office, where he could smoke his Camels, swear, and expound his racist theories. "What have you clowns got for me today?" he asked.

After the prosecutor had given him the policeman's version of the case, the judge turned to me. "Well, counselor, sounds like your man's headed to the crowbar hotel. Hope he brought his toothbrush."

"Presumed innocent," I responded. "He's already lost his job. If you stick him in jail, he won't be able to get another one. Can't we get a break?"

"Tell him that in my dictionary, sympathy's right between shit and syphilis," he said. "If he wants to get out of jail in time for Christmas, he'd better plead guilty. If he puts us through a trial, he gets the max."

I blurted out, quite imprudently, "I'll try my own case, thank you."

Instead of the explosion I expected, Judge Warfield seemed puzzled, even impressed, by my defiance. "Well, let's get started then."

Jury selection was the first event. When it was my turn to question the potential jurors, my inexperience became obvious. A pleasant looking middle-aged woman's number came up, and I started off by asking her, "So, are you a housewife or do you have a job?"

Even the judge's cranky disposition was broken by this mistake. He chuckled, "Counsel, did you think before you said that?"

The courtroom, including the twenty or so potential jurors watching the show, broke into laughter. Trying to be the good sport, I joined in, but my heart sank.

Once the actual trial started, things got worse. The arresting officer, a handsome, square-jawed young man, laid out the facts.

It was 1:00 a.m. at the Boat House bar. The establishment was located next to the bridge over the Mississippi River. The officer was parked nearby, looking for possible drunk drivers. He spotted Ed staggering to his car, urinating in the parking lot, then peeling out, burning rubber. As Ed drove over the bridge, his car crossed over the center line four times, almost colliding with another vehicle. When the officer was finally able to stop him, Ed stumbled out of the vehicle. He flunked the straight-line walking test and couldn't get beyond "Y" in reciting the alphabet backwards. When asked how much he had had to drink, Ed said, "Maybe five beers." What's worse, he blew a .18 on the breathalyzer, over twice the legal limit.

I cautiously peeked at the jurors. They were looking Ed over, and not in a friendly manner.

By the time the policeman was done, the judge called the noon break. The court reporter, John, and I headed to the nearby Smuggler's Inn – a hangout of the legal and business community. It was dimly lit, with thick carpet, leather-padded booths and dark, textured wallpaper. A pall of cigarette smoke hung in the air. If you had been there for a couple of hours, perhaps enjoying a few drinks, you'd be rudely awakened by the light of day as you left.

Judge Warfield was seated with three other men. "Business cronies," John told me. "They're all partners in a shopping center development."

In the company of his fellow capitalists the judge was quite jovial. It looked like they were daily customers, since a round of martinis was already set out at their table. Soon enough they were calling the comely young cocktail waitress for another. What these old farts thought they had to gain by flirting with her was beyond me, but I didn't begrudge her for trying to get a tip out of them.

John and I refrained from imbibing, and instead talked about the ongoing trial.

"It's a long-shot, but maybe you could try the venue defense."

The venue defense says that the police officer is beyond his proper jurisdiction. When Ed entered a different county by driving over the Mississippi River, the officer didn't have the power to arrest.

It's a bullshit defense, a meaningless technicality -- like saying the defendant should get off a murder rap because someone spelled his middle name wrong on the indictment. In a case like Ed's, there's an exception when the offender purposely crosses the county line to flee arrest.

"Give it a try," John said with a wink. "When you've got nothing – you've got nothing to lose," quoting the Janis Joplin song.

I finished lunch quickly in order to get to the law library and research the venue issue. Before leaving I took one last look at the judge's table. The waitress had returned with yet another round of martinis.

At the library, I discovered that the boundary between the two counties was the center of the channel of the Mississippi River. Armed with this information, I returned to the courtroom, anxious to try out my last-ditch strategy.

Ed was already sitting at the table. I noticed his hands had stopped shaking, and I could immediately tell why. He'd been back at the Boat House again.

This happens frequently with guilty parties. "I'm going to jail anyway, so why not feel good when they lock me up?"

I should have had a mint for Ed, and vowed to thereafter always keep a supply available in my briefcase. "Don't breathe on anyone," I told him.

The jury filed in. They were staring at Ed. Finally, Judge Warfield entered. His face was florid, quite a contrast with his white hair. His doughy nose had a purplish tinge. As the prosecutor rattled on, I watched the judge, wondering how long our insignificant drunk driving case was going to keep him awake.

When my turn to cross-examine the police officer came, I didn't waste any time.

"Officer, what's the boundary between Hennepin and Anoka County?"

"The bridge?" His eyebrows raised as his voice wavered.

"What if I told you it was the center of the channel of the Mississippi river, and that you had passed beyond your jurisdiction?" I showed him the relevant provision from the statute book.

The officer gave me a bewildered look, but Judge Warfield was on it before he could offer a response.

"Counsel, to the bench!" he bellowed.

Lowering his voice to avoid the ears of the jury, he whispered, "Okay, Jeff." Suddenly I was on a first-name basis with him. "You've muddied the waters. I'm going to dismiss the case."

"Wait a minute!" the prosecutor blurted. "You can't do that – I object!"

"You can object all day," the judge snarled, "but you'll be doing it in the jailhouse after I find you in contempt."

Turning to the jury, the judge said, "Who's the foreman?"

A gentleman rose, looking mystified.

"The court reporter is going to bring you a verdict form finding the defendant guilty of speeding. Sign it."

John walked up to the foreman and handed him the document, giving me a surreptitious wink. I glanced at the policeman. He was livid.

Turning to Ed, Judge Warfield said, "It's a fifty-dollar fine if you pay it today." That was the end of the trial, if you want to call it a trial. After the judge and the jury departed, Ed turned to me, grasping and pumping my hand.

"Wow, you did a great job!" he said. "Do you have some business cards on you? I've got lots of friends."

Off he went, probably right back to the Boat House to brag about his good fortune. For a long time thereafter, I'd get calls from more losers with their DUIs. They were Ed's buddies. Mostly low-lives who couldn't afford to pay me, but enough of them were good for it that my cash flow impressed the boss.

A week after the trial, the receptionist buzzed me, "It's Judge Warfield on the phone for you."

"Hello, Jeff," he said. "I was impressed with how you handled that trial last week. Could you meet with me tomorrow at the Smuggler's Inn? I have a matter I need a little help with."

CHAPTER 9

The Long Road from Buffalo

Fran's client questionnaire said she was forty, but she looked closer to fifty. Her salt-and-pepper hair was in a bun, her complexion a gray pallor. Her face sagged, which made for a hollow-eyed appearance. Fran rose as I approached, and forced a smile.

I greeted her, inviting her back to the office.

"Guess I'd better," was her curt response.

As she settled in, an image flashed in my mind. It was from those photos you see in Time-Life books of women during the Depression. Fran could have been a character in *The Grapes of Wrath*.

"How can we help you?"

"I wasn't always like this," she said. "I was a strong woman. Grew up on a farm. Raised two kids when I was still a teenager. Now, this."

She reached into her purse and passed me some papers. It was an OFP (Order for Protection), together with her supporting affidavit. The order was against her husband, Norbert Bleeker.

The case was venued in Wright County, Minnesota, of which the county seat is Buffalo, located out on the western edge of the judicial district. Back in those days, the urban sprawl had yet to take over. It was like Buffalo was halfway to North Dakota.

"You started the case yourself?"

"The gals at the shelter helped me. They said I need a lawyer for the first hearing. Norb controls all our money, so they staked me the retainer fee."

The hearing was scheduled for the following week. Fran had an *Ex Parte* OFP, which a judge will sign if there is an immediate danger. She had recorded a phone call from Norbert, in which he threatened, "Get off my fucking back, or I'll get you before the cancer does."

The drawback of the *Ex Parte* process is that the order is issued before the adverse party gets to tell his side of the story. Due process requires an accelerated hearing so each party can be heard.

I wasn't surprised by the cancer reference, because in our questionnaire we ask about health status. Fran had written, "Not good. Will be discussed."

"Let's talk about the big picture, Fran. If we prevail in this hearing, the judge could continue the order for up to a year, and we could get financial support for you. Is that what you want, or do you think your difficulties with Norbert could be patched up?"

She rolled her eyes. "Patched up? I wouldn't take him back in a hundred years. Got himself shacked up with that skank down the street!"

"What happened?"

"Long story short, it goes back to my diagnosis last year. It's cancer of the uterus, one of the worst kinds. He was supportive at first. Went to my appointments with me." Fran's eyes were misting up, so I passed her the Kleenex box.

"I had to have female surgery, then chemo and radiation. It dragged me down, really down, but Norb couldn't wait for me to recover. He wants sex. I'm just not able."

"Of course not. Then he threatened you?"

"It wasn't the first time he did that. Last month, he cleaned me out of my meds and said that I'd get them back when he got a blow job. He backed down, but then he took up with Rosie."

"Who's Rosie?"

Fran's face reddened. "The town whore, that's who. Rosie Deschanes. She hangs out at the Buffalo House Bar. Gives it up to any guy who asks. Norb decided it was his turn, so that's where he headed. Funny thing, he's decided they're in love, even though he knows her history."

"He's with her now?" Our noisy air conditioning blower clicked on as I asked. "Norb tells people he's living with his brother across town, but I know better. His car's parked in her driveway every night, three houses down my block."

"So, you want to go for a permanent order?"

"I suppose. Nothing's for sure with me anymore. I'm going to get my post-chemo results Friday."

* * * * * * *

After Fran left, I met with my assistant to put together a financial analysis for the judge. Fran was unemployed and would need spousal support. Norb had a decent job with the highway department, so he could afford to pay.

Fran called late Friday morning.

"I thought I should give you an update. The test says I'm stage four. They're recommending another round of chemo, but it's up to me whether to take it. As far as I can tell, they can't really do anything that'll help. Don't know if I want to prolong it."

I couldn't think of a way to respond, so I gave her a brief pep talk. "You don't deserve this, Fran. We'll go to bat for you."

"All right then, do the best you can."

An hour later, a call came from another lawyer in town, Bill Daby. "I'll be representing Norbert Bleeker next week at the OFP hearing. Want to meet for coffee and talk about it?"

Bill had opened a solo practice the previous year. Most of the lawyers in town were older and well-established, and he had felt shunned by some of them. I was a young lawyer myself and knew what he was going through, and had been able to steer a few clients to him when my firm had a conflict.

We met the following Monday at a local café. I wasn't about to mince words about his client. I updated him on Fran's most recent diagnosis.

"Bill, I like you, but this guy is the biggest jerk I've come across in my career. I'm going after him."

"That's harsh. He's been through a lot with this cancer thing, too. He admits he lost his cool during that phone call, and he'll apologize for it. Why don't we continue the case and have them do some counseling?"

"Did he tell you he was screwing the neighbor woman?"

Bill didn't know, so I passed on the whole story.

"I'll take it up with him," Bill said. "I believe in the Sixth Commandment, and this is a serious transgression. But, as they say, 'Hate the sin – love the sinner.'"

Bill was a PK – a preacher's kid. Although he had long hair, dressed modishly, and enjoyed quaffing cocktails at bar association events, he was quite traditional. We were discussing politics once, and he said, "I would never allow my wife to have an abortion." We concluded our meeting on friendly terms, but without a resolution. As we parted Bill said, "It's a long drive over to Buffalo. Let's carpool. I'll pick you up." Sure, I thought. Why not?

* * * * * * *

As planned, Bill stopped by my office early Wednesday morning. I was able to enjoy the countryside as Bill drove. After a few miles, we were free of the suburban traffic, cruising along country roads. The terrain became rolling, dotted with small bodies of water, what the locals call "pothole lakes." It was late May, just after the fishing opener, so lots of boats were in the water. As we approached Buffalo, we saw the old stucco courthouse, the tallest building in town.

"I've never been here. Do you know anything about the judges?" Bill asked.

"Couple of old Norskies," I said. "One's Olson, and the other's Swenson.

* * * * * * *

Once inside, Bill and I climbed the rickety stairs to the main courtroom. The sign on the door announced, "Judge Swenson, presiding." I saw Fran at one end of the hallway. A man down at the other end, who must have been Norbert Bleeker, waved to Bill. Shortly thereafter, a bailiff emerged from the courtroom, summoning us in.

As we sat at our respective counsel tables, I got my first good look at Norb. He was balding but sported a scraggly, unwashed ponytail. His smile revealed missing teeth, and the survivors were a moldy yellow. He wore a suit, but it must have dated from years earlier since his soft belly flowed over a too-tight waist.

The bailiff cleared his throat and stood. "All rise for the Honorable Glenn W. Swenson." A door opened, and the judge lumbered in, a cane in one hand and some files in the other.

"I've read the petition," he growled as he finally sat at the podium. "Let's get on with it. Counsel for the Petitioner?"

I called Fran to the witness stand. She shuffled over, her gait almost as halting as Judge Swenson's. I asked her to relate Norb's threats. She eventually got to Norb's withholding of her medications, but at the mention of the word "blowjob" the judge pounded his gavel.

"Stop there, young lady. Respect the dignity of these proceedings."

An uncomfortable pause followed, finally broken by the judge. "You will refer to this as 'the sex act.'"

I caught Bill's eye as he said it. We exchanged subtle smiles.

Despite his admonition, I sensed that Judge Swenson was on our side, so I went for the kill.

"Mrs. Bleeker, has your husband kept his distance from you since the *ex-Parte* Order?"

"No. He set up housekeeping with the neighbor lady, Rosie Deschanes."

The judge perked up with sudden recognition. He lowered his eyeglasses and looked at Fran. "Rosie Deschanes?"

Fran nodded.

I was finished with Fran, and it was time for Bill's cross-examination. Before he could get out a word, Judge Swenson pointed to Norb. "The bailiff will swear you in. Sit there." He gestured to the witness stand.

Bill rose to object, but the judge banged the gavel again. "I'm in charge here," he barked. Once Norb was seated, the judge stared at him. "Explain yourself, sir."

It would have been the time for contrition, but an apology wasn't in Norb's frame of reference. "The blowjob? Op, I mean the sex act." Norb smiled as if he had made a joke, but all he got from Judge Swenson was silence.

"Well, your Honor, I didn't think it was too much to ask. She hadn't been a wife to me for five months. You know, I could've demanded more."

The judge maintained his silence but nodded to Bill for follow-up.

Bill did his best to rehabilitate Norb with some leading questions.

"Now Mr. Bleeker, you've been a good husband to your wife, isn't that true?"

"Yes, sir."

"And you stayed at your wife's side through sickness and health, correct?"

All Norb had to do was answer with a simple yes, but he was too dense to get it.

"That's right, except it's taking forever."

Bill knew when it was time to surrender. "No further questions, your Honor."

Judge Swenson announced a recess. "When we return, I'll hear counsel's arguments on what order I should make."

* * * * * * *

Twenty minutes later, we resumed. I was full of righteous indignation and could sense Judge Swenson was on the same page. It was time to make Norb pay.

"Your Honor, we propose a one-year order restraining Mr. Bleeker from any contact with my client. She should have exclusive use of the home and the contents thereof."

Judge Swenson nodded, "And what about the matter of support?"

"The financial report we submitted shows that Respondent has a net monthly income of three thousand dollars. My client has none, and with her health, no prospects. In light of the heinous nature of Mr. Bleeker's acts, we propose support of twenty-five hundred per month."

The judge nodded again. "That's interesting, counsel, I had the same number in mind. So ordered."

Bill leapt to his feet. "Your Honor, we haven't even been heard yet. You're taking eighty-five percent of my client's income!"

"That's what I meant to do, counsel," Judge Swenson said. He grabbed his cane and tottered out of the courtroom.

I quickly ushered Fran out. It's what you do when you're winning. "Go home,

Fran. I'll get a deputy to deliver the written order to you."

"You don't think Norb's going to be too angry?"

"Sure, he'll be upset. He got what he deserved." I expected a smile, or even a thank you, but Fran just turned around and left.

Bill and Norb were at the other end of the hallway. Norb was yelling at Bill, stabbing his finger in his chest. There was a torrent of four-letter words, loud enough for everyone to hear.

* * * * * * *

I decided to leave the building and wait by Bill's car. After what must have been ten minutes he approached with a hang-dog expression on his face, avoiding my gaze.

"Let's get out of here," he said.

There was silence for the first several miles of the trip. By then, it was late morning, and the fisherman had mostly pulled their boats out of the lakes. The walleye bite vanishes when the sun is high.

The tension in the air played havoc with the pleasant view. Finally, Bill broke the silence.

"You really took us to the cleaners, man. Eighty-five percent? What did I do wrong?"

I couldn't help feeling smug. "I've learned to be more aggressive with these judges. Don't just sit there and take it, Bill. Couldn't you see I had that old fossil eating out of my hand?"

More silence ensued, as Bill lapsed back into his funk. I tried changing the subject to the Vikings' upcoming game against the Bears, but it was like Bill hadn't heard me. "When I graduated from college, my dad lined up a fellowship for me at divinity school. He wanted me to take over his church when he retired. I wouldn't have it. I had to go to law school. My client fired me, and he stopped payment on his retainer check."

"Then sue him. Hell, I'll represent you."

Bill shook his head. "I don't know if I'm cut out for this."

At last, Bill dropped me off at my office. The forty-five-minute drive had seemed more like two hours, but I was still feeling pretty good about myself.

* * * * * * * *

A week later I got a call from Fran. "I've decided to switch lawyers."

"Switch lawyers?" I was incredulous.

"Things just went too far in that hearing. I know you wanted to punish my husband, but I didn't want to ruin his life. I hired an experienced attorney here in Buffalo. He settled everything with Norb in a couple of hours."

* * * * * * * *

The next month, I ran into Bill before a bar association meeting. He was sitting alone at a table with two Manhattans in front of him. One was almost empty.

"How'd things work out with your case in Buffalo?" he asked.

"It's not my case anymore," I confessed, and went on to tell him what had transpired with Fran and Norb.

He looked up with a whimsical smile. "Guess we've both got a few things to learn."

CHAPTER 10

"In the Best Interests"

In 2018, 2.7 million grandparents were engaged in raising their grandchildren, a number that has increased by 7% since 2009. Reasons normally cited are the increasing amounts of men and women who are incarcerated or with drug or mental health issues. Even military deployments can be a factor.

You'd think that laws would be changing so as to accommodate this trend, which provides a safety net for millions of needy children. In fact, the legal system seems to be fighting it. Troxel v. Granville, decided by our Supreme Court in 2000, created the "superior rights" doctrine. This says that -- except in the worst cases - efforts by grandparents to intercede in the relationship between children and their biological parents should be denied.

"My clients are quality people," my lawyer friend Gus said over the phone. He's from a small county-seat community an hour from the Cities, one of those towns struggling to maintain an identity separate from the rapidly-approaching exurbs.

"They're fighting with their daughter over the two grandkids – Joey and Jamarr. The custody study isn't going well. The trial's in the Cities. I hate going to court there.

Think you could help us out?"

"Sure, Gus," I said. "Sounds like they're good for the fees, too, right?"

"Of course," Gus said. "Ralph Johansen owns the biggest farm implement business in the area, and he's on the board of one of our local banks. His wife Emily is an assistant principal and the girl's junior varsity basketball coach."

By the next day I had the file. It was well-documented -- a good thing since the trial was only three weeks away.

The custody evaluation had been submitted the previous week by Joyce Steiner, MSW, the social worker appointed by the judge. I didn't know her, but her competence was obvious as I read through her summary.

Joey was nine and Jamarr was seven. Lexi was twenty-nine. She had a checkered history, having lived at multiple addresses over the lifetimes of the boys. The boys themselves had separate fathers. Joey's father, an undocumented Mexican immigrant, had been imprisoned and ultimately deported when Joey was only two years old. Jamarr's situation was different. Lexi refused to identify his father for the evaluation, and his name wasn't on Jamarr's birth certificate, but Lexi implied that he was part of his son's life.

Lexi was afflicted with addiction and mental health issues. Alcohol and more serious drugs – including meth – had led to multiple treatment programs, both voluntary and via the commitment route. She also had had a succession of relationships with men – some of them abusive.

Ms. Steiner reported that, during the preceding three years, the boys had lived primarily with Ralph and Emily, attending school in their community. On an irregular basis their daughter Lexi would appear, unannounced, and take them to her home in the city. Days or weeks later, she would re-appear at her parent's home, dropping them off, without explanation.

Lexi claimed sobriety for almost a year and had passed two unannounced urinalyses, the most recent of which was about two months before the report. She had also acquired employment at a furniture rental company near her apartment, which was located in a somewhat sketchy part of the city. Lexi had indicated her intention to move to

California with the boys, which triggered Ralph and Emily's petition for grandparent custody.

Ralph and Emily, Ms. Steiner correctly observed, did not qualify as "*de facto*" parents of their grandsons, which would have placed them on a more or less equal footing with Lexi. To qualify as "*de facto*" parents, Ralph and Emily needed to have continuous residency with their grandchildren for an extended period of time, with their daughter's consent. Instead, Ralph and Emily were "interested third parties," which meant that, even if it was in the "best interests" of the children to live with them, they had to establish that the boys were "endangered" if they remained with Lexi. It was a difficult burden of proof.

The report concluded that although Joey and Jamarr's home with their grandparents was the most stable and secure place for them, there was insufficient evidence of endangerment to them to justify overcoming the so-called "superior rights" of their mother. In her cover letter Ms. Steiner stated, "This is a preliminary conclusion. We await the completion of background investigations and any new evidence."

The following day I had my first meeting with Ralph and Emily. Emily's athletic build and graceful gait made her appear ten years younger than her age of fifty-four. She wore a smart beige suit with a rose-colored scarf, and flashed a toothy smile as she was introduced by her husband.

Ralph was a handsome guy. Attired in a blue sports jacket and khaki slacks, he had curly salt-and-pepper hair and a ruddy complexion. His expansive stomach didn't deter from his looks. In older times, men would point to their tummies and refer to them as their "corporation," the girth being emblematic of success. I could picture Ralph doing that.

"The custody report says that we give our boys a better home, but somehow that isn't as important as Lexi being the biological parent," Emily said. "I thought this was about the best interests of the child."

"Is there any middle ground?" I asked. "Maybe we could achieve a compromise that works for everyone."

"I don't think so," Emily said. "Lexi . . ." She stopped, tears brimming in her eyes.

Ralph sensed her distress, and he gently took her hand, which seemed to help.

"She was a beautiful child," Emily continued. "We doted on her. She was smart, too. Then about junior high school age, she started lying about things and rebelling. By the time she was in high school, she was totally defiant. We never knew where she was staying or even if she was going to school."

Ralph jumped into the conversation. "Then she got mixed up with this Carlos guy. We tried to be nice to him but he was bad news all the way. He got her pregnant with Joey. Then the cops nailed him for selling drugs and deported him to Mexico. Joey was only two when it happened."

"And she didn't tell that social worker the truth about Jamarr." Emily said. "His father's married and has his own family. He gives Lexi money under the table, so the status quo's okay with her. She covers up for him. He's an okay guy – I've met him -- but Jamarr thinks his dad's just some special friend who drops by every once in a while. "

"I've got to be honest with you," Emily said. "They love their mother even though they're starting to figure out what her problems are. It kills me that they see their role as her defenders."

Ralph was getting steamed up. "Another thing. It makes me mad that this social worker – Ms. Steiner – says it's better for the boys to live in the Cities because they're mixed race."

"The custody law gives preference to the 'cultural and ethnic background of the child' and the ability of the parent to raise the child in their 'community,'" I explained.

"But our home is their community!" Ralph said. "Our town's changed a lot in my lifetime." He chuckled, "It used to be that you were either a Swede or a Norwegian. Now we've got a big turkey processing plant in town, and we've got Latinos, Chinese, you name it out there. They even have Spanish-language services at the Catholic Church. We've done everything we can to make people feel welcome. Besides, we need them to stay viable – too many of our own kids leave town for the Cities."

"And Jamarr's not the only African-American kid at his school," Emily said. "I bet there are at least ten. I've got three black girls on the Jayvee basketball team. We've always loved these boys like our own. We don't care what color they are."

"The social worker's completing her background checks on everyone. Is there anything I have to worry about from our side?" I asked.

"Certainly not!" Emily said, shaking her head. But our eyes didn't meet, arousing my suspicion. Denial happens a lot in family law.

About a week before the trial, I returned to my office from a court hearing. My assistant saw me walking by, and said, "Ralph Johansen is on his way. He said it's urgent."

Within a few minutes, Ralph was sitting in my office. When he reached into his jacket pocket, I noticed that his shirt was stained with sweat. He handed over a wad of papers, which appeared to have been folded over numerous times. It was a faxed letter from Joyce Steiner, accompanied by a police report.

"Dear Mr. Johansen," the letter said, "The enclosed report was received in connection with the background check I am doing for the custody evaluation. Please review and respond. It will be necessary to include this in my evaluation."

It was a report from the Minneapolis Park Police Department:

I, Officer David Small, was on routine patrol at 2200 hours in Theodore Wirth Park when I observed a late-model Cadillac parked in an area we had been patrolling because of suspected drug activity. I approached the vehicle with my flashlight and observed a partially clothed man and woman engaged in a sex act. I requested that the male, who was in the driver's seat, exit the vehicle. He identified himself as Ralph Johansen, age 61. The woman (name redacted) was identified as age 28. I could detect the odor of an alcoholic beverage emanating from Johansen's breath and requested that he undergo a breath test, which resulted in a BAC (blood alcohol content) of .09%. Since the female was a licensed driver and appeared to be sober, I issued Johansen a citation for DUI over .08% and released Johansen to her. Also, since there were people in the vicinity, I issued both parties citations for indecent exposure.

You've got plenty of money, Ralph, I thought to myself. Couldn't you have paid for a motel room?

Since it had been six months, I asked Ralph what happened to his case.

"I hired this criminal defense lawyer in the Cities," Ralph said. "He told me that we should push it to trial because my reading on the breathalyzer was just barely over and I wasn't driving, plus the prosecutors were overwhelmed there. He was right. We showed up for trial and the prosecutor had ten cases set for trial, so he dismissed the DUI and the indecent exposure. I pled guilty to disorderly conduct, and I just got a fine. Emily doesn't know anything, but it gets put in this report, I'm screwed."

"Look," I said, "I know it's tough, but maybe you should tell Emily yourself. Say you just got drunk and you're sorry."

"Are you kidding?" he said. "Emily caught me with the same gal before, about three years ago. She said if I didn't stay away from her, she'd divorce me for sure. Can we talk to this social worker? Maybe you can convince her to make it go away.

I called Ms. Steiner. "This isn't really relevant," I said. "It doesn't involve the kids, and you know from the chemical dependency evaluations that he's not an alcoholic."

"That's not the point," she said. "It's my ethical duty to treat them all equally. If I had the same information on Lexi it would be in my report, too. Sorry."

I called Ralph back and broke him the bad news.

"Then we'll drop the case. I'll tell Emily that we had a setback at work and we lost a lot of money and can't afford it."

"What about the kids? They'll get moved to California."

"Yeah. That'd break my heart. But if Emily finds out, I'm ruined. I'll lose everything – her, my money, my business. Look, maybe I can talk to this woman, Ms. Steiner. Could I offer her something, do you think?"

"You mean a bribe? I'm going to forget you just said that." I let it settle in for a minute, then said, "I don't care if you talk to her. You can beg her. You can charm her. But no money or I'm out."

A couple of days later, I got a call from Joyce Steiner.

"Counsel," she said, "I've changed my mind. I hate this anti-grandparent law. It's bad enough that these kids might have to go with their mom. I don't want to make it worse by breaking up a marriage. I'm going to keep Ralph's arrest out of my report." I wondered what Ralph had said or done, but I wasn't going to look a gift horse in the mouth.

A week later the trial started. As I was walking over to the courthouse with my assistant, I saw Lexi getting out of her car. She was her mother's daughter, for sure -- pretty and athletic -- dressed provocatively, but not indecently.

Two things stood out. The first was an expansive tattoo of a dragon, which started on her shoulder, extended under her dress through regions unknown, then continued on to her lower leg. The second was her bright orange hair. She was finishing a cigarette, which she threw, unextinguished, on the grass in the median.

In the courtroom, I sat at the counsel table with Ralph and Emily. Joyce Steiner was several rows behind -- in a neutral corner, as they say.

Lexi entered with her lawyer, who was an angry-looking younger woman. Lexi locked eyes momentarily with Emily, shooting her a nasty smirk.

The judge took control immediately. "Counsel and parties, I've read the custody evaluation, so Ms. Steiner can testify last, if necessary. First, I would like to hear from the mother. Then we can proceed with the grandparent's case."

Lexi took the stand. Her lawyer led her through the case, putting the best spin possible on Lexi's tortured past.

"Yes," Lexi said, "I've made mistakes." She looked directly at her parents. "But I'm not the only one."

Did she know about Ralph? I wondered.

She went on to blame Ralph and Emily for the estrangement. "They were verbally abusive when I was young," she said. "They never accepted Joey and Jamarr into their lily-white home. I need to get away from their constant interference in my life – to California, where we can have a fresh start.

I noticed as her testimony continued that she was getting increasingly fidgety – even flushed.

Finally, her lawyer asked, "Ms. Johansen, have you been clean and sober, and if so for how long? Have you been law-abiding?"

"Yes," she said. "Sober for almost a year, and I haven't been convicted of anything for two years."

Her response made me suspicious. Why had she said the word "convicted" instead of simply answering her lawyer's question as to whether she'd been 'law abiding"? A person can be charged before being convicted.

I was ready for cross-examination, but Lexi asked for a second with her lawyer first. After a few whispered moments, the lawyer said, "My client's feeling ill. Can we have twenty minutes?"

During the break, I walked over to the window overlooking where Lexi's car was parked. She was walking quickly toward it. I couldn't see what she was doing inside the car except that there seemed to be a lot of movement.

How to proceed? I wondered.

As I've said many times, a lawyer never asks a question unless he already knows the answer. Was this an ambush? Were Lexi and her lawyer waiting for me to accuse her of lying about her record so they could throw it back to me that they knew about Ralph and his escapade?

On the other hand, we stood to lose the case without something dramatic, and Lexi had made me suspicious with her equivocal answer.

After the recess, Lexi resumed her position on the witness chair. The fidgeting was gone. She appeared confident and ready for me. I wished I'd had more time, but plunged ahead anyway.

"Ms. Johansen," I said, "you may not have been convicted yet, but you're under charges, aren't you?"

"Objection!" her lawyer said. "She's presumed innocent even if she's under charges."

"Now, wait a minute, counsel," the judge said to Lexi's lawyer. "This is a civil trial. She may be presumed innocent in criminal court, but I'm trying to decide about the best interests of these children. Now, tell me what happened."

I cringed internally at the judge's comment, wondering what he would say to me if he found I was concealing Ralph's story.

"Well, if you must know," Lexi's lawyer said, "she's under federal indictment for distribution of methamphetamine. Her defense is that her boyfriend was the perpetrator, and she was just an innocent bystander."

"Your Honor," I said. "I request that you order Ms. Johansen to undergo a urinalysis immediately. I believe she might have been using during the break."

"I wouldn't do that normally," the judge said, "but based on her deception I will grant that request. Bailiff, escort her to the Sheriff's Department and get her tested." Lexi's lawyer glared at me, then at the judge.

Lexi tested positive for meth, which ended our trial. The judge awarded permanent custody to Ralph and Emily.

Lexi did a plea bargain in federal court for delivery of methamphetamine and served a year and a day at the Women's Correctional Institute in Shakopee. Then she was placed on probation for ten years.

She never made it to California.

Eventually, curiosity got the best of me, and I called Ralph.

"How'd you ever talk Joyce Steiner out of putting the arrest report in her evaluation?"

"It wasn't me who called her. It was Emily. I figured the news would get out eventually, so I fessed up to Emily about it. She thought Ms. Steiner would be more likely to listen to her than me."

"You said she was going to divorce you for sure."

"She decided the best interests of the kids come before anything else. Though, to be honest, I had to sleep on the couch for months."

Joey and Jamarr? They're happily living with their grandparents in a small town in Minnesota.

CHAPTER 11

A Sure Bet

It was 1982, but her style harkened back to the sixties. Instead of the popular high waisted pantsuit, she had chosen a black skirt with a revealing slit. Fish-net stockings. A deep-neck purple blouse. Her black hair was long and swept over a shoulder, reminiscent of the hippie-style ironed look. She was probably in her late thirties, although she had striven for a younger appearance. Roni Weiss, her intake slip read.

As she took her seat, Roni reached to place her large purse on the chair next to her but missed. The contents fell to the floor. A half-empty pack of Virginia Slims, a wire hairbrush in need of a cleaning, a disk of birth-control pills.

"My God. I'm so nervous," she said.

I moved to the scene of the accident to help, but she waved me away and blocked my view, as if to erase the revealing clues that had spilled.

"Don't feel bad," I said. "Our clients come to us in stressful situations."

"You're right. I'm totally stressed, and this is embarrassing. I thought I was done with my ex. But, since my divorce, my friends have been telling me I got screwed, so I thought maybe someone could help me make it right." She handed me her divorce decree. At first glance, it seemed she was right. Her ex-husband, Marc, had received a settlement of almost a half-million dollars, whereas Roni got only a hundred-fifty thousand. Still, she'd had a good lawyer, and the judge who decided the case was highly-respected.

While I read, Roni became increasingly agitated. She drummed her manicured nails on the desk. "Three times what I got! That's just wrong."

"Give me a minute," I responded. "Let me check out the judge's reasoning." I turned to the part of her divorce decree entitled "Findings of Fact." Paragraph 12 read as follows:

> *12. Non-marital claim. Respondent entered the marriage with an inheritance of $350,000. He invested $200,000 of this sum in the marital homestead. Over the course of the four-year marriage, the home increased in value as the result of market factors. The remainder of the inheritance remained intact. Each party is entitled to one-half of the increased value. The Court awards Petitioner $100,000 plus an additional $50,000 in lieu of spousal maintenance.*

"Roni, your friends are wrong. The judge's logic conforms to our law."

"That's what my first lawyer told me. The problem is, I'm out of money. Can't I get more from Marc?"

"Probably not," I said. "The decree is final. The judge gave you a settlement for spousal maintenance, and, frankly, you were lucky to get that much in a short-term marriage. Why are you broke?"

"Well, it took me money to set up a new household. You wouldn't believe how much it costs for furniture and appliances and even kitchen utensils. I needed a new car, too."

"But that didn't take a hundred-fifty grand, did it?"

"You're right." Her face reddened. "Okay. Here's the truth. After we separated, I was really pissed at Marc for dumping me for another woman. I wanted revenge. At about the same time, my girlfriend set me up with this younger guy, Billy. He's really good-looking. He drives a new Porsche. Billy came to one of the court hearings with me and Marc was super jealous."

"Sure," I said. "I understand."

"I really fell for Billy. One day, I got up the courage to ask him about his job. He said he didn't have regular work but lives off his winnings from sports betting. I've never met any guy like that."

Uh-oh, I thought.

"Billy said he had some inside information on this year's Super Bowl. The 49ers against the Cincinnati Bengals. The Niners were favored by six points, but Billy had it that Joe Montana got a hamstring injury during practice for the big game. He said I should put money on the Bengals. He'd match my money and we'd both come off winners."

"How much?" I asked, knowing that the Niners had won.

"Seventy-five grand."

If I wasn't better at controlling my emotions, my jaw would have dropped. "What happened?"

"I lost all my money. Billy said he'd make it up to me by winning some bets, but it's been a month and we haven't talked about it since then."

She started to cry. The tears smeared her mascara. She blew her nose.

"The thing is, I love Billy. That's why I'm here. I figured it was a long shot going back after Marc, but maybe you'd come up with a plan."

"I'm sorry Roni. There's no chance the judge is going to re-open your case. As a matter of fact, once he heard about what happened, he might even make you pay Marc's attorney fees for bringing it back to court."

It was as gently as I could put it, but the truth was unavoidable. Her tears continued as I escorted her to the elevator.

* * * * * * * *

A year later I heard again from Roni. As a matter of fact, it was right before the Super Bowl.

"Hello. We talked last year," she said.

It would have been mean to joke about the game, but I was tempted.

"You kicked me out of your office, remember? I didn't have a case, you said."

"I was just being straight with you. Can I help you with something else?"

"Actually, it's about the same thing, but I've got some new information."

I agreed to see her, and she was in the next day. She'd changed her appearance. Her hair was shorter, lighter, and permed. She wore a burgundy midi-skirt and boots. It was a good look.

"You remember I had this boyfriend, Billy?"

"Yeah. The young guy with the Porsche. Are you still together?"

"I just broke it off with him. He's an asshole. By the way, he doesn't have the Porsche anymore. He sold it and bought a Ferrari. With my money!"

"Wait. He lost the bet, didn't he?"

"That's what he told me, but I got suspicious when he got the new car, so I started talking to some people we both know. Turns out, he did very well on the bet."

"How do you know that?"

"He was two-timing me with Sandy, this college girl. I talked to her after he dumped her. She said he bragged about how he cheated me."

"Did he?"

"Sure did. He bet on Cincinnati, like he told me, but he bet the spread. The odds were that the Niners would win by six points, but they won by only five. He'd taken the Bengals, but with five points."

"So, he won?"

"Yup. He doubled my money – into a hundred-fifty thousand"

"And, he said it was all lost?"

"Exactly. It wasn't just Sandy who told me. There was his ex-friend Brad, who he cheated on a different deal. He filled in the details."

"Did you confront Billy?"

"I did. We had a date to a concert last month. On the drive there, I asked him point-blank. He denied it then, but later, after we did a few lines and drank some cocktails, I asked him again. He fessed up. I recorded it on my cassette."

She reached into her purse, pulled out a tiny device and played the two-minute conversation. She had Billy, dead to rights.

"See, I'm not the same naïve gal you met last year. No more young guys. No more life in the fast lane. You'll help me get that hundred-fifty, won't you?

"We'll sure try."

"How about that we don't have anything in writing? Can we still go after him? "

"We can, Roni. It's true that we have a rule in the law about hearsay, so under normal circumstances we couldn't use what Sandy and Brad said to you, but in your case, you have the tape. When Billy confessed, he made what we call an 'admission against interest,' which is an exception to the hearsay rule."

I quickly drafted a summons and complaint against William Kronholm, the boyfriend. I was concerned that, even if we got a judgment against him, it would be hard to collect, so my staff contacted the Department of Motor Vehicles to check the registration of the Ferrari. Billy was listed as the owner. Our clever investigator found Billy at a club in Uptown Minneapolis and served him the papers. We were in business.

The summons gave the defendant twenty days to contest the case, so I was expecting to hear from Billy or a lawyer on his behalf. Nothing came. After allowing a few days to transpire beyond the deadline, I filed a Notice of Default with the court and entered judgment against Billy for $150,000, together with additional costs of service and filing fees.

Armed with our judgment, I contacted the sheriff's department to seize Billy's Ferrari. The next day, Roni called.

"Billy stopped by my place this morning. He heard that a deputy was nosing around, looking for his car. Now he says he doesn't own it anymore, cuz he's in hock to some 'bad guys' in Chicago, and he signed it over to them."

"That won't work," I said. "It's a fraudulent transfer. Tell Billy to turn it over to the cops."

Roni said she would, although her spirit seemed weak.

That night, I got a call at home. "This is Billy Kronhom."

How could this happen? My number was unlisted. I jealously guarded my privacy. The staff at my office was under instructions to release no personal information about any of the lawyers at the firm.

"How'd you get this number?" I asked Billy.

"Let's just say some people I know are really skilled in technology," was his answer.

"Then speak."

"It's too bad things didn't work out for Roni and me. I really care about her. That's why I called, to warn you. If you guys don't lay off me, there'll be consequences, not just for Roni."

"So, you just threatened me. As soon as we're off the line, I'm calling the police. "

"That's your choice, but if it was me I'd think again. This is coming from some guys who stop at nothing."

I hung up on him, but immediately had second thoughts. Calling the police could set off unintended consequences. Would the sinister forces Billy alluded to act out, endangering Roni or myself?

When I got to work the next morning, there was a note on my desk asking me to call Roni. "Urgent," it said. I called.

"Sorry," she said, in a strange voice. "I've got a bad case of the nerves and started the day with some Bloody Marys. I had a visit last night. A man and a woman. From the FBI."

"Are you sure that's who they were?"

"They showed me their badges, and once they started talking it was obvious they were legit. They had a letter from their director, saying that I could get immunity if I cooperated with them."

"Immunity from what? You didn't do anything."

"Well, I guess I did. There's more to the story than I told you last time."

"Tell me now, Roni." I felt like reading her the riot act, but I'd become so accustomed to dishonesty from clients that I let it go.

"Billy used to take me in the Ferrari on his rounds. He'd go all over the Cities. Mostly to north Minneapolis, but also to some nicer parts of town. He'd pick up packages from people, or drop them off. He never told me what was in them, but I snooped a bit when he wasn't looking. Money, sometimes drugs, like coke and meth. I guess that makes me an accomplice. Right? That's what the FBI people said. I wanted to explain, but told them I had to meet with you first."

"They're trying to intimidate you, Roni. Assuming you're telling me the truth this time, and there's not more to it, I'm sure they consider you a small fish. Don't talk to anyone. I'll do some checking and get back to you."

I wasn't experienced in dealing with the FBI, or gangsters either. I met with my law partners. We drew up a short list of lawyers I might call. The next day, serendipitously, I got a call from someone on the list. It was Mickey Silver.

"Hello, old friend," Mickey said.

Mickey started his career as a humble assistant prosecutor in the city attorney's office, turning to the defense side after being overworked and underpaid by the government. He'd made friends with cops while prosecuting, and it paid off, as he specialized in representing them when they found themselves on the wrong end of the law. After a few notorious cases, his fame spread. We'd gotten to know each other over the years, and had even socialized outside of the legal world.

"I understand your client is Roni Weiss, right?" Mickey asked.

"How'd you know that?"

"Your name is on the default judgment you just filed. Wow, you did a number on her poor boyfriend."

"Did he even read the summons, Mick? Why'd he let the twenty days go by?"

"Because he's not the brightest bulb. You could say that about a lot of my clients."

"Okay. What are you asking me for?"

"I'd like to meet with you and Ms. Weiss. Get this whole thing resolved. Coincidentally, I have a court appearance in your neck of the woods tomorrow morning.

How about 11:00 a.m. at your office."

"As long as it's just you, Mickey."

* * * * * * *

I had Roni meet me in our conference room a half-hour early. She was a wreck, but she was sober.

"Can't I stay in your office while you talk to him? I hate this."

"Roni, I'll be next to you the whole time. We'll have Mr. Silver on the other side of the table. I want you to be aware of what happens, instead of having you wondering what we were really talking about in your absence. If it's unbearable, just tug on my sleeve and I'll get you out."

I glanced out the third-story window and saw Mickey pull into our parking lot. He drove a bright red Mazda Rx-7, with customized plates – MGS. As I suspected, there was no other reason for his coming. If he'd had a hearing, as he told me the day before, he would have walked over, since the courthouse was right next to us.

Roni wanted to get a look at Mickey, so I let her peek through the curtains as he waited in the lobby for us. He fit the image of a high-powered criminal defense lawyer. Slim and balding, he wore an Italian silk suit, red tie and highly-polished black loafers. When I went out to greet him, he handed me a yellow envelope. As we shook hands, his diamond cufflinks gleamed.

We all sat at the boardroom table. Mickey started.

"Look folks, I know your client wants to get the FBI off her back and squeeze some money out of Mr. Kronholm."

Under the table, Roni grasped my wrist.

"What do you mean, the FBI?" I asked, feigning ignorance.

"My client is very resourceful."

"Resourceful enough to get my unlisted home phone number and call me at home last night, it seems."

"He did that? I'm sorry. What a dumbshit!"

"Interesting. You just said he was so resourceful. Mickey, who are you really representing?"

"Let's not go there, my friend. Instead, look in the yellow envelope." Ronnie leaned over as I unsealed it.

"It's a bank money order made out to you and your client for ninety grand. Seventy-five for the money she lent to Mr. Kronholm and fifteen so she can pay your fees. I worked hard for that last part because we're friends."

"Seventy-five? She owes him twice that." Mickey gave a non-committal nod.

"Look, pal. I stuck my neck out to get this for you. You don't know how far."

"And this contract?" I asked.

"Just an NDA for Ms. West to sign."

At that moment, the receptionist buzzed me on the intercom. "There's a gentleman out here who's demanding to talk to Mr. Silver, immediately." I could detect concern from the tone of her voice.

Mickey heard this on the speaker, and excused himself. "Ten minutes. Please." I peeked through the curtain again. Mickey talking to younger man, attired in a red track suit. He towered over Mickey. Moments later, I spotted them below in the parking lot, engaged in an animated conversation.

* * * * * * *

While Mickey was gone, I perused the money order. It was drawn on Wells Fargo, and there was a branch right across the street. I called in an assistant and asked her to take it over and verify that it was genuine.

Next, I went through the non-disclosure agreement with Roni.

"Roni, it says that in agreeing to accept the payment, you promise not to discuss the subject matter of our case with any person or agency. That would include the FBI, do you understand?"

"Sure, but that's just a piece of paper. What if they try to indict me or something? "

"You're just a minor player in whatever is going on with these people. You can always plead the fifth. Anyway, someone seems to have an inside track on the FBI, so I wouldn't count on them to keep things confidential."

"Okay. I'll sign it. It's the only way I'll get my money back."

I asked Roni to sit outside while I talked to Mickey, who had just returned. Mickey looked upset. His eyes darted back and forth. "Lemme take a look out your window," he said. "Good, he's gone."

"What was that about?" I asked.

"Better you don't know."

"Okay, then. We've got a deal." I handed him the agreement and the release. "Mickey, on the money order you gave us, it names the remitter as 'WCIP.' Who's that?"

Mickey gave me a wry smile. "Don't know. It could stand for West Chicago Partners, but that's just a guess on my part."

After Mickey left, I walked over to the bank with Roni. We endorsed the money order and a teller issued us separate checks - $75,000 to Roni and $15,000 to my law firm.

"It's time to say goodbye, Roni. I hope you have a good life."

"Oh, I will. Things are already looking up. I started seeing my ex again. He got rid of that slut who broke up our marriage. As a matter of fact, we're going on a Caribbean cruise next month."

"Have fun, but take my advice."

"What's that."

"Steer clear of the casino."

* * * * * * * *

Some months later, I noticed an article in *Finance and Commerce*, a weekly publication subscribed to by many lawyers. "Disbarment proceedings instituted against Minneapolis lawyer."

It was Mickey. He had been cited by the Board of Professional Responsibility for filing false affidavits. I called him.

"Anything I can do to help? Do you need a character witness?"

"Thanks for the offer," he said. "You don't know how much that means to me, but I just signed a consent decree with the ethics people. I'll give up my license rather than have it go any further."

"Meaning?"

"Meaning that I got involved with the wrong people and that the more that comes out, the worse it'll be for my family and myself."

I never saw Mickey again, but every year or two, a new client would call me. "Mickey Silver told me to say hello." At first, I was skeptical, but they were all good people.

CHAPTER 12

Chisago Lakes

Two eighteen-year-olds were seated in front of me. Mark spoke first. He was beanpole-thin, with scraggly, unwashed blond hair. "It was my car. That's why I'm the one who got charged. But I wasn't the driver. That was Duane." Mark nodded toward his friend, Duane Williams, who was seated to his right.

"That's what I told them," Duane said. "I was willing to take the rap for it, but they wouldn't listen to me."

"I don't think either one of you wants to do that," I said. "See this complaint? It charges you with Aggravated Assault, Mark. That's a felony, which can result in prison, even for a first-time offense."

Their mouths dropped. "No! That can't be!" Mark gasped.

"We're here to help you," I replied, "but you have to tell me everything. The truth."

Mark sighed. "It was the Vikings' last game of the season. You know, against the Packers.

We thought it'd be more fun to watch it in Hudson."

He was referring to Hudson, Wisconsin.

"I'm guessing you weren't there just because it was Packer territory," I said with a smile.

Every night, but especially Sundays, when the liquor stores are closed in Minnesota, young people flock across the St. Croix River to

Wisconsin. At the time, Wisconsin had a legal drinking age of eighteen, which made the problem even worse. It's a major source of revenue for some small towns like Hudson, but it's also a source of heartache for the families who lose their sons and daughters to fatal traffic accidents as they return home.

"I take it you guys were drinking."

"We got to the bar three hours before the game started," Mark said. "Duane was having schnapps and Coke. It was beer for me. He stopped at halftime, but I kept pounding 'em down.

By the end of the game, I handed Duane the keys."

"Were you drunk, Duane?"

"I was half-buzzed, for sure. But Mark could hardly stand up. I should've taken the time to get sober. On the other hand, I was hot to drive Mark's Trans-Am."

I took a closer look at Duane. Where Mark was tall, he was short. Where Mark was thin, he was fat. Neither of them impressed me with their intelligence, which led to my next question.

"How did you come by that car, Mark? I bet it cost a pretty penny."

"I got it through my Uncle Ed. He works at a bank and it was a repo. He swung a loan for me."

"How much is the payment?"

"Five-fifteen a month. It's almost a third of what I make. And now it's decorated with bullet holes."

"What?" I asked.

"Things got a little out-of-hand," Mark replied.

After Mark and Duane left, I called the Chisago County Attorney. He was Jim Clancy, a young lawyer like me. I'd crossed paths with him before, and liked him. When I told him that I represented Mark and passed on the "wrong driver" theory, Jim wasn't happy.

"He's a lying sack of shit. We've got a solid ID. I'll send you the police report." It arrived two days later. Submitted by Deputy Sheriff Adolph Bohaty, it read in part:

An alert was received at 2130 hours, Sunday, 11/26/75, from Highway Patrol of a late-model sports car crossing the I-94 bridge into Minnesota at a high rate of speed. MHP activated lights and siren, but vehicle headed north, eluding pursuit. Contact was initiated by Chisago Sheriff as vehicle was spotted on County Road 35 but subject continued at high rate of speed. I, Deputy Bohaty, directed set-up of a roadblock by two squads. Vehicle approached but deviated from road into ditch. I and Deputy Swenson, in fear of bodily injury due to actions of subject, deployed our weapons and discharged them toward vehicle. In doing so, we clearly saw driver, later identified by license tag as Mark Allen Johnsen (dob 01/08/57). Vehicle eluded roadblock but was found abandoned one hour later in rural East Bethel, Anoka County. Officers, based on vehicle registration, proceeded to home of Johnsen. When confronted by myself, Johnsen denied being driver and to provide further information. The next day, I was called by an individual, Duane Johnsen, who claimed he had in fact been driver of the vehicle.

Our case was scheduled for a probable cause hearing in Center City, the county seat. In felony matters, the defendant has the right to challenge the state's case to determine if there is sufficient merit to subject him to a jury trial. However, it is rare to achieve a dismissal at this pretrial proceeding. Many defense lawyers use the hearing as an opportunity to hear the state's evidence in order to prepare for the main trial.

Judge Carroll Larson was assigned to our case. He was an elderly man, on the cusp of retirement, and was known to be tough on criminal cases. His court reporter was Einar Eeg, a storied character in legal circles.

Einar, of Swedish heritage, was about the same age as his judge. A burly fellow, he looked somewhat ridiculous as he held his tiny steno machine between his meaty knees, hunching over it as he tapped away on the keys. Occasionally, he'd bark out directions in the midst of a trial.

"Louder!" He would shout if a witness was too soft-spoken. We lawyers speculated as to who was really in charge in the courtroom, referring *sotto voce* to Einar as "Judge Eeg" and to Judge Larson as "Grandpa."

I met with Mark and Duane to prepare for the probable cause hearing. Duane asked me point-blank. "Why can't I just walk into the courtroom and plead guilty? "

"No, Duane. Actually, I want you to stay away. It's the state's burden to prove their case.

Let's not make it any easier for them."

* * * * * * *

Chisago County is off the beaten track. An hour north of Saint Paul, it encompasses a lovely rolling countryside, dotted by pristine lakes. It was settled in the nineteenth century by Swedish immigrants. The traveler progresses through quaint villages: Lindstrom (with its coffee-pot shaped water tower), Scandia, and Taylor Falls, on the shore of the rushing, pure waters of the St. Croix River. The Swedish writer Wilhelm Moberg, wrote of it in his *Emigrants* trilogy. A statue of his fictional immigrant couple, Karl Oskar and Christina, stands along the main route.

The hearing convened on a gray, cold day. Winter had come early that year. I told Mark to bring his wounded Trans Am, for a demonstration I had planned.

Just before court was convened, I noticed Deputies Bohaty and Swenson in the hallway. Unlike most cops, who despise defense lawyers, they were friendly. "Your client could've been me twenty years ago," Bohaty said with a smile.

"Then why not give him a break?" I asked.

"Not for me to say," he said, nodding his head toward Clancy, the prosecutor. As he did so, Clancy approached me.

"Let's go somewhere and talk," he said. We found an available conference room, and he set his file on the table. He looked at me directly.

"Look, my friend, I know what your client and his friend are saying, but they're playing you for a fool. "

"How so?" I was bit offended by that.

"The reason they conjured up this story is because your man Johnsen's got a record. Drugs. Possession of marijuana and peyote. He gets convicted here, and his felony sentence gets enhanced by three years. So, he gets his buddy, who has a clean record, to take the rap. He'd only get probation."

I was dumbfounded. Why hadn't I checked Mark's history before? Maybe I'd been hoodwinked by his claim of innocence, or was just naïve.

Before I could react, our conversation was interrupted by Einar, who stuck his head out the courtroom door. "Let's get going!"

Judge Larson took the podium, and asked Clancy to make his opening statement. "Your Honor, we who live along the Wisconsin border are in constant danger from these young drivers who carouse at the bars in Hudson and other towns. Some of them don't make it home due to their drunkenness and negligence. He turned toward Mark. Just as bad, innocent citizens of our own county have lost their lives. This defendant, in particular, caused great harm, using his vehicle as a weapon to threaten law enforcement personnel who were safeguarding the public."

"Call your first witness, Mr. Prosecutor," the judge said.

"We call Deputy Adolph Bohaty."

It was obvious that Bohaty had been through this routine before, as he carefully read through his report, pausing for effect and maintaining eye contact with the judge. When he concluded, Clifford had a question.

"Is it fair to say, deputy, that when the Trans Am approached the roadblock, you and Deputy Swenson were in fear of your life?"

It was a leading question, but I let it go without objection, because it played right into my strategy.

"Yes, we were both scared."

It was the end of the afternoon and time for my demonstration. The four of us, Judge Larson, Einar Eeg, and prosecutor Jim Clancy, assembled in front of the courthouse atop the peninsula overlooking Chisago Lake. The late afternoon darkness had set in. Out of the northwest, and crossing the ice-covered lake below, the wind lashed our faces. The subject of our attention was Mark's Trans-Am. Bright orange and highlighted by blue racing stripes, its driver's side was peppered by fresh bullet holes.

"I asked you to come out here," I said, "to show you how incredulous the eyewitness testimony was. The roadblock was in conditions like we have here now, but on an unlit county road. The officers were hiding behind their own car. Bohaty testified that they were in fear of their lives and they started shooting. All in the dark. Under such circumstances, how certain can their identification of the driver be?"

I had hoped for a reaction from the judge. Even a question. But he was stony-faced and silent, bundled in his winter coat.

"We'll resume the trial at 9:00 tomorrow," he said.

* * * * * * * *

We started late the next morning due to some perfunctory matters that had already been scheduled before the judge. It was my turn to cross-examine Deputy Bohaty.

"Deputy," I asked, "wasn't it unusual to set up a roadblock under the circumstances of this incident?"

"Yes, but I felt it was justified due to the danger of the subject's driving behavior."

"But, if the driver hadn't evaded the squad car that was blocking the road, there would have been a possibly fatal collision. There would be an inquiry, maybe a lawsuit, and you would have to defend your decision, right?"

"I give you the same answer."

"You discharged your weapon, directly into the Trans Am. Why was that necessary"

"We were trying to disable the vehicle."

"How long did the confrontation at the roadblock take place?"

"It was over in seconds."

As he said so, I noticed Einar looking at Judge Larson, raising an eyebrow. "Yet," Deputy Bohaty, "you say you are certain that the driver of the Trans Am was Mark Johnsen. "Yes. Totally certain."

"It's time for the lunch break," the judge announced. "We'll resume at 2:00." Things had gone well so far. During the break, I called Duane, telling him to be on call for the afternoon session. First, though, I had to have a word with Mark.

"Mr. Clancy tells me you have a prior conviction for a drug offense. Is that right?"

"Oh, he knew about that?"

"Of course, he knew. He's the prosecutor! Why didn't you tell me about it?"

"Well, you didn't ask."

That made me so angry, that I lost my train of thought for a few moments.

"So, did you make it up that Duane was driving?"

"No way. He was the driver. We didn't make anything up." I took it with a pinch of salt.

* * * * * * *

I arrived early for the afternoon session. As I walked into the courtroom, I saw Judge Larson and Einar enter through a side door. The judge went into his chambers, but Einar went over to his desk.

"Did you have a nice lunch, Einar?"

"Sure did. Whenever the judge and I come over here for court, we drive over to St. Croix Falls and eat at the Swedish Family Inn House." It was a well-known spot on the Wisconsin side.

"So, is your case going to go long this afternoon?" Einar asked.

"I'll have my client and another witness, but it could take a while depending on what Mr. Clancy has in mind."

"Do what you want," said Einar, "but here's some advice from an old veteran. Things will go your way unless you screw it up by trying to do too much."

At that moment, Judge Larson opened his door and asked Einar to come into the chambers.

What did Einar mean? It seemed that he was telling me I had the case won. I remembered the way he and Judge Larson looked at each other when Deputy Bohaty testified. If that was right, I could waive my side of the case and move for a directed verdict of dismissal, but it was a major risk. If I did that, the judge wouldn't hear Duane's admission of guilt, and the case could be bound over for trial, putting Mark at risk for prison. On the other hand, if we put on our case, Clancy would reveal his theory that Mark and Duane were conspiring to evade the truth.

I took Mark back to a conference room to explain the situation, since it was ultimately his decision, but he was no help. "Do what you think is right," was all he would say.

The clerk rapped the gavel, calling the hearing to order. "Counselor," Judge Larson said, "Proceed with your case."

"Your Honor, the defendant will rest on the record and not present a case beyond that."

Clancy leaned over to me. "Are you serious?" he whispered. "You're setting yourself up for a malpractice suit."

Judge Larson responded quickly, though. "The court finds that the prosecution has failed to meet the standard of probable cause. Even in the light most favorable to the state, a reasonable jury could not convict the defendant. Case dismissed."

I quickly gathered my papers, grabbed Mark's arm, and left the courtroom. This is what you do when you win. Get out before anything changes.

The next day, back in the office, I got a call from Jim Clancy. "Congratulations," he said.

"Just curious. How were you so sure Judge Larson would grant your motion?"

"Just my intuition," I said.

"Well, for your information, I'm not going any further with this case. If the other guy did it, I couldn't ever prove it, after Bohaty said he was so sure of what he saw."

Still, there was doubt in my mind about how it all happened. Did I really get played by these two kids?

Later that day, Duane called me. "Are they gonna come after me now? I'm ready to face up to it and plead guilty." I explained what Clancy had said, but Duane had set my mind at ease.

Several months later, I had another case in Chisago County. It was easy, and I had some extra time afterwards. Before heading home, I stopped at the Swedish Family Inn.

Aunt Lena's krumkake.

It's to die for.

CHAPTER 13

Cord of Deceit

My fellow lieutenants and I had finished our Signal Corps training. I'd sleepwalked through the extended course on radios, barely passing. We had three months of active duty left. The colonel said, "We'll find an assignment for you, but if you've got a plan of your own, let us know and we'll consider it."

I'd learned the hard way not to let the Army decide what was best for me. If you let that happen, you'll get screwed. I heard through the grapevine that there was an opening at the Public Information Office and that it was an easy job, so I went for it.

What a sweet gig! While my companions were out in the Georgia sun training recruits, I was sitting inside the General's office in an air-conditioned building, writing speeches for the Old Man and giving the occasional tour of Fort Gordon to high school groups.

After the three months were up, I was released to my civilian lawyer job, obligated for six years in the Reserves. I was a "weekend warrior," required to show up in uniform one weekend per month and two weeks in the summer, and, once again, I was given the chance to find a "slot" on my own. It was an easy choice when I discovered an opening for a Public Information Officer (PIO), directly under the State Adjutant General. Unlike my unit at Fort Gordon, though, the troops under my command had full-time civilian jobs in the media – radio, print, and television.

A sergeant in our unit, Bob, who was a producer at the ABC affiliate in the Twin Cities, called me up one day. "There's a gal in our art department. Her name is Sue. Her husband just got out of prison and she needs a divorce lawyer. That's what you do in the real world, right? Would you take her call?" I agreed to meet Sue the next day.

"Your new client is here," our receptionist said as she stuck her head in the door. She gave me a look as if to say – wait till you see this!

Sue's thick mascara and green eye shadow overwhelmed her face. She wore high, jeweled boots with spiked heels. Her long, red hair was swept over her shoulder, but not too much to conceal a plunging V-neck silk blouse. She definitely added an exotic air to our white-bread suburban office.

"I met Jack in a bar," Sue said. "I was a struggling actress living in a dump with another gal, doing auditions, trying to get work in commercials and productions. Here was this big guy from Wayzata."

It's a swanky village in the Lake Minnetonka area west of the city, home to the Pillsburys, Cargills, Weyerhausers, and others of the super-rich.

"He was driving this classic 1937 Cord convertible," Sue said, "flashing his money around."

I'd heard of Cord automobiles, but did some research after Sue left. The remaining Cords are true classic American cars. They were manufactured only from 1929 to 1932, and then again in 1936 and 1937. Cords have been featured in many films, including "The Godfather." They were sold new for $2,500, but are now valued in the six-figures. "It seemed like Jack knew everybody," Sue told me. "I loved riding around in that Cord. I knew he'd been to prison, but that sort of made him more exciting to me. It was the rebel in him. I'd had enough of those 'warm and sensitive' guys. Then, when I got pregnant, he married me to give our daughter his name. "

"So, what's wrong?" I asked.

"He got caught selling stolen jewelry and coin collections and was sent to prison a second time. He just got out last Fall. While he was away, Bob got me a job at ABC. I don't know how I would've gotten through it without Bob. He's been such a friend – always ready to come over and help me through the worst days." She blushed, then added quickly, "Of course, we're just friends."

My bullshit-detecting radar snapped to the alert with a flashing red echo that said – Lie in progress! Bob was sort of a big shot at Channel 11, and a family man to boot, but I wouldn't put it past him for a minute to take on an emotionally fragile woman like Sue. Bob was a bit of a renegade himself. He'd been suspended the previous year for cutting loose with a string of profanities that ended up on the public airwaves thanks to an untended live mike.

"Since he's been out of prison, Jack comes and goes," Sue said. "Sometimes I won't see him for a week or two. I'm sure he's out there selling stolen stuff again. What really scares me is that he makes jokes about doing a killing for money. I know him. He's not joking."

This was new ground for me. I'd done scores of divorce cases, but never one involving a killer.

"You have a five-year-old daughter?"

"Asia," Sue said. "She idolizes Jack. He puts her in the front seat of his Cord and drives her around day and night. No seatbelt. Plus, he takes her into bars to show her off to his friends." She conspicuously re-crossed her legs, then glanced at her watch. "Hey, I forgot to tell you, Jack's gonna call you right now. That's okay, isn't it?"

It was not okay. I hadn't even spent an hour with Sue. I didn't know yet whether her husband had a lawyer. I wondered why Sue thought it was a good idea to spring this on me. Was there some hidden agenda between her and Jack?

Almost immediately, the receptionist buzzed me.

"There's a Jack Ratner on the line. He said you're waiting for his call."

I decided to take the call but raised an eyebrow to Sue as I did so. I asked Mr. Ratner if he had his own lawyer.

"Don't need one," he said. "Look, I don't know who you are, but you better talk Suzie out of this. Go through with it and you'll both regret it."

His voice had a feral edge to it, and even though I'd held the receiver close to my ear, I'm sure Sue had heard every word.

Ratner went on, laughing. "Didn't someone say we should kill all the lawyers first?"

I knew the line. It was from *"Henry VI,"* by Shakespeare, a frequently misused literary allusion. Maybe he'd picked this up in prison. I wasn't going to debate the meaning of it with him. "Get a lawyer," I said. "I'm not talking with you again. See you in court."

"Fine with me," he said. "You tell your client I've got my sources over at the station, and I know all about her and her fuck buddy. She pushes this divorce and I'll call up the station manager and get them both fired."

Undeterred by Ratner's threats, I went ahead and filed the case. It was no big surprise that the process server tracked him down in a bar.

Although I got a few worried calls from Sue about Ratner's visitations with Asia, nothing much happened until the pretrial conference, which was to occur at the towering Government Center in Minneapolis. We'd filed our exhaustive statement of the case, as required by court rules, but nothing had been filed by Ratner, so we had no idea what would happen in the courtroom.

As the bailiff called the case, in walked my old friend Mickey Silver. He was my age, though prematurely bald. Like a lot of criminal defense lawyers, Mickey got his start at the county attorney's office as a prosecutor. Many lawyers who work hard for government pay get tired of watching opposing defense lawyers pulling down big fees for doing the same work. Mickey, like many others, switched sides, and although he hadn't reached the top echelon of the criminal defense bar, he was already living the life -- Italian silk suit, Rolex watch, a flashy sports car.

"Ratner hired me this morning. Haven't done a divorce case in years, but he insisted," Mickey said. "Sorry. I don't have a Statement of the Case for you."

He said it with a smile, because that was Mickey's nature. "I had a talk with Ratner," Mickey said, "I told him to lay off with that crap about getting Sue and your friend fired."

"Where is Ratner?" I asked.

"He doesn't want the divorce, so he thinks he can stop it if he doesn't show up. I'm instructed to say he's sick."

"You're a lousy liar, Mickey," I said. "Try selling that to the judge."

Sue heard it all, and as I walked back to counsel table, I could see her trembling, and madly scribbling on her notepad. Grabbing my arm, she said, "He can't get away with that, can he?"

The judge entered, and as he approached the podium my heart sank. It was Ed Dworsky. I'd appeared in front of him before. He was a slight, older man with a ring of curly gray hair encircling his bald dome. Although he was experienced, he was an introvert, susceptible to being bossed around by aggressive lawyers.

"Where's your client, Mr. Silver?" he asked in his thin, reedy voice.

"He's ill, your Honor, so we're going to need a continuance."

"Any objection, counsel?" the Judge asked me.

"Certainly," I said. "Mr. Ratner has told me directly that he'll do anything to stop this case, and it's clear this is part of his strategy."

"What if he's really sick?" the judge said. "We have something in this country called due process. I'm going to grant the continuance. We'll reconvene one month from today."

The next day, I got a phone call from Sue. "Call up the judge and get him to reverse the continuance. My friend saw Jack driving the Cord around town last night, hitting the bars and bragging about how he beat the system."

There was nothing I could do. The decision had been made already. It's hard to explain to a client that justice can't be accomplished on demand, but that's the way the system works.

I promised to bring it up at our next court appearance. Maybe, I told Sue, we could get an award of attorney's fees because of yesterday's fiasco.

Eventually, the day arrived for the rescheduled pretrial. It was the same scene – Sue and I, Mickey Silver, and no Jack Ratner.

The judge entered. "This looks familiar," he said. "Where's your client this time, Mr. Silver?"

"I know this sounds fishy, your Honor, but he's not able to be here today. He injured his back."

"How long are we going to put up with this, your Honor?" I asked. "He wasn't sick last time. He was seen that very night, driving around town in his 1937 Cord."

"Do you have proof of this, or is it just hearsay?"

"We don't have pictures because my client doesn't have the money to hire a private detective to trail him around, but what's happening to-day is consistent with what I told you last time. It's obvious he's trying to manipulate the system. We move the Court for a default judgment. Grant us the divorce and award us attorney's fees."

The judge was momentarily silent, and I wondered if he would summon up some fortitude, but we were disappointed again. "To deny Respondent his standing in court when we don't know all the facts would be a miscarriage of justice." He turned to Mickey. "Mr. Silver, I am frustrated with your client. I'm setting the case for a final trial in six weeks, and if your client doesn't appear, I'll consider counsel's motion for a default.

I couldn't believe it. Any other judge would have thrown Mickey out of court over this. Glancing at Sue, I saw dark rivulets of mascara running down her cheeks.

"He just pulls the strings. Asia and I don't mean a thing, do we? I'm paying you thousands of dollars that I can't afford, and we're no better off than if I'd done it myself."

Mickey must have overheard this, because he walked over to our table and said, "I'm really sorry about this. Next time – no more games."

Six weeks later, it was the day of the trial. We had our exhibits ready and Sue's testimony had been rehearsed. Again, Jack was a no-show. This time, though, the result was different.

"Mr. Silver, where is your client?" the judge said. "What's the story this time?"

"I can understand why the court might question this, your Honor," Mickey said, "but I assure you that Mr. Ratner is in the hospital for his back injury and isn't able to be here."

I protested, "Your Honor, this is another scam, just like the last time. Grant our motion for default judgment!"

It seemed that the judge had discovered his spine. "Which hospital is he at, Mr. Silver?"

"Glenwood Hills, your Honor."

"Court will re-convene in your client's room, in one hour. If he's not there, I'm granting default judgment."

One hour later, we were in Jack Ratner's room, and there he was -- in traction. If he really wasn't injured, it was a pretty elaborate ruse.

It was the first time I'd seen Ratner in person. Thick as a linebacker, his oily black curls lay below his shoulders, and his body hair grew in unsightly tufts, peeking through the hospital gown. He had an angry sneer on his face.

The judge, who looked even less imposing without his judicial robe, entered the room with his clerk and court reporter. After calling the case, the judge gestured to me to start.

"I call Jack Ratner," I said, standing next to the bed. It was a first for me –cross-examining a witness lying on his back in a hospital bed, a leg hoisted up by pulleys.

"What is your occupation, sir?"

Ratner turned his head toward his lawyer. "Do I answer this, Mick?"

"It's not for Mr. Silver to decide," I said. "If you don't answer, I'll get the judge to hold you in contempt of court."

He ignored me, waiting until he got a response from Mickey, then said, "Professional gambler."

"And what's your income?"

"Lose more than I win," he said.

"How do you support yourself?"

"Loans from friends," he said with a chuckle.

"You are observed driving a classic car on a daily basis. How do you afford that?"

"Not mine. Take care of it for another guy."

It continued like this, with his evasive, impudent responses. I complained to the judge, but to no avail.

"Let's get through this. Do your best," he said.

Sue held up well through her testimony. The trial finally concluded in the early evening, when the judge announced, "Evidence is closed and the case is under advisement."

What does "under advisement" mean? In Minnesota, the judge is given ninety days to make a decision. Some do it sooner. Others wait until the last day. The good thing is, if it goes beyond the ninety days, the lawyer can get the judge's pay suspended. With this judge, I had no expectation of a quick result.

A couple of weeks after the trial, I was informed that Mickey Silver was on the line.

"Where's the money?" he said in a loud voice.

"You got anger issues, Mickey? I'd have thought you'd call me to apologize again.

Anyway, you know there's no money in this case."

"You don't know? Ask your client. She'll tell you."

He wouldn't say anything else, so I called Sue.

At first, she professed ignorance, but she finally opened up. "Jack showed up last week with a suitcase full of cash -- $50,000. He told me to hold it for him. He said it was his biggest score yet, but he was afraid he was going to be arrested. I could keep $10,000 for myself and take $5,000 to pay you, and Jack would drop his side of the case." She paused, "Yesterday he called me and said the heat's off, so I have to give it all back, but I don't want to. I've never had this much money in my whole life."

"That's crazy, Sue," I said. "Why do you think it's his biggest score? You yourself told me he said he'd do a murder for hire. This is blood money."

"Why should I care? They wouldn't come after me."

"Sure, they will. You could go to prison as an accessory, and I won't take a dime of it."

"That's easy for you to say," she said. "You're a rich lawyer. I have to worry about me and Asia."

I sure wasn't getting rich on this case, I thought. The hassle of dealing with the cast of characters wasn't especially pleasant, either.

The next day, Mickey was on the line again. "Sorry about yesterday, my friend. Everything's okay now."

"What happened?" I asked.

"Sue and Jack got it worked out between themselves. I'm happy, too. He dropped off a fat retainer for me."

"How so?"

"It happens all the time in my line of work. All of a sudden, a client drops a big load of cash at my office, for 'future services to be rendered.' Of course, they just made some kind of heist and before it runs through their fingers, they pay me in advance for the next time they get in trouble. Works for me. No questions asked."

That was it for Sue and I.

Ratner dropped his case and the divorce was granted on favorable terms to Sue. I never asked Bob if he continued to provide "counsel and guidance" to Sue. I assume he did until she moved on to greener pastures.

I never got paid. Chalk that up to experience. Playing it down the straight and narrow cost me, but in the long run I think it made me a better lawyer and stronger person because of it. At least I never had to wait around for criminals to drop off unexplained piles of cash.

A few years later Bob called me, inviting me to dinner with some Army friends at a restaurant in Wayzata. As I pulled into the parking lot, I saw Bob, but then I noticed a stunning cream and red colored classic car. The license plate read – '37 Cord.

Time to find a different place, we decided.

CHAPTER 14

Rooftop Redemption

If I had one word to describe him, I'd say "scraggly." It looked like he'd made an effort to make himself presentable, but his hair was an improbable yellow. It was the year everyone from Vince Vaughn to Tiger Woods was a blonde. For him, though, his brown mustache made it look even more incongruous. His complexion was marred by pimples and sores, even on his lips. I guessed he was fifty, but he could have been younger. When I introduced myself, he smiled, but he kept his mouth closed. He handed me the divorce papers, and we walked back to the office.

Finally, he spoke. "Gus Michael," he said as he thrust his hand forward. "It's my mom's fault I have two first names." This time when he smiled, I could see that his teeth were rotten, a condition my police friends refer to as "meth mouth." He handed me his card, which read, "Michael's Roofing – 24 Hour Service."

"You work at night? On roofs?"

"People get leaky roofs all the time," he said. "Especially in the spring, like now, with all the freezing and thawing. We're the only company around here that'll do emergency nighttime calls. Had to invest in a lot of lighting equipment, but it's paid off." He said it with pride. Perhaps I had jumped to the wrong conclusion about him based on his appearance.

He handed me the papers his wife's attorney had served on him, and I paged through the documents, finally settling on his wife's affidavit. She'd pulled no punches. "I married Respondent twenty years ago. Although we were blessed with three children and he was a good supporter in our early years, he has become more and more selfish. He gambles daily, both on-line and at the casino. He is a hard worker, but our financial security is in jeopardy because of his neglect."

Gus was ready to admit his shortcomings. "I bet you hear all kinds of excuses around here, but I deserve this – 100%. I totally fucked up my life. My wife finally gave up on me. She looked up her old high school boyfriend on Facebook. Flew down to Texas last month to hook up with him. That sucked, but I'm not blaming her."

He got up from his seat and started pacing back and forth. I noticed his eyes darting from one side of the office to the other.

"Relax, my friend," I said. "Do you need a break? Maybe you want to go out for a smoke?" I'd seen a pack of Marlboro's in his shirt pocket.

"Thanks," he said, and he was quickly out the door. From my third story office window, I looked down to the parking lot. Gus was in his car with the windows closed for at least fifteen minutes. Why so long? What was he smoking?

I took advantage of the interlude to go through the rest of the lengthy affidavit. It was strange that, as much as his wife disparaged him, there was no mention of drugs or addiction. Instead, she concluded with the self-righteous statement, "His God is money – mine the Almighty."

When Gus returned, he was much calmer. I decided to deal with the elephant in the room.

"Gus, is there a problem with drugs or alcohol here? I don't see it mentioned, but sometimes I can sense when it's an issue."

"Oh no," he said. "Kandy and I both do some stuff every once in a while, but nothing's out of control."

Denial, I thought. There were all the classic signs – a crumbling marriage, a chaotic life, and his beleaguered physical appearance. On the other hand, he seemed like a nice guy, almost too eager to accept the blame for the divorce. Why was his wife getting off so easy?

The case was venued in a rural county fifty miles north of the Cities. It was the kind of town where everyone knew everyone else's business.

I first saw his wife, Kandy, in the courtroom, at the preliminary hearing. She too was an unconvincing blonde, but she didn't share Gus' slender physique. She had stuffed herself into a too-short lavender dress. She wore matching eye shadow and was weighed down with glitzy silver costume jewelry. It might have worked at a different place on a different person, but it didn't suit her, especially for such a formal proceeding.

Kandy wanted Gus out, her lawyer said, but not without a goodly share of the family income.

"Your Honor," I argued, "the family business is on the homestead property. The trucks are in the pole barn and the materials are in the shelter – he's got to have access. There aren't any allegations of abuse. It would be a disaster if you kicked him out. Besides, the children need both parents."

"Well, they'd better start paying attention to their family," the judge said.

I was mystified, and my face must have shown it.

"Don't you know?"

I shook my head.

"Their sixteen-year-old got caught selling marijuana in the school parking lot last week. I had him in Court yesterday."

Gus jumped out of his chair. "Wait a minute! Why didn't someone tell me about this?" He glared at Kandy and her lawyer.

"If you were ever home, you'd know," Kandy shot back. "To you, it's all about money."

"Quiet!" said the judge. "I'll listen to the lawyers – not you two."

It was an excruciating hour-long hearing.

Finally, the judge said, "Folks, this is only a temporary order. If the case goes to the end, you'll both be unhappy with my final decision. For now, there's no alternative but to leave the status quo. You'll have to live together, and respect each other and help each other with these kids. Court is adjourned."

As the judge walked out Kandy grabbed her lawyer's arm. "That's it? He gets to stay? Aren't you gonna do something about it?"

I suspected he'd stoked Kandy's unrealistic expectations. As they walked down the crowded courthouse hallway, everyone in earshot could hear her giving him hell.

Gus gave me a pat on the back. "Thanks for everything, pal. Look, I'm going to make it up to her and the kids. Mark my words, I'll change. What she said about me being a selfish man? That's true. You won't hear it again."

A couple of months went by without word from Gus. One morning, I got a letter from Kandy's lawyer. It contained a single sheet of paper, entitled Notice of Dismissal. "Comes now the Petitioner, and of her own volition, does hereby dismiss the above-referenced proceeding."

Since we hadn't filed a Counterpetition, this immediately ended the case. I sent a copy to Gus, asking him to contact me if he had questions. He didn't. It seemed his efforts to change and save the marriage had worked. Was that the end?

* * * * * * *

Two years later, I saw Gus's name on my calendar again. When I went out to the lobby to greet him, I was astonished. His hair was a natural brown and neatly groomed. His face was full, and his complexion was clear. This time, when he cracked a smile, his teeth were white and even.

"Wow, Gus, you look great," I said.

"Thanks for that," he said. "A lot's happened in two years."

Once again, he'd been served with divorce papers by Kandy, but first, he wanted to talk about something else. "Take a look at this."

It was a clipping from his hometown paper. "Local man wins huge jackpot at Grand Casino."

Gus was standing with a large replica of a check from the casino, and the amount of the check was $955,000! The article was dated shortly after the court hearing we'd had two years before.

"Hard to believe, but I won it on a high-stakes slot machine."

Gambling isn't my thing, but I congratulated him. "You had some good fortune, so why the divorce papers?"

"Yup, you're right. The money was a mixed blessing, but mostly for the good. Of course, a lot of it went right to the IRS, but that still left plenty. I paid off my business debt, which was a bunch. Then I bought a new Mercedes for Kandy. I thought it was the least I could do."

"You still had plenty left, right?" I said.

"Well, 'had' is the right word. About half of it went up the vein," he said, pointing to his arm. "I guess I wasn't fooling anyone about my addiction. I kept on using, kept on gambling, and before I knew it I was almost broke. Kandy decided she'd had enough and she skedaddled down to Texas to take up with the old boyfriend again, this time for good."

"What about the kids?"

"The girls are at home with me. They're okay, thank goodness." Gus paused, with a frown.

"I wish it was that easy with Jimmy. I guess it's like father like son. He got busted for selling meth. He's been in prison for almost a year. I blame myself for that, but he joined an NA group there, and I think he's seen the light about addiction. They let me attend the meetings with him at the prison. "

"You kicked the habit?" I asked.

"Sure did," he said. "When Kandy left, it woke me up. I've been sober for eighteen months. Went through treatment, spent a fortune getting my teeth done. How do you like these choppers?" He flashed me a smile. "I go to group therapy every week, and -- guess what -- I met a gal who actually likes my ugly old mug. She's been doing some accounting for me and I told her to come here to show you the books."

He pulled his phone out of his pocket and tapped out a text. "She's sittin' out in the lobby right now. Lemme go get her."

Gus walked back in with a pretty, well-dressed thirty-ish woman. "This is Naomi," Gus said. "She's been helping me organize the company – no one ever did that before. Show him what you've done, sweetheart."

Naomi opened her briefcase and handed me a neatly organized folder, a corporate balance sheet, income statement, and another section setting out Gus's living expenses and budget.

"I gotta make a call to a customer," Gus said. "You two carry on – I'll just go out to the lobby."

After he left, I took a closer look at Naomi. She was fit, stylish, and professional looking. Not beautiful, but warm and engaging. After a few more minutes of financial discussion, she looked up. "I was in the recovery group because I did a horrible thing. I got drunk and drove my car off an exit ramp into a pond. When they found us, my best friend was dead in the seat next to me. I was convicted of Criminal Negligent Homicide and served two years down in Shakopee." She was talking about the state's women's prison.

"They put me into a treatment program. I felt like a piece of shit for what I'd done. That's when I met Gus. He was putting his life together, too, but he sorta took over the group. He convinced me – actually everyone -- that our lives were worth living." She set the papers aside and leaned her elbows on the desk between us. "Gus visits his son in prison every week. He's there for his girls at home. I don't see how he manages it all. We probably look like a strange couple, but I really fell for him."

With Naomi's help, we put together the financial part of the case. The divorce wasn't going to be easy.

Gus had been running the roofing company for twenty years. It was successful, and he wanted to grow, so every time he could, he bought new equipment, hired more people, and plowed the profits back into the company. When the business was appraised in the divorce case, it was worth more than anyone thought – a million dollars. They had equity in their home as well as the business. You'd think it would be easy – each person gets half -- right?

Not so easy.

Where would Kandy's money come from? Not from the house. Gus needed to keep the home for the family, so he would have to pay

Kandy for her share of the home as well as the business. If Kandy got a lump sum, Gus would have to borrow the entire amount, but his income would be eclipsed by the debt service on the loan. What would be left for the family? On top of that, would Gus have to pay alimony to Kandy?

At the end of the trial, her lawyer addressed the court. "Your Honor, my client is entitled to a new start in life. She's a high school graduate and the world's full of educated millennials. She needs to go back to school so she can compete, but to do that she needs alimony. Otherwise the money from the property settlement is going to be gone in a couple of years and she'll be on welfare." I had to stifle a laugh.

"Welfare, your Honor?" I responded. "Let's get serious. She's asking for alimony on top of the property settlement. Totally unfair. He won the big jackpot, and what did he do? He paid off their debts, paid the taxes – even bought her a fancy car. That would be punishing him for succeeding."

Fortunately, the judge saw it our way. "Madam, do you want me to kill the goose that laid the golden egg? If he gets hammered too hard, he's got no reason to get up in the morning. Nope. I'll let him keep the house, and he'll pay you fifty thousand dollars a year, with interest, for the next ten years. You should be grateful that I'm not making you pay child support for those children you left him with."

Gus was happy with the result, although I could tell the burden of paying the settlement was going to weigh on him. "It pisses me off that her boyfriend's driving around in that Mercedes," he said with an ironic chuckle.

"It's going to be tough, especially in those first few years while the kids are still at home," I said.

"Yup. I'm going to have to live another ten years to pay her off. Guess that Hep C will have to take a back seat till I'm done."

"Hep C? What are you talking about?" I asked.

"Hepatitis C – it ruins your organs. That's what I get for sharing those dirty needles. The doc says I've only got half a normal liver function."

"That's terrible, Gus. Why didn't you tell me about this before the trial? We could have used it."

"Oh no," he said. "It's not her fault I'm sick. It's my own doing."

I was shaken by this, and could only conjure up a "Good luck, then."

Gus drove off in his pickup truck. He and Naomi gave me a friendly wave.

* * * * * * *

About three years later, I was scheduled to meet a new client named Kurt Swanson. The receptionist rang and said, "Your new client's here, along with an old friend."

The old friend was Gus. He had changed again. Like the first time I'd seen him, he was gaunt and sickly looking. It wasn't the same as when he'd been using --no blemishes, no nervous tics – but he'd aged a dozen years.

"This here's one of my best workers, Kurt," he said. "His girlfriend's got an Order for Protection against him. Now she wants to renew it. I got him into the Domestic Abuse Project, and he hasn't had a drink for six months, so he wants it off his record. Deer hunting's coming up and he can't get a license til it's cleared up."

Kurt spoke up. "Before anything, I've gotta say this. There aren't many bosses that would've put up with me like Gus has for all these years. I was nothing but trouble. He rode herd on me and finally got me into that program. Thing is, he was honest about his own mistakes. Instead of giving me some phony lecture, he showed me by his own example that I could turn my life around. What a guy!"

Gus was beaming. I wanted to talk to him, so I asked Kurt to excuse himself.

"How you doing, Gus?"

"Oh, the business is booming now that the recession's over," he said. "We doubled our employees and -- guess what -- I managed to pay Kandy off early."

"I was asking about you -- not the company."

"You can probably tell by looking at me. I have end-stage liver disease. The Hepatitis C progressed to cirrhosis. They're just giving me a few months. That's what I get for all that wild living, I guess."

"How about you and Naomi?"

"She got her law degree last year. Then she ran off with my best foreman. It hurt, but I was fooling myself by thinking that she'd stay with me."

Wow! First, his wife, then his girlfriend. It seemed so wrong, and I was disappointed in Naomi for being so shallow.

"What happened?" I asked.

"I guess she had too much energy for a sick old man like me."

A couple of months later I was in court for Kurt's hearing. He'd stayed sober and his sponsor had sent a glowing letter about his progress.

"Kurt," I said as I spotted him outside the courtroom, "where's Gus?"

"He passed last week," Kurt said, his face contorted with emotion.

The judge was impressed by Kurt's progress. He dismissed the petition to extend the restraining order, so Kurt would get to go deer hunting after all.

"Gus would have been proud of you," I said.

"He saved a lot of people," Kurt said, "not just me."

CHAPTER 15

Mamma Bear

She rose from her chair in the lobby to greet me with a friendly smile. She wore a nameplate that said "Betty", and below it was inscribed with the name of her establishment – "Gordy's Hi Hat Café." I knew it-- so does anyone else who heads up to their cabin in the Northwoods --it's noted by a big billboard - "Famous Sunday Brunch".

Betty must have driven the seventy-five miles down right after work, because the stale grease from breakfast cooking permeated the sterile office air within seconds. She must have known it. "Sorry there wasn't time to clean up," she said, "but I didn't want to reschedule. There's only two weeks before the trial."

In spite of it, she made a pleasant impression. Her permed hair was red – or I should say it probably once was red but was now bright red – and was enhanced by copper accents, and, although the mascara was a bit over the top, it was clear that she cared about her appearance. Her thin blue polyester utility shift zipped down the front. Perhaps a good friend would have suggested it was a bit too tight for her figure, but maybe she'd already considered that.

"My family calls me Mamma Bear," she said. She was young to be a grandmother, I thought. I put her in her early forties. These days most people wait until their thirties to marry and start a family, but perhaps she'd been a teenage mother.

"He's my pride and joy," she said. She pulled out a snapshot of a toddler opening his Christmas presents. "He's Tommy, and he just turned two. After my daughter got divorced and Bill kicked me out, we all moved into the same double-wide. "

"What brings you down here to the Twin Cities?" I asked.

"Another screw-up," she said, "It's the story of my life. I just fired my lawyer."

"Two weeks before the trial? Why?"

"Oh, it's not his fault, really. He's a regular at the café, and he's young and cute. He helped me start my case when no one else would listen to me, and I thank him for that, but when we went to Court for the pretrial conference Bill's lawyer just outclassed him. When you're the richest guy in town you get the best lawyer, I s'pose. Yup, Bill Johansen, my ex, mister big shot."

I noticed that she was holding a satchel full of legal documents, so I asked her to let me see.

"They call it a palimony case, I guess," she said. "My first lawyer said there's a law against them but my case might be an exception."

This was generally true. In the 1970's, actor Lee Marvin had a long-term live-in relationship with his girlfriend, Michelle Triola. When they broke up, she sued him for support on a theory of cohabitation rights. The tabloid press ate it up, plastering pictures of them that were displayed by the supermarket counters and calling it a "palimony" case.

After protracted litigation, she won a generous settlement.

Perhaps because Marvin was such a popular actor, and Ms. Triola wasn't very photogenic, or maybe because there were religious and moral undertones to unmarried relationships, politicians reacted negatively. "Anti-palimony" laws were enacted in many states, including Minnesota. According to our statute, a lawsuit could not occur in a meretricious relationship (another word for cohabitation) unless the parties had entered into a written contract, "prior to a cohabitation in which sexual relations are contemplated."

You heard me right. According to this law, a man and woman would need to sit down and draw up a legally binding document before they had sex. How often does that happen?

I read through Betty's Petition. It said that Betty and Bill had lived together at his house for seven years. During that time, Betty had quit her waitress job to keep Bill's house and support his quest to patent an invention of his. "Heat's On" is a system that keeps construction equipment operable during cold weather, and it had made him rich.

"He was already well-off," Betty said, "he's got the biggest house in town out there on Long Lake (note to reader: there are probably two hundred Long Lakes in our state), and there's a five-car garage full of pickup trucks, snowmobiles, fishing boats, and hunting equipment. He had a prototype for his heating machine when I first met him," Betty said, "and after I moved in he was going all over the country showing it to manufacturers. After a year or so, he hooked up with a guy he trusted and they started producing them. I'd go to the Cities with him when he met with the patent lawyers and bankers. That's when the money really started rolling in."

Betty shifted in her seat, self-consciously straightening her tight clothing. "Even so, he was chintzy about his money, unless it was for something he wanted. I told him I'd help redecorate the house, cuz his ex-wife had terrible taste, but he made me do it with my own money – my life's savings. I said, 'I'm not going to do that unless you marry me,' and he said he would."

I winced inwardly. "What happened?"

"Well, he said we'd go on vacation to Las Vegas and have one of those Elvis weddings. But it never happened. He was always too busy, or so he said. So here I am with this palimony case.

"I think I put a lot into this relationship – my savings, my labor, and I helped him with his invention and his investments, and now I'm back in the double-wide, waiting tables. He's got another girlfriend with him now and he comes into the café all the time with his buddies, and they have a good laugh at my expense while I'm fetching their coffee for them."

"Betty," I said, "I'd love to help you, but I've got a trial starting tomorrow that's supposed to last into next week. Why don't you let me get another lawyer for you? "

"Oh, please," she had tears in her eyes. "I paid the retainer fee that your paralegal quoted me. My friends all say you're the best!".

As usual, flattery, money, and tears got the best of me. Against my better judgment, I said yes. My assistant procured Betty's file from the former lawyer.

As it turned out, the proceeding I already had didn't end until the day before Betty's trial. It was a lawyer's worst-case scenario. I was tired, and unprepared, and would have to learn the case as it unfolded in the courtroom.

The courthouse was a pre-WWII relic, with beige brick and corroding concrete trim. and the hallway was jammed with the usual Monday morning "drunks and disorderlies." Walking by them in my three-piece suit, I could sense their resentment of the interloper from the Cities. When I entered the courtroom, I saw Bill's lawyer cheerfully chatting with the judge. They probably played in the same foursome at the local country club.

"Hello counselor," the judge said. "I'm Judge Larson. Let me introduce you to your adversary, Mr. Knutson."

They were friendly enough, but I had to wonder whether they'd been discussing the case already. My suspicions were confirmed right away.

"The judge and I were thinking you'd want to call your client as your first witness," Knutson said. "Then your case could be over by lunchtime so the judge's court reporter can get to her doctor's appointment on time".

The judge leaned over and spoke to me in a hushed tone as if to imply confidentiality. "I was a little surprised to see you coming up from the Cities for this case. I thought her first lawyer was doing right by her, but of course, who she hires is her choice."

In a regular tone of voice, and said with a chuckle, "Well, bring your client in here so we can get our little drama underway."

I was relieved to see Betty wearing a conservative and tasteful blue pantsuit, although it looked like the hairdresser had given her an extra shot of copper accents and the mascara was still an issue. Her ex was sitting at his counsel table. He was a handsome, fiftyish guy wearing farm jeans and a Carhartt jacket – a simple touch for a multi-millionaire, I thought. Seated a few rows behind Bill and his lawyer were two women. One was middle-aged, perhaps five years older than Betty. Like Betty, she was a redhead, but she had a dark, angry countenance. Next to her was a younger woman, who looked to be her daughter.

"Who are they?" I asked Betty.

"Oh, that's his ex-wife and his stepdaughter," she said. "I didn't have a chance to tell you before, but she's trying to re-open her divorce case against Bill. She says he was hiding money from her when she settled with him and she wants part of the invention money. That's her daughter from a previous marriage, and she's here because she's a hateful bitch."

What other surprises were in store? I wondered. But it was time for the trial to start. Betty was my first and only witness.

"I was working at the Hi-Hat," she testified. "Bill used to come in after church for the brunch, and after a while he made it known that he wanted me to be the one waiting on him. He'd wink at me and say, 'Red, how about that coffee?' It was sort of a secret code we had. He always called me 'Red,' on account of my hair, and everyone could see something special was going on between us." She smiled at Bill, but he ignored her with a vacant stare.

The silence was interrupted by a loud and sarcastic snort from one of the women behind us, and tears started rolling down Betty's cheeks. "Now, settle down folks," the judge said. "This is a court of law, not a reality show. We all have to see each other in church next Sunday. Let's show some respect for each other."

Betty bounced back quickly, describing her efforts over the years of her relationship with Bill. She included a quantification of the hours of sweat equity she'd put into Bill's house, the number of business trips she'd gone on with him, and the income she'd given up when she quit her job at his request. My paralegal had obtained real estate tax statements showing the increase in value of the home over the seven years of her cohabitation, and we'd subpoenaed financial statements Bill had submitted to the local bank to support his loan portfolio. We calculated that his net worth had increased from a little over a million dollars at the beginning of their relationship to more than ten million at the end.

"Did you keep records of your personal savings?" I asked her.

"Yes," she said as I handed her the exhibit we'd prepared.

"I'm showing you Exhibit D. Can you tell us what it is?"

"Yes," she said, "These are all of my bank statements for the past ten years. I kept them for my taxes. It says that I'd saved over fifty thousand dollars up to the time that Bill asked me to help him with the remodeling. Of course, it all got spent on the project. "

"How were you save that much on a waitress' salary?" I asked.

"Cuz I lived simple. I lived in a double-wide. I made my daughter pay rent. I didn't travel. I didn't go to the casino and I drove a crappy car."

"How much is in your account now?" I asked.

"In the year since he kicked me out, I managed to save another $6,000, but then I had to give $1,000 to my first lawyer and $5,000 to you, so I'm broke again," Betty said. "And what's your living situation now," I asked Betty.

"I suppose you could say I'm right back to where I was seven years ago, but I'll never get those years back. All that time Bill was puttin' sixty hours a week into his invention, and traveling around promoting it, and wheeling and dealing with the investors. I stood by him, keeping his house and giving him moral support, and on top of that I was his lover. He'd say, 'Red, I couldn't do this without you.'

"Then, after everything I did for him, he just dumps me for someone else like I'm a used tire. If he's gotten that much richer, then I think I've earned some of that."

"So," I said, "what do you think would be a fair remuneration?"

Knutson was on his feet immediately.

"I object, your Honor!"

"The question invades the province of the court. It's not for her to decide what's fair – that's your job, your Honor."

"Of course you're right, Mr. Knutson," the judge said. "but I'm a big boy - -- I can make up my own mind. Why don't you answer the question as best you can, Missy."

"For my time, valued at $15.00 per hour, that would be $200,000, Betty said. "But then his net worth has gone up so much, and the value of his house too, so I think I'm entitled to my fair share of that."

She said it with a quiver in her voice, but she looked Bill straight in the eye. This time he met her gaze.

We were done. After a rocky start, Betty had finished strong. It was time for the cross-examination.

Attorney Knutson approached Betty.

"Just to be clear, Ma'am, there was never anything in writing between you and my client, correct?"

"No, but he promised he'd marry me," she responded.

Attorney Knutson made a pleading gesture to the judge. "Your Honor . . . "

"Just answer the question, young lady. It's yes or no," the judge said.

"I'm sorry," Betty said, chastened by the warning.

"And, also to be clear, my client was married when you undertook your relationship with him, correct?"

"Yes, but," Betty said. Then, catching herself, "I mean yes."

"As a matter of fact, he was happily married to the woman in the back of this room, and you broke that marriage up, correct?"

What the hell? She hadn't said a thing about this to me. I've never understood why I don't get the straight story from my clients. I guess they want to put their best foot forward, but this was a perfect example of why you should tip off your lawyer to the bad news. I had to stop this.

"Objection, your Honor, irrelevant," I said. "This case is about the financial value of my client's participation in the relationship – not whose fault it was."

"Not correct." Knutson said, "Not long ago his client was on the stand talking about their secret code, implying that she was lured into this. She opened the door to this issue, and now that it's coming out that she's the aggressor and she doesn't like it."

"The objection is sustained," Judge Larson said. "Proceed."

"The fact is, Ma'am, that during these seven years, you lived in luxury, keeping a five-bedroom house and driving my client's cars. That's a pretty far cry from your previous life."

"Yes," Betty said.

"The 'Heat's On," invention – that wasn't your idea, was it?"

"I didn't say that," Betty said. "But I helped him indirectly . . ."

"Answer the question!" Judge Larson snapped.

"No," said Betty, looking miserable. She cast a pleading look at Bill. He squirmed in his chair.

"Okay, folks," the judge said, "Time for our morning break. We'll resume in thirty minutes."

Betty made a bee-line for the outdoor smoking area as I called my office. As soon as I hung up, the ex-wife and her daughter approached me.

"Looks like your client caught you by surprise," the older one said with a nasty laugh.

"That figures," the younger one chimed in. "She's a lying, cheating, homewrecking slut. I guess you thought you could come up from the Cities and blow everyone away. Good luck with that."

Then it was back to the ex-wife. "My lawyer says I'm going to get a piece of that invention, so you guys are arguing over the crumbs. Loser!"

There wasn't anything to be gained by participating in a conversation with these two, so I turned around and walked away.

I looked out the second-story hallway window, and noticed that the two women were approaching Betty from behind. In short order, the three of them were engaged in an angry shouting match with her. Suddenly, Betty pushed at the ex-wife. The stepdaughter pushed back and delivered a hard fist to Betty's face. In a moment, they were all on the ground, rolling on the asphalt. A female bailiff, also in the smoking area, rushed to the scene and separated them.

I ran out the door, but as I reached the scene two deputies had arrived with handcuffs. The shouting continued. Betty was bleeding profusely from her nose – there was already a large bloody stain on the front of her pantsuit.

The Sheriff arrived. After a quick look, he announced, "All three of you are going to jail, right now. Separate cells."

Shortly thereafter, the judge's law clerk approached me. "The judge wants all parties and lawyers in Court tomorrow at 9:00."

I called a bail bondsman, and Betty was released a few hours later. The next morning I waited for her in the courtroom.

She was a sight. There was a large gauze covering her nose, and she was sporting two black eyes. The ex-wife and her daughter were again in the rear of the courtroom, also looking worse for wear. The judge entered.

"Let me say how disappointed I am in you ladies," he started. "I've looked at the videotape of what happened and I've asked the County Attorney to prepare charges against all three of you for Disorderly Conduct. But, I'm not going to let you hijack this trial. Mr. Knutson, it's your case. Go ahead."

"Before I start our case, your Honor," he said, "I'm moving for a directed verdict."

At the close of the Plaintiff's case, the judge can decide that there isn't sufficient evidence to require a trial to go forward. If Bill's motion were to be granted, the case would be over and Betty would get nothing.

"When our anti-palimony law was passed, it was to prevent cases just like this," Knutson said. "Our country has succeeded because men like my client have had the innovative qualities to take an idea forward and make it succeed. Now the vultures are circling, trying to suck away the fruits of his endeavors."

"And don't forget about the Internal Revenue Service," the judge said.

He and Knutson shared a chuckle, as if they'd had the same discussion over cocktails last night, while perhaps enjoying a laugh about the fracas outside the courthouse. At that moment, I knew we were sunk.

"That's right, your Honor, and if he wanted to share the bounty, he would have married this woman. But he didn't, and because of that this case must be dismissed." The judge allowed me to give a rebuttal, but it was like talking to a brick wall. "Case dismissed," the judge said. You ladies will need to be here tomorrow for your arraignments."

As the courtroom cleared, Knutson walked over, extended his hand, and said, "Nice try."

I shook, but responded, "It's not over yet. I'm going to appeal."

Four months later, I was standing in front of a three-judge panel at the Court of Appeals in Saint Paul. I was familiar with two of the three judges, and sensed they were with us as I spoke. The third judge, though, was a little hostile.

"You've heard the adage that good cases make bad law, haven't you counselor?" He said.

He was referring to a theory that cases that beg for justice (a "good case") can induce a court to make an exception to a law, so as to do justice. But then when too many exceptions are made, loopholes expand, and the law becomes worthless – or a "bad law. "

"I agree with the principle, your Honor," I said, "but the Supreme Court has already made an exception in the case of In re Ericksen, and others as well, where a party like my client has made identifiable contributions to the meretricious relationship. My client had documented the economic contributions she had made."

Two months later the opinion arrived. "Reversed and remanded" – it said. It meant that Judge Larson was overruled and that the case should go forward. It didn't mean we'd win, or how much Betty would get, but it meant we would return to finish the trial. It's always awkward to appear in front of a judge against whom you have successfully appealed, and it was no exception with Judge Larson as court was reconvened. The friendly interlocutor who had introduced me to my opponent on the first day of the trial was no more.

"I don't know why we even show up for work when the geniuses down in Saint Paul reverse every decision we make," he snarled. "I'm ordering the parties and their lawyers to go over to Attorney Knutson's office for the rest of the day and see if it can be settled. court is adjourned." Without another word, he stalked back to his chambers.

When I drove into Attorney Knutson's parking lot, I saw Bill's fancy pickup, with the "Heat's On" logo painted on the side. Betty's old green beater was parked next to it. When I walked around the corner, I was shocked to see Betty and Bill standing together in front of the office, sharing a cigarette.

"Are you all right here, Betty?" I said.

"We're good," she said with a smile. "Go in and talk to the lawyer now, okay?" Knutson was waiting for me as I entered. "We're going to make a cash offer to your client right now. I've got a release prepared – all we need is a number. Would you tell my client to come back here?"

Bill and Betty were still outside smoking. I told him he was needed back in the office.

As he left, he smiled at Betty, and said, "Good luck, Red." She smiled back.

"What was that about?" I asked Betty.

"He's going to give me $150,000, and we're done."

"No, Betty," I said. "We can do way better than that. We got our case reversed. "He's worth $10 million – probably more by now. You deserve more than that."

"I knew you wouldn't like it," she said. "Listen, $150,000 is more money than I've ever had. I can pay you and still have more than $100,000 left. He's broke up with his new woman, and I think we've got a future."

I gave it another try, but she'd hear nothing of it.

"I'm the client, right? It's my decision."

The papers were signed. Bill got out his checkbook.

"I'm going to talk to the lawyer for a few minutes about the case dismissal, so wait for me out in the lobby, okay, Betty?" I said.

When I walked back to the lobby a few minutes later Betty wasn't there. Maybe she was in her car, I thought. When I went out to the lot her green beater was still there, but Betty had left with Bill.

CHAPTER 16

The Family Jewels

The message popped up on my computer screen – it was from my law partner Mike. "Could you stop by my office right now?"

Walking in, I observed an attractive woman sitting in a client chair, talking to him. "Oh, here he is," Mike said, introducing me to Nancy. Looking at her again, it became obvious that Nancy was more than attractive. She had wavy reddish-brown hair, emerald eyes and creamy white skin, and the stature of a fashion model. She was a real beauty. "I'd handle her case myself," Mike said, "but her husband is headmaster at the school my kids go to, and I'd feel conflicted doing it." It was the premier private school in the city - where the progeny of the well-heeled elite learn the rules of the rules of the privileged world they will inherit. Nancy's address spoke of the tony neighborhood nearby.

Back in my office, she said, "I want a divorce. My husband cheats on me. Last week, he got back from a trip and told me that I should go to the clinic and get myself checked out."

"What for?" I stupidly blurted out, instantly wishing I could grab the words back out of the air. But if she was chagrined, she didn't show it. Instead, she handed me a small, but weighty silk purse and a sheet of paper with the names of seven or eight women.

The purse was full of rings and jewels as well as several $20 gold coins from the nineteenth century.

"This is his family fortune – he cares more about it than me, and that's a list of the women I think he's slept with. I want you to offer his things back to him in return for his admitting to these names."

"What makes you think he'd agree to that? And, why would you want to know?"

"Oh, he'll do it if I promise to keep it secret – it's just something a woman wants to know," she went on.

"By the way, I don't have access to the cash so I can't pay you a retainer fee, but can't we work something out?"

It was against my better judgment, but another look at her tipped the scales. "Okay, I can take an attorney's lien against your property." That was fine with her.

I called the husband's lawyer and passed on the proposal. And, despite his initial incredulity, acceptance of our proposal arrived the next day by courier. His client would do the deal, but only if an iron-clad confidentiality agreement, which was enclosed, was signed. We signed the documents, and soon enough Nancy's husband got his jewels back and we had the list. Five of the names were circled, each initialed by him.

Soon it was time for the temporary hearing, the purpose of which was to determine an Order for the next six or so months until the trial. Nancy walked into the courtroom in a stunning but demure cashmere navy dress. As I stood to make the opening statement, Nancy grabbed my sleeve, "Get him!" she said. It was more of a command.

I was taken aback. What is this, I thought? She's the master and I'm the attack dog? It took a minute to regain my composure, but then I launched into my statement, scolding the husband for his infidelity and the resulting indignities Nancy had suffered, all the while carefully honoring the confidentiality of the agreement we had. I thought it was going well, and I peeked up at the judge to gauge his reaction. He was nodding his head, sure enough, but his gaze was directed not at me but beneath our counsel table. Curiously, I looked down myself, realizing that what I had thought was Nancy's demure dress actually had a long slit which was offering a generous view of her lovely thigh. The lawyers eventually finished their presentations and it was time for the judge's decision. I always advise my clients that everyone loses in divorce. Financially, a whole pie is cut in half at the same time that a marriage begun with such high hope is cast on the rocks.

This was, however, was a complete and unconditional victory for us. She got the home, the lake cabin and a more than generous – indeed almost usurious – award of alimony. As we walked out of the courtroom I saw the husband and his attorney shaking their heads. Nancy suddenly, and in full view, threw her arms around me. "I couldn't have a better lawyer than you!" I reveled in her warm embrace, the sweetness of her scent and the thrilling win in court.

Six hours later I was in the shower room at the health club, relaxed by my tough workout and enjoying the ablution of the steaming water. The animated conversation nearby barely registered.

Suddenly I was interrupted, "That's the guy I was telling you about," I heard. Looking up, I saw that it was him – Nancy's husband! He was with a friend, and I was standing directly in front of them, defenseless in my nakedness. What's worse, he was taller than me, placing me in awkward proximity to his – tool of adultery.

"I suppose you think you're hot shit after court today," he said, "but you'd better watch out for that client of yours."

"Thanks a lot," I shot back with a dose of sarcasm, "Especially when it's coming from you!"

The next morning as I walked into my office, there was an array of pink "Please Call" slips on my desk. They were from opposing counsel, and the most recent indicated "Urgent!" I returned to call.

"What the hell?" Her lawyer was angry. "You signed an agreement. Now I'm getting calls from some woman who says your client's harassing her and accusing her of adultery. I'm holding you responsible for this!" I recognized the woman's name from the list and promised to get to the bottom of it.

"I didn't do a thing - I promise," Nancy said when I called her. "I just wanted to know who these women were. Maybe my husband told her about the list. Who knows if she's even telling the truth? I'd never lie to you . . ." she said, stifling a sob. Even though her explanation defied logic, I wanted to believe her, so that's where we left it.

The reprieve was short-lived, though. As I walked down to hallway for coffee, Mike called out to me, asking me to join him in his office. There was a couple in his office.

"These folks have two children who go to school with my kids," he said. The husband shot me an angry look. Glancing at his wife, I could see that she'd been crying. The husband thrust a letter into my hands – it was signed by Nancy. "Your wife had sex with my husband," it said. "My lawyer will be starting a lawsuit against her." It went on, mentioning my name.

That did it. I called Nancy and told to come in immediately, and showed her the letter. She owned up to it. "I'm so sorry. I hope I didn't get you in trouble because you're the best lawyer I could ever have. It's just that – well, you know what he put me through."

"It's not that easy!" I was incensed. "You promised. Now I get to pick up the pieces because you lied. I wonder if that wasn't your plan all the way through."

Tears filled her eyes. "I thought you were on my side."

The next morning I got a call from a lawyer I didn't know. "I'm going to be Nancy's new lawyer," she said.

"What? Why?" I said.

"She just said she's lost confidence in you," was her response.

It's not unusual for divorce clients to change lawyers and we get used to it. But that this beautiful woman, for whom I'd gotten such a great win in court, had fired me really hurt.

After that, the months rolled by and I heard nothing more about Nancy or the case, and was actually starting to forget about it – other than a monthly reminder when my bill was returned as undeliverable. Then one day my assistant came in with the mail. "Looks important," she said.

There were two letters. The first was from the State Judicial Center, marked "Personal and Confidential." I drew a gasp, because that's how letters from the State Ethics Board are labeled. We divorce lawyers are the frequent recipients of these complaints and they're normally dismissed, but it's never a good feeling to get one. With a tremor in my fingers, I opened it. But, to my surprise, it wasn't from the ethics committee. Instead, it was from the State Board of Judicial Standards – the agency that polices judges.

"Your testimony is hereby requested at the hearing associated with the enclosed order," it said.

The order mentioned Nancy and the judge in our case – "Probable cause has been found an inappropriate sexual relationship between the above-named judge and party litigant in a proceeding for dissolution of marriage."

The other letter was from Twin Cities Title. Addressed to me, it also referenced Nancy, and stated, "At the sale of her lake cabin, your former client assured us that it was free and clear of encumbrances. However, our search determined the existence of your lien."

Enclosed was a check, marked "Paid in Full."

CHAPTER 17

Mark of Shame

Every year, a leading publication in our state bestows on a few young lawyers the designation "Rising Star." That's a term that would have aptly described my friend Mark. He was five years younger than me, a "home town boy done good." Mark had been a big wheel in high school – president of the student council, quarterback of the football team, valedictorian. He went on to be a top student at the premier law school in the state, returning to his suburban community to open a law office.

Mark was stunningly good-looking. You could tell by the way women acted around him. The middle-age ladies at the clerk of courts office were enthralled by Mark. Though he was twenty years younger, they'd shamelessly gush, "You look just like a young Paul Newman," when he flashed a smile at them. This would often be followed by an inquiry as to his marital status, presumably on behalf of their daughters – but, based on the way some of them behaved around him, I'm not so sure of that. If Mark needed a favor from the Assignment Office, such as to move up a trial date, he'd quickly secure a friendly accomplice.

Mark was married, and the father of two boys. His family lived in a big house he'd recently built in the nicest part of his otherwise blue-collar town.

Mark was also popular with men. He had a charming, friendly manner. So, when he said no to your settlement proposal, he'd wink his eye and soften the blow with something like, "You had a great idea and I'm with you. It was my client who refused it. What an asshole!"

We had many cases against each other over the years, and built up a friendly, but professional, relationship. One day he made an appointment to see me about a "private matter." That could have an ominous portent, but didn't turn out to be directly about Mark.

"I'd like you to do a big favor for me," he said. "My parents are getting divorced. What a shock that was. I'd appreciate it if you'd be Mom's lawyer."

I said okay, and he added, "You're good friends with Mickey Silver, right?"

I nodded. Mickey was a trusted colleague.

"Great. He's a friend of mine, too, and I'm going to ask him to take on Dad's side. Maybe the two of you can get together and make it as easy as possible for them."

After Mark left, one of our secretaries burst into my office. She was young, and although she was a good technician, she was painfully shy – so much so that I was considering letting her go. This time, though, she was beaming. "Who's your friend?" she asked. "Is he ever handsome! I about fell off my chair when he walked in." It was the longest conversation I ever had with her.

Mark's mother, in her sixties, was a nervous wreck, and a real challenge to represent. She would pace back and forth in the office – ignoring my repeated requests that she relax and sit down.

I asked her when she had first considered divorcing her husband. "Right after the honeymoon," she said.

Maybe her strange personality was the consequence of so many years of regret. "He's had a life-long love affair with himself," she added.

After an hour or so, she demanded to look at my notepad. I'm not a big note taker, preferring to keep eye contact with the client, and following up later by dictating a memo of the conference. Occasionally, I'll make a note, especially if my client says something really dumb.

Fortunately, in Helen's case, I hadn't written anything, so I agreed – just for that one time. She insisted that I tape my phone calls with the other lawyer so she could listen to them. "I want to know what you're saying about me," she said. That one I refused.

Mark's father was an accountant. He was a good-looking fellow, like his son, but was consumed with his spreadsheets of the family finances. He had the personality of a dead fish, and I wondered how Mark, with his boundless confidence and outgoing demeanor, could be a product of these two. At a settlement conference, I suggested to both of them that they must be proud of their son. All I got was a silent acknowledgment. The whole experience turned out to be frustrating and unpleasant, but Mickey and I got the job done and we settled the case.

Shortly thereafter, Mark and I were on the opposite end of a divorce case. He was representing a local lawyer, Lawrence Janssen -- one of the courthouse regulars whom I tried to avoid when possible. Unable to make a go of it with conventional, quality clients, Janssen sought out bottom feeders by offering cut-rate legal services. If you were at a social event, looking to enjoy yourself with friends and cocktails, you'd cringe if you saw him walking over, knowing you were in for a long, boring story about some dreadful case of his.

My client Kirsten, on the other hand, was lovely and intelligent, with blue eyes, blonde hair, and pale skin. She was reserved and demure. Not sexy – just beautiful. What had she seen in Lawrence?

The case was complicated by the fact that Kirsten's father had made Janssen his law partner. Neither one of them was a shining beacon in the legal community.

One day I got a call from Kirsten. "The police found Lawrence's car rolled over on the highway last night, but they couldn't find him. I hope he's all right."

I called his lawyer. "Oh, he's fine." Mark said, "See, he isn't as dumb as we thought." We had a good laugh about that. In the shorthand that lawyers use when they talk to each other, he didn't have to add anything else. When you roll your car and you're okay to walk away, if you're smart, you get lost. You can take care of things twenty-four hours later when the booze is out of your system. That's what Janssen did. The fool is the one who sits in the car, waiting for the cops to show up, resulting in a DWI and the world of pain that accompanies it.

I passed on the news to Kirsten. She was relieved that her husband was okay, but not so impressed with his conduct. "Get this over with. Let's sell the house and split up the money – ASAP."

That's what we did, and shortly thereafter we had the closing at my office. It was a sad commentary on their marriage that the twenty-thousand dollars they got from the sale was the sum total of their net worth.

It's standard to place the proceeds into one of the lawyer's trust accounts until the divorce judgment is final, and I was prepared to do that went Mark pulled me aside. "I don't know why, but Janssen's insisting we put the house money in my trust account.

Okay?"

"Sure – no problem," I said.

"This is another no-fee deal for me," he said. "I get tired of doing these freebies."

That was another of Mark's traits – he'd be the one to open his bill-fold and pick up the tab -- whether it was for his family, friends, or even, sometimes, a client. As successful as he appeared to be, you'd wonder how he could afford to do business this way.

Perhaps it was because of Mark's charming manner that it never occurred to me to be suspicious of his insistence about the trust account.

A couple of weeks later, my phone rang. "It's your client Kirsten," the receptionist said, "It's urgent."

"I just got a call from a friend. She's getting divorced too, and Mark represents her husband. She says Mark's in trouble – the Ethics Board just called about her case. I think it's about money." I promised Kirsten I'd follow up, and called the Board of Professional Responsibility that afternoon.

When I did, I was referred to a lawyer at the Board – a guy who played things strictly by the book. He confirmed that Mark was the center of an investigation, but refused to elaborate. When I explained that my client's entire settlement was possibly at risk, he'd only tell me that they were near completion of their case and would announce the results when they were done.

I decided that I had to be proactive, and drove the twenty miles or so over to Mark's office.

"I'm sorry, he can't see you at the moment," his secretary said. "Could you come back tomorrow?"

"No. I'll wait," I told her. I sat there, stewing for an hour – maybe longer. I could actually hear Mark through the door talking on the phone, so when I noticed a pause in the conversation, I barged in.

He looked up, and on seeing me flashed a smile. I hadn't been to his office before and took a look. It was nice, but his desk was stacked with files. It was before the days of voicemail, and phone calls were noted by those pink "While you were out" slips. I hated them, and if I'd get five or more, I'd get nervous enough to start working on them, but Mark had two huge piles of them – each six inches high. He also looked like he hadn't slept much the night before.

"I just talked to the ethics investigator." He nodded.

"Look, no matter what happened, you're still my friend."

"Thanks," he said. "It really sucks, but I'll come through it okay."

"I'd be glad to help you if you need it," I said, "but I'm going to have to have Kirsten's money, right now."

"Sure," he said, "I'll write the check, but I have to post-date it. The bank has the account all screwed up. It's okay if she waits a few days, right?"

"Mark," I said, "you know as well as I do that our clients come before everything, including friendship. I'm not leaving till I get the money. No post-dated check. Make it out to me, and I'm going straight over to the bank to cash it."

He wrote the check, although I could detect a tremor in his hand as he did so. The bank was within walking distance, and I was there in an instant. Because I didn't have an account with the bank, I was put through the third degree -- I had to give an imprint of my thumb, and then I was interrogated by a loan officer. She hemmed and hawed about the trouble they were having with Mark's account and tried to get me to return later, but eventually, I walked out with a bank check for half the homestead proceeds.

What happened then? I can tell you firsthand because I had hired Mark's secretary not too long after my confrontation with him. She replaced the shy young woman who was bowled over by Mark. She'd been left with a paycheck from Mark that was drawn on a closed account.

According to her, Mark came in the next day and spent the morning in his office. Then he said, "I'm going to lunch. I won't be back."

No truer words were spoken. He might have gone to lunch, but he didn't come back -- ever. He disappeared, leaving his family, his clients, and his creditors in the lurch. The local media ran feature stories on him, describing his history, his story, and the massive theft. The specifics were set forth by the Supreme Court, in 408 N.W.2d 574 (1987). Summarizing the decision, the Court found that Mark had stolen approximately $450,000 from numerous (mostly female) clients. The Court concluded, "We find no relief to be appropriate other than disbarment." Kirsten's money was the last anyone got out of him.

As a result of Mark's escapades, the state established a client security fund to ensure that his clients, and future victims of other lawyers' dishonesty, were compensated for their losses.

At the time of the decision, Mark's whereabouts were still unknown. Six years later, a headline in the local paper announced the news – "Disbarred lawyer found, arrested in Taos, New Mexico." It was Mark. He'd been on the lam all the time, having adopted an alias incorporating a first name of one of his sons and a surname based on his wife's maiden name. He'd been living a high-profile life as a host for a well-known resort. There was even a picture of him on a promotional brochure – sitting in a hot tub with a beautiful model, each of them holding a glass of wine, as if to say – "If you stay at our hotel – you'll be just like us!" However, proving that there is no such thing as a perfect crime, Mark had used his real social security number on his bank account, resulting, eventually, in detection.

A year or two later our family was in Taos on vacation. It's an artsy, bohemian place, where you could well imagine conjuring up a fake identity to conceal your secrets. We went on one of those white-water rafting adventures on the Rio Grande. Afterward, as we were waiting around to be picked up, I asked our guide if he'd ever heard of Mark – the lawyer who'd fled from the law and ended up in Taos.

He gave me a blank look for a moment. Then the recognition lit up his face. "You mean Judd Pratt?" He bellowed it. "That son-of-a-bitch! He dated my sister. Screwed her life up and stole her money!"

Years later I was walking through the courthouse when I noticed a vaguely familiar face out of the corner of my eye. I heard my name called out from behind me. It was Mark.

He was older and worse for wear, as you might expect from someone who'd spent years in prison. He'd gone gray, and I noticed a spare tire hanging over his belt. Still, he flashed me his winning smile and asked me about myself and my law partners.

"I miss you guys," he said.

"What are you doing here?" I asked.

"Paying my real estate taxes." Then he added, sheepishly. "Also, I'm making my monthly report to the parole office."

The conversation went on for a while, but it was awkward, interspersed with pregnant pauses.

As he bade me goodbye, he said, "Tell Kirsten I'm glad she got her money."

CHAPTER 18

The Magazine

People think that lawyers are just in it for the money. Sure – the pay's okay. But for me, it's all about going to bat for your client, and sometimes it feels so good.

A demure woman in her early forties had already been seated in the office. She was conservatively dressed in a blue pin-striped suit. She had a shy countenance, but a pretty, kind face.

"I never thought I'd be in a lawyer's office."

She wanted to go on, so I let her.

"My husband's an executive at the local munitions plant. They employ hundreds of people in our town. He's on the church board. Chairman of the country club. And, he's rich. He knows everyone, even the judges. They all think he's the Great Man."

"I'm sure he didn't do it alone," I said. "You should get credit for his success as well."

"He doesn't see it that way. Everyone assumes we're the perfect family, but they've never seen behind the curtain. She clutched a Kleenex with both hands as the tears welled up in her eyes. "He's so stubborn. He says he won't give me a divorce."

I tried to re-assure her. "It's not up to him to give you a divorce – you have the right to it if you choose. We have no-fault divorce. You don't have to have grounds."

Something important was coming. "I'm going to be honest with you. A couple of years ago there was this young man at work. He was so nice to me – my husband had been so mean – and, well, we had an affair. I cut it off, but the guilt was killing me. I decided to clear my conscience and tell my husband. I was hoping that maybe we could start counseling. What a dumb idea that was."

I wondered what compels people to make these confessions. Do they think of the consequences? A lot of good it did her.

Her words came in a rush. "Ever since then, it's been unbearable. He's threatened to tell my parents and the people at church. If I try to divorce him, he'll tell the judge. He's on me every day about it, and" – she blanched -- "he humiliates me. You know . . . sexually."

I called up the husband's lawyer to inform him that I was on the case. He was a good guy. One of the courthouse regulars.

"Oh, him," he said, referring to my client's husband. "Number one on my list of the top ten assholes of the year!"

We agreed to schedule a mediation conference the following week, as the trial was looming. Mediation is a court-mandated meeting involving the parties and their lawyers and is chaired by a certified mediator, usually a lawyer.

My client and I arrived early. The atmosphere, already tense, thickened as the husband and his lawyer walked in.

"Ah, counselor, your reputation precedes you," the husband said with sarcasm as he eschewed the customary handshake. "Do you enjoy making a fortune off other people's problems? Well, no one's getting rich off me. Alimony? Never! She'll be lucky to get out of this with her wedding ring."

"We'll see about that," I shot back.

He wasn't finished. "Have you screwed her yet? You wouldn't be the first. She usually goes for the younger guys, though."

We made a settlement proposal, but he clung to his threat.

In another week it was time for the trial. My client and I met in one of the anterooms outside the courtroom to go over her testimony. She handed me a canvas bookbag. "I don't know if this matters, but my sister said I should show it to you. My husband doesn't think I know about them."

Gazing inside the bag, I saw a stack of pornographic magazines -- the most graphic variety. I picked one off the top. On the cover was an attractive young couple engaged in an act which may still be illegal in some Southern states. "I'll keep this," I said as the clerk summoned me to report to chambers for a last-minute meeting with the judge.

The other lawyer and I stood in the corridor outside the judge's door waiting to be called. As we did so, I reached into the bag and flashed one of the offending magazines at him. Pointing to the banner above the picture, I said with mock indignation, "Look, your client reads Cocksucker Magazine!"

Any pretense of propriety immediately dissolved as we broke into unrestrained giggles. The clerk opened the door and we were escorted into chambers like two sixth graders hauled into the principal's office.

"What's so funny?", the judge demanded. He wasn't kidding, either. He was a prudish, fussbudget man. I wondered if he'd ever laughed.

His question only made us laugh harder. "Well, you'd better compose yourselves, because the trial is starting now!" the judge said.

Everyone was seated and ready as we entered the courtroom. The gallery was peppered with the usual assortment of family, friends, and supporters, divided, as we lawyers say, between the "groom's side" and the "bride's side." I noted a man in a ministerial collar was seated directly behind the husband.

As we took our places at the adjoining counsel tables, I discreetly but clearly displayed the bookbag, and its contents, to the husband. I tried catching his lawyer's eye, but he was evading mine, intent on avoiding another meltdown of guffaws.

The husband, however, had seen a ghost. His previous stubborn demeanor had evaporated. His shoulders slumped and I noticed that sweat was forming above his lip, Richard Nixon style.

Could I have used the porn stash in the trial? Probably not. What relevance did it have? But he didn't know that and his lawyer didn't have an opportunity to tell him.

I rose and said, "We call the Respondent."

The husband shuffled up to the witness stand and took the oath. I walked to the front of the counsel table to face him while, just a few feet away, my hand clearly rested on the book bag.

"I want you to repeat what you said last week before the mediation. You know, about the alimony."

He was stricken. His eyes shifted from me, to the judge, to the bookbag, to his lawyer, and finally to the gallery and the minister. For a while, it seemed he'd lost the power of speech. Finally, he replied softly, "Oh, that. I think I was confused. No, she has every right to alimony."

CHAPTER 19

The Friendly Divorce

They had made their appointment as a couple. "Bill and Jenny Bednarek -Divorce," it said. When I went out to the lobby to greet them, they both rose up to shake hands.

"This is a friendly divorce," Bill said as we sat down in my office. "We want you to represent both of us." Jenny nodded her agreement.

Bill was tall, pale, and had a sizable paunch. He looked to be in his late forties. As is often the case, his comb-over made the encroaching baldness look worse.

He had a habitual snort. It was like he needed to blow his nose, but he chose to keep it for himself instead. When I slid the Kleenex box over to him, he ignored it. Jenny rolled her eyes.

She looked years younger than Bill, although the questionnaire they had filled out said that they were the same age. She wore Lycra tights, and had bleach-blonde permed hair.

She and Bill wore yellow t-shirts with an image of a weightlifter, bearing the logo "Iron Works Gym." I was familiar with the place because it was on my way to work.

"You belong to Iron Works?" I asked.

"Actually, we own it," said Bill. "Bought it ten years ago."

"Looks like it's doing well," I said. "The parking lot's always full."

Jenny handed me a promotional flyer. There were numerous photos of the club, and information about membership rates. There was an enlarged photo of Bill and Jenny holding a certificate from the city, congratulating the company for its contribution to community causes. Standing between them was a younger, muscular middle-eastern looking man. He had curly black hair and dimples. White teeth were offset by his olive skin.

"Who's that in the photo with you?" I asked.

"Oh, that's Habib," said Jenny. "He's from Iran. Habib's our main attraction. He's been with us for five years. Before he came to us, most of our members were musclehead guys, but Habib got the women to join up for his fitness classes. They love him."

Couples often seek out lawyers for a "friendly divorce." Some do it to save money, while others believe it will help them remain on good terms after the marriage ends. Perhaps Bill and Jenny had heard of cases where couples had waged war in divorce court, wasting their assets and creating permanent rifts among family and friends. Some guidelines apply, though.

"The Lawyer's Code of Professional Responsibility doesn't allow me to represent both of you," I said. "However, if you agree on the terms of your divorce, I can prepare the necessary legal documents and go to court to finalize the case. One of you will be my client, and the other represents himself or herself."

"That sounds sort of silly," Jenny said. "You lawyers always make things so complicated."

"It's really for your protection," I said. "Otherwise, I'd have a conflict of interest. Let's say we were halfway through, and one of you had a change of heart about the terms, or the divorce itself. Then I'd be in the middle and I couldn't help either one of you. "

"I guess that makes sense," Bill said. "Why don't you be the client, dear?" he said to Jenny.

"I suppose," she said.

"Now, what do you have in mind about the divorce?" I asked.

"We don't really want to be divorced," Bill said. "The problem is that I just got diagnosed with rheumatoid arthritis. They say it's a serious case and I'll need treatment for the rest of my life. We don't have insurance. I checked into getting Medical Assistance, but we've got too much money. If we were divorced and Jenny got everything, I'd be eligible and all my expenses would be paid by the government."

Jenny spoke up. "It's just not fair that we work hard to build a business and pay taxes all our life, then when we need help, we get punished for being successful. Those politicians make sure they have insurance for themselves. They're a bunch of greedy bastards, excuse my French."

Although their scheme may sound unethical, it's actually legal, as long as the eligibility guidelines are followed. I'd handled a couple of similar cases before.

Some judges refuse to go along with the scheme, reasoning that it's a form of welfare fraud. From a moral standpoint, it's hard to disagree with that analysis. Why should well-off people be getting money meant for the poor? That's a philosophical argument, though. Lawyers are obligated to get the best result for their clients, so long as it's within the bounds of the law.

"I can help you," I said. "We'll create an agreement where Bill is given some of the property, just enough so he still qualifies for medical assistance. That will make it easier to sell it to the judge. Let's look at your financial statement."

Bill handed me a packet that had been prepared by an accountant. It described a net worth for he and Jenny of about one million dollars. Half of the value was in home equity and most of the remainder was in the business.

I was curious about the $400,000 value ascribed to The Iron Works. It was in a separate appraisal, addressed to a local bank. Obviously, Bill and Jenny had applied for a loan, and the appraiser had puffed up the numbers to impress a banker.

"It says here that your fixtures and equipment are worth a hundred grand, but the rest is in 'goodwill?'" I asked.

"The accountant told us it's the capitalized value of our member-ship list," Jenny said. "In other words, a buyer would pay us that for an ongoing business."

"But you said that Habib is your main attraction. What if he leaves and sets up a gym of his own down the street?"

"Oh, he'd never do that. He loves us and we just paid him a big bonus," she said.

While she was talking, I noticed a footnote in the report:

"The appraiser makes no representation as to the income reported by the business in its federal and state income tax returns. Equipment and fixtures have been depreciated to almost zero and inflated personal expenses of the owners have been deducted as costs of doing business. An adverse response by taxing authorities is possible."

I chose not to pursue this red flag, although I would have if I was advising a potential buyer of the company.

A few weeks later, Bill and Jenny were in to sign the proposed Judg-ment and Decree. There were some important issues to discuss.

"This agreement designates me as the lawyer for Jenny only," I said. "Bill, you have to sign a waiver." I showed him the pertinent clause:

I, William Bednarek, acknowledge that I am waiving my right to legal representation, and that counsel for Petitioner does not represent me in this proceeding. "Do you understand this? Any questions about it? "

"I'll sign it. Doesn't change our plan," Bill said.

"Yes, the plan's the same, but, in the worst-case scenario, it means what it says." I also explained how I'd drawn up the settlement. Bill was awarded the minimum assets allowed by the guidelines at the time: a motor vehicle, a lien on the homestead of a hundred-fifty thousand dollars, payable on its sale, and a small amount in bank accounts. Jenny was given title to the home and the business.

We all signed the judgment and sent it to the court. After the re-quired thirty-day waiting period, we appeared before the judge. He was an old hand – a libertarian of sorts. Jenny and I sat at one table and Bill at the other.

The judge pored over the agreement, then looked up with a wry smile. "I wasn't born yesterday."

He turned to Bill. "Do you understand that you are permanently signing away your rights to these assets, Mr. Bednarek? If things don't work out with you and your wife, you can't come back and change your mind?"

"Yes, your honor," Bill said without hesitation.

"Then, if you want to screw over the government, that's no concern of mine. Judgment granted."

Shortly thereafter, I received a check from Jenny for the bill. In keeping with the terms of the Judgment, I had insisted it come from her only. I heard nothing more from either of them for over a year, until I was informed that Bill was in the lobby, unannounced, wanting to see me.

He looked better than I remembered. There was some color in his face, and he'd shed some pounds. He still snorted, though.

"How are you doing with the rheumatoid arthritis?" I asked.

"Really good. Those treatments they gave me worked. I've stabilized and I just have to show up once a year for a check-up. Looking back at things, that divorce we did wasn't really necessary."

"What brings you here, then?"

"This!" He pushed a document across the desk.

It was a DANCO – a Domestic Abuse No Contact Order. Jenny was the Petitioner *pro se*, meaning that she had proceeded without a lawyer.

"It says I'm out of the house, and the gym, too."

Bill was right. He was excluded from both properties for a couple of weeks until there was a hearing.

There was an affidavit from Jenny supporting the order. It claimed that Bill had thrown some dishes against the kitchen wall during an argument, and said, "If you call the cops, you'll live to regret it." Based on these events, Jenny had "reasonable fear for her life."

"They can't call that domestic abuse, can they? I didn't touch her, and I said she'd "live to regret it" – not that she'd die."

"The definition of abuse is pretty broad," I said. "It's not the strongest case, except for one thing."

"What?"

"She owns the house and business. You've been there only because she gave you permission. She can kick you out if she feels like it, and she did."

"Bullshit. I never stopped living with her, and nothing changed at the gym, either. "

"Remember when I warned you about this when you signed the divorce agreement? Then, when we were in court, the judge gave you the same warning, but you were so intent on doing your scheme that you ignored the consequences."

"I don't care what you think, I'm going to fight it."

"You're welcome to. I'll give you a list of lawyers you can call. I'm out, though. I could even be called as a witness."

We were done. Bill shook my hand and left, but his red face belied his anger. A week later, I heard from him again, when he called the office.

"Hey, I did a little detective work and I found out what's been going on."

"Okay, what is it?"

"I went into the house when she was at work, and it's obvious she's been entertaining a guest."

"In the house? You can't go in there. It says so right on your court order, and a violation is a gross misdemeanor. That's a year in jail."

"I don't give a shit. It's Habib. After all I did for him. His stuff's in the living room and his pecker tracks are on the bed!"

"I don't want to hear another word, Bill. Get your own lawyer," I said, hanging up on him.

I didn't hear from Bill again, but I did from Jenny. Like him, she showed up without an appointment.

She looked different. She'd let her hair out, and wore more makeup. Instead of the bulky Iron Works sweatshirt from last year, she wore a tight, sleeveless top that flaunted her buff body.

"I'm hoping that this was another of Bill's lies, but he said you were going to be his lawyer and he was fighting me in court."

"Not true, Jenny. I can't be his lawyer, and even though you were my client before, I can't be your lawyer now."

"Well, okay, but I want you to hear my side. This is all about Bill and his threats."

"You mean throwing the plates?" I asked.

"That didn't really scare me, but it was a convenient way for me to get the court order. The real problem is our business plan. Since the beginning, we've been taking hardly any taxable income out of the gym."

She didn't seem bothered by disclosing this obvious fraud.

"So, that's why the accountant flagged your appraisal."

"Big deal. They had no business sticking their nose into it. They'd known for years that we'd dummied up invoices from make-believe vendors, then paid them by sending the money to bank accounts that we set up, so we could pull cash out of the accounts. Now, Bill's threatening to spill the beans to the IRS because of his jealousy."

"What good would that do? You'd both be in trouble."

"I know, but he's just in a rage. He accuses me of having an affair with Habib, but I'm innocent. Habib's a friend, but there's nothing between us. He's never even been at our house."

The more she said, the more her eyes evaded me. Mendacity is a regular occurrence in my work, so I've become something of an expert in detecting it. Jenny was a lousy liar.

I gave her the same lecture about needing to find her own legal representation, and escorted her out to the lobby. After the elevator doors closed, our receptionist caught my attention.

"A guy came in with her." As she spoke, she exhaled, fanning her face with her hand, as if she were cooling herself off.

I took a look out my third-floor window on the parking lot below. Jenny was getting into a sports car with Habib.

I never saw Bill or Jenny again, although I still drove by the gym as before. One day, after a mid-winter vacation, I noticed that the Iron Works sign had been turned off.

There was a foot of unplowed snow in the empty lot.

A couple of days later, there was a front-page article in the local paper:

LOCAL BUSINESS SHUT DOWN BY IRS

The Iron Works Gym was closed by order of the U.S. District Court this week. The owner, Jenny Bednarek, and her former husband Bill Bednarek, have been charged with tax fraud and remanded to federal custody.

I followed the story with great interest. Eventually, both Bill and Jenny pled guilty and were incarcerated for several years.

As springtime rolled around, I detected some activity at the Iron Works building. A paint crew had spruced up the exterior. One day, a temporary banner was placed over the old sign. It read: "Coming soon. Habib's Fitness Club."

CHAPTER 20

Happy Father's Day

I've written about the drama that one finds in family court – divorce, deprivation of parental rights, avarice, and betrayal. You might wonder – what could be worse? Let's throw death into the mix.

Jason and Michael Nordberg were accompanied by their mother, Myrtle. She was in her sixties, it seemed. A stout, gray woman with a stern countenance, her frumpy attire and lack of make-up led to a mannish look. Her sons sported more stylish clothes – one in jeans and the other in a black motorcycle jacket.

Before I could speak, Myrtle turned to Jason, "Tell the man about your father." It was a demand – not a request.

"Okay," he said, "Dad died last month." He handed me a picture. Looking at it, I could see where the boys had gotten their narrow-set eyes and receding chins.

"He had cancer for about a year. It was sort of sad to see him waste away. Anyhow, he had a will that left everything to Michael and me, but now this lawyer, who happens to be his cousin, says he tore it up and left everything to some other woman." Myrtle jumped in. "I told the boys that's not legal. Clarence couldn't cut them out – they're his sons, right?"

"Actually, he could cut out his sons," I said, "but not you, Myrtle. As his surviving spouse you can elect against the will and take a widow's share."

"But I'm not his surviving spouse. I divorced him. He took up with this bimbo a few years ago. I gave him a month to get rid of her, but he wouldn't, so I got rid of him." She said it as if she were proud of herself.

"Funny thing is, not too long after the divorce she dumped him and married this rich old guy for his money, then that guy died and she came out smelling like a rose. Then as soon as Clarence gets sick, all of a sudden, she's back with him and he's under her spell again. What a bitch!"

The propensity of men of a certain age to jump into such relationships never ceases to amaze me. The old adage that "There's no fool like an old fool" is so true. I asked them about Clarence's financial status.

"He was an insurance agent, but he never did so well, plus he was a cheapskate," Jason said. "We always lived in this crappy crackerbox house and he hardly ever took us on vacation. Then when Fannie – that's his girlfriend - showed up he started spending all his money on her. Mom got the house in the divorce and that's about it."

Then Michael chimed in for the first time. "A couple years after the divorce, our uncle Richie died and left Dad a lot of money – like a million dollars. Dad told us he made his will out to us boys and that we'd be in good shape when he passed on, but first, he was going to live it up himself. He retired and started going on cruises and bought himself a new car, but he put Jason and me on his checking account cuz' he was gone so much and he wanted us to take care of his bills and stuff. Then he got sick and this Fannie woman showed up again and started calling all the shots."

"Show him the letter from the lawyer," Myrtle said to Jason. Another demand. He handed me a thick envelope, addressed to himself and Michael, which I opened. There was a cover letter. Although it was on embossed paper, it was easy to see that it was the product of an old-style manual typewriter. It read:

Dear Sirs:

The enclosed testamentary document was executed by your father, Clarence Nordberg, one week prior to his passing, during his residency at the Good Shepard Hospice.

Since each of you is mentioned in the will, I am obligated by law to provide you with this copy. It is our intention to file the will for probate forthwith on behalf of your late father and his sole beneficiary, Fannie McMurtry.

Sincerely,

William Hansen, Esq.

Enc.

Enclosed in the envelope was a two-page, handwritten document entitled "Last Will and Testament." It was in shaky, cursive writing, but it clearly stated the wishes of Clarence Nordberg.

"So," Myrtle said, "That's not legal, is it? I mean, his old will was typed in a lawyer's office and looked professional. This thing's a piece of crap."

"I've got more bad news, I'm afraid," I said. "It's what we call a holographic will – meaning that even though it's handwritten, if it's properly witnessed, it's legal. I pointed to two signatures at the bottom of the page. Looks like some staff people from the hospice helped out."

"Well, there's gotta be some way around this," Myrtle said. "That woman wrecked my marriage. Now you're telling me she's taking my sons' inheritance. What if you can prove she tricked him into changing his will?"

"Proving undue influence is hard," I said. "Basically, you have to show that the decedent lacked testamentary capacity."

"You mean he was crazy?" Jason said. "He was, you know. He was seeing things – they even called him 'Crazy Clarence' over at the nursing home. Just ask his doctor." Myrtle dug into her purse and found a card – Alan Boyer, M.D. I gave him a call and set up an appointment at his office for later in the week.

Dr. Boyer was friendly, a slight fellow, but he seemed extremely nervous – throughout our conversation he shifted in his chair; drumming his fingers on his desk. But he had read his charts and was ready to talk about Clarence's case.

"He presented with symptoms of a persistent cough and breathing difficulties, and had difficulty swallowing," he said of Clarence. "The x-rays and CT scan clearly revealed squamous-cell carcinoma. Not surprisingly, he had been a lifelong smoker. Because he was in his early sixties, we treated him aggressively, first through removal of the affected lobe, then with chemotherapy. He tolerated it well and improved for some time, but, as is often the case, the cancer eventually spread to the brain."

I explained that, as attorney for the family, my interest was in Clarence's competency to make a will. He had a definite opinion.

"In his last months, his behavior changed drastically. For example, he told me that he was being spied on by the CIA. He thought there were little men living in his refrigerator. Is that when he made out his will?"

I told him he was right, and that Clarence's prior will had left everything to his adult sons, but that he'd changed it shortly before he died in favor of Fannie. "You mean that woman who was with him all the time?" I nodded yes.

"Well, I hate to say this about him, but I don't think he was competent to make any decision, especially a will. For one thing, this woman was running the show. She was with him for every conference we had – he insisted on it. A couple of times she wanted to talk with me afterwards. She was always asking how much time he had left. Of course, I couldn't say for sure, but she said she needed to know to help him get his affairs in order. Now that I know about him changing his will, it all fits together."

I told Dr. Boyer how important his testimony would be for our case, but he was unhappy about the prospect, to say the least.

"Look – I don't want to be a witness. Can't I just send a letter to the judge?" I explained that only with his in-person testimony, which would be subject to cross-examination, would his opinion be evidence in the case.

"Then you'll have to do without me," he said. "Present company excluded, of course, I don't care too much for lawyers and courts. I got called as a witness in a malpractice case against another doctor once – it was terrible."

His attitude was not uncommon and I understood it. But I was ready to play hardball.

"To be frank with you, sir, I could serve you with a subpoena and make you testify. You'd receive the statutory $25 fee plus your mileage. Or, we could pay you well for your time if you came on a voluntary basis. Plus, this is probate court, so it's just a judge trial – not a jury case like that malpractice proceeding. It won't be so hard, I promise."

He eventually came around, and, with Jason and Michael, our witness list was complete. The case was set before the Honorable William Cuthbert for a one-day trial the following Monday.

The courthouse in downtown Saint Paul, constructed in 1932, deserves mention. It is a twenty-story building in the art-deco style, featuring limestone on the outside and dark marble and wood on the inside. The entrance is dominated by a thirty-eight-foot-high white onyx statue called the "Indian God of Peace." Even at the time of our trial, in the 1980s, the elevators were manned by human operators, mostly older pensioners, who would click their castanets when the elevator was to depart.

The throw-back atmosphere of the courthouse was complemented by Judge Cuthbert's chambers. He had his office done up in an "Old English Men's Club" motif. There was a deep red carpet, and wall hangings depicting the royal family, Winston Churchill and Lord Wellington, as well as pastoral scenes.

"So you're an Anglophile," I said to him as opposing counsel and I took our seats. I shuddered as I thought what my mother would say. She was a product of generations of wild Irish revolutionaries hailing from County Kerry, a woman who would hurl anti-British slurs at my English father in the heat of argument.

"True," the judge said. "My parents both hail from the mother country. I'm proud of my heritage. As it is said, 'The British do not expect happiness . . . they do not want to be happy; they want to be right.' That is my expectation for my courtroom as well. I just want to be clear about that."

Opposing counsel was Salomon Cohen. He was a stooped-over octogenarian, and was friendly -to a point. His diction was old-style, formal.

"Your Honor, I represent the estate by way of the last will of the decedent, and I am also here on behalf of my life-long friend, William Hansen, who drafted the will, as well as Miss McMurtry, the sole bene-ficiary. Mr. Hansen, who has been a lawyer of good standing for fifty-five years in this community, is highly offended that his integrity as a scrivener has been challenged by young counsel and his clients. Further-more, there is the cost – I charge two-hundred and fifty dollars a day for my time in court."

I had to pinch myself. Two-hundred-fifty? Even at this early point in my career, I would rack up several times that in fees. Judge Cuthbert was ready to start the trial.

I entered the courtroom. It was paneled in dark rosewood and, dimly lit with rounded fixtures, it resembled the inside of a coffin – a fitting venue, I thought, for a probate proceeding. I was surprised to see Myrtle and her sons already sitting at the counsel table. She projected a proprietary air, like the dowager queen with her two princes, but I told her to move back a few rows since, although she was paying the bill, she wasn't a party. Shortly thereafter, the opposing entourage made its en-trance. Mr. Cohen was accompanied by his friend and the drafter of the will, Mr. Hansen, a white-haired gentleman of the same approximate age, who supported himself with a cane.

However, the scene was stolen by the beneficiary – Fannie Mc-Murtry. She appeared to be in her late fifties but it was obvious that she had had some "work" done. Although she was free of wrinkles, a face-lift had stretched her mouth uncomfortably wide, making her smile appear almost painful. Her breasts were, as one of my law partners would say, "store-bought," projecting forward at a perpendicular angle to her otherwise slight frame. This presentation was enhanced by a tight, orange dress that featured a plunging neckline. The bailiff was distracted by the latter to the extent that, for a moment, I feared he might drop his clipboard.

Glancing back at Myrtle, I saw that she and Fannie were engaged in a death stare. It persisted for an uncomfortably long interval, and I was reminded of the Roadrunner cartoon when Wil E. Coyote was so furious at being foiled again that steam was shooting out of his ears.

Judge Cuthbert took the bench and convened the proceedings. "Ladies and gentlemen, as Lord Kingston said on the BBC, 'Everyone wants peace – but they will fight the most terrible war to get it'. I ask that you treat this proceeding not as a war but as a quest for the truth."

William Hansen was called as the first witness. After being sworn in, he was asked about his legal background.

"I was admitted to the bar in 1925," he said. "I was one of the earliest tenants of the Foshay Building."

He was speaking of the famous first skyscraper of Minneapolis, which was constructed in 1929, only three years before our courthouse.

"Now, the will that you drafted was in your own handwriting. Is that unusual, sir?" Mr. Cohen asked.

"No," he said, "I let my secretary go many years ago, so I do all my own documents, except for the long ones, which I send to a printer. "

"Describe the scene when the will was drafted," the lawyer asked.

"The charming young lady sitting behind you," he nodded to Fannie, "had called me the night before and asked me to meet with my cousin Clarence in his room. She said I was the one lawyer he would trust. When I arrived, I asked her to leave the room, since it wouldn't be appropriate for the beneficiary to be present at the execution of the will. Clarence and I had a nice, long talk and then I started on the will. When it was done, we read it out loud together, and then enlisted a couple of lady nurses to sign as witnesses."

"Did the decedent appear to be of sound mind? Or was he, as his sons contend, under the undue influence of any person?"

"He was certainly not under the influence!" Hansen said, in anger. "That this will is contested is an effrontery to myself and the court."

"Now, sir," Cohen said, "please read the testamentary portion of the will." Hansen fumbled for his glasses, which were suspended by a band around his neck, and stated, "I, Clarence Nordberg, renounce my previous will and testament, and in so doing, it is my intent that by this will, my sons, Michael Nordberg, and Jason Nordberg, take nothing. Instead, I leave the rest, residue, and remainder of my estate to my good friend, Fannie McMurtry."

Fannie McMurtry testified next. Considering her flamboyant appearance, she was surprisingly poised. Clarence had good days and bad days, she explained, but was consistent in his desire to have her be his sole beneficiary. Casting a malevolent glance at Myrtle, she said, "He told me that I'd opened his eyes to happiness after the hell of his marriage."

The final witness for the estate was Rose Jordan, a licensed practical nurse at the hospice where Clarence spent his last three months. She was asked about the will signing. "I remember it well," she said. "Miss McMurtry had been a constant companion to Clarence during those last few months, but the gentleman here," she pointed to Mr. Hansen, "had requested that she go down to the cafeteria. He asked Clarence if he had read the will and if he understood it, and Clarence said he did. Then he asked if I or the other nurse had any concerns or questions and we didn't. Clarence went ahead and signed the will and we signed as the witnesses. We do that a lot at our jobs."

It was my turn next, and I got right to the point. Based on what I knew, I figured we had a good case that Clarence was subject to Fanny's influence.

"Ms. Jordan, since Ms. McMurtry was always with Mr. Nordberg, as you say, did you ever observe them going through financial matters together?"

"Oh, yes," she said. "She'd write up his checks for him and he'd sign them. When his broker came to visit him about a month before he died, she was at the meeting, too."

"Isn't it a fact, Ms. Jordan, that you and others on the staff referred to the decedent as 'Crazy Clarence?'"

She stiffened as if sensing the need to defend him.

"Yes, we did," she said.

"And why was that?"

"Well, it's just that he was sort of a flirt with us gals. Death is a daily visitor to us, so we don't get many patients like him, you know – a person with a feisty, positive attitude. Actually, one time when I reached over to fluff up his pillow he pinched my butt." She paused, noticeably reddening. "I suppose I could have reported it to HR but, to tell you the truth, he was harmless and I didn't want to get him in trouble. So, yes, we called him 'Crazy Clarence' but really he was okay."

That hurt us, big time, and it was my own fault. When a lawyer asks "Why" during cross-examination, he's just opening the door for unexpected damaging testimony.

It was time for the noon break. The afternoon was for our side of the case. Since we were paying Dr. Boyer by the hour, I had arranged for him to be our first witness. We were to meet at 1:15, fifteen minutes before the trial resumed, for one last review of his testimony, but at 1:25, I was still waiting. Just a minute later, he arrived with a woman.

"This is my wife," he said. "As long as I'm taking the day off for this, we decided to come down and have lunch, then go shopping later."

The judge granted us a short delay and I got a conference room for us, but when we entered the close quarters it immediately became evident to me that these two were "in the jar" – an old southern Illinois expression for those who've been imbibing.

"Here, you'd better take one of these," I said, handing him a mint.

"Oh, is it that obvious?" he said. "Sorry, but I told you how much I hate doing this. I guess I felt the need to fortify myself for it."

At that moment, the bailiff popped into the room, demanding that we start immediately. I called Dr. Boyer to the witness stand.

"Doctor," I said, "please describe your relationship with the decedent."

"Well, I first became acquainted with Charles Nordling..."

I interrupted. "Would it help if I reminded you that the decedent was named Clarence Nordberg?"

"Oops, yes. Thank you," he said.

For some reason, this seemed to get Dr. Boyer on track, and he did reasonably well in describing the history of his treatment of Clarence, concluding that Clarence lacked testamentary capacity, and certainly could have been influenced by Fannie to sign his estate over to her. He attributed some of Clarence's behavior, such as imagining living beings in the refrigerator, as being related to his palliative treatment, including the administration of opiates, in his final months.

Then it was Mr. Cohen's turn, and he rose. "Your Honor, may I approach the witness to review the decedent's chart with him?"

The judge granted his request and Cohen walked up to the witness. He stood next to Dr. Boyer, asking him some medical questions, then stopped, and said, "Sir, have you been drinking?"

"Yes, I have," Dr. Boyer said, "but it was only a cocktail with lunch."

"Your Honor," Cohen said, "This is an outrage and an insult to the court, and I request that this witness be excused and his testimony entirely disregarded."

The judge only smiled and said, "This reminds me of a story about Oscar Wilde. He was at a party and talking to a woman. She was offended by something he said and exclaimed 'Sir, you're drunk!' Mr. Wilde responded, 'That may be true, my dear, but you are ugly, and the difference between us is that when I wake up in the morning, I will be sober.'"

I had to admit – it was a good story. The judge continued. "In the Old Bailey, the barristers often take a whiskey during the lunchtime hour, so I will not begrudge the witness for doing that."

My final witness was Jason Nordberg, Clarence's oldest son. He got through the direct examination well enough, although he frequently glanced up to his mother, as if seeking reassurement. It was a shame, he said, for his father to have suffered as he did, but he could not forgive Fannie for her actions.

"That woman," he pointed at Fannie, "she twisted our father around her finger. Just look at her, all gussied up. You can tell how she snared him in."

It was attorney Cohen's turn.

"Mr. Nordberg, how many times did you or your brother visit your father during the last year of his life?"

"Probably twice," he said.

"Just twice?" Hansen said with mock surprise.

"Well," Jason said, "it was her fault. She shut us out."

"Sir," Cohen said, "I am showing you what has been marked as Petitioner's Exhibit 14. Do you recognize was this is?"

"Yes," said Jason.

I was handed a copy. I read through it with horror. It was a page from a spiral notebook.

"Now," Cohen said, "This is what some might call a 'Father's Day' card, correct?

Did you send this to your father?"

"Yes," said Jason. He looked awestruck. "We left it in his mailbox."

HAPPY FATHER'S DAY – it read, but each letter was followed by other words.

"Read the card for us, Mr. Nordberg," Cohen said.

Jason's hands trembled as he held the card.

"H – Here's your card.

A – Asshole is what you are.

P – Piss on you.

P – Pussy face.

Y – Your a loser"

I noted the ungrammatical use of the possessive pronoun "your." Jason continued, "F – Farting is what you do best . . ."

It went on from there, getting even worse.

"So, is this an example of how much you loved your father?" Cohen asked.

"Okay," Jason said, "I guess we were mad at him for a while after the divorce. "

"It's interesting that you say that, sir," said Cohen, "since you delivered this only a year ago – three full years after the divorce."

"I suppose," Jason said. He had a defeated look.

"There was another reason for it, wasn't there?"

Cohen picked up some financial documents and approached Jason, showing them to him.

"Isn't it a fact that for some time you and your brother were on your father's checking account, and you each made significant withdrawals from it?" Cohen asked.

"Well yes," Jason said, "he told us that since he'd inherited a lot of money from his Uncle Richie, he wanted us each to have a new car, so I got a new Mustang and Mike got a Camaro."

Like most unpleasant surprises that happen in the courtroom, my clients had given me no idea it could be coming.

"I would suggest to you that you are lying," Cohen said. "I submit that these withdrawals were wholly unauthorized and that, on learning of them, your father cut off your access to the account and put Miss McMurtry's name on it instead. It was only a few weeks later, sir, that you and your brother delivered this despicable so-called 'Father's Day card.'"

Jason mumbled a weak denial, but the damage was already inflicted. I could have attempted to rehabilitate his testimony, but who knows where that would lead, so I let it be. After the final arguments were made, the judge retired to his chambers, informing us that he would return shortly with his decision.

Fifteen minutes later, Judge Cuthbert returned. "As General MacArthur announced at the signing of the Japanese surrender on the *USS Missouri*," he said, "'These proceedings are closed.'"

He's finally quoting an American, I thought.

"The court finds that, although the decedent suffered from delusions related to his medications, he had a rational basis for the changes he made in executing his new will. The will was signed during a lucid moment – as we say in the law, and it will be sustained."

My clients were furious, of course, demanding that we appeal the decision, but I declined, giving them the name of a colleague. As I walked out of the courthouse past the Indian God of Peace, I thought to myself – You win some and you lose some. Then it occurred to me – Father's Day was next week!

CHAPTER 21

Take a Chance on Me

The client questionnaire said Shannon was forty-six years old, but she looked like sixty. Her slumped posture suggested the onset of a "dowager's hump." Wrinkles were etched deeply around her eyes and cheeks. Sallow, jaundiced skin added to the unhealthy aura. Her thinning gray hair was brushed straight back into a bun, exposing her scalp. The pungent scent of tobacco smoke followed her in from the hallway.

"He finally did it," she said as she handed over the divorce petition her husband had initiated. "He's been threatening this for years, but now he's got his honey so it's time to dump the old lady."

"Let's talk about your marriage," I said.

It was an oft-told tale of a couple that wed early in life -- college sweethearts. "Once I met him, all I wanted to do was get married," she said. "He was the one with the big ambitions. Maybe it's his family name – Grandison."

Once their undergraduate studies were over, Shannon got a job doing data entry for the school district while her husband, George, went on to graduate school.

"It was a crappy job," she said, "but I really didn't mind because I was crazy in love."

After getting his MBA, George went on to get a specialized degree in Medical Management. Shannon never stopped working, even when they became parents of a boy and a girl.

"He said we had to work hard to get ahead, and we did. He got a job as an assistant manager for a medical clinic in the city. Ten years ago, a large group of emergency physicians hired him to manage their professional association. Things got good for us financially, but his big fat ego got in the way."

"He outgrew the marriage?"

"Right. I'm not good enough for him. It was gradual. At first, he took me on some of his business trips and even some of those 'drug dinners', as he calls them. You know, when the pharma companies wine and dine the doctors. We traveled a lot, and I loved it. After a while, he started leaving me home. I asked him why. He just blew me off at first, then he said that it embarrassed him to be seen with me. Look, I know the years haven't been kind to me, but I don't deserve this. I came through for him when he needed me early on. I guess I don't matter anymore."

I sighed. "Sure you do, Shannon."

"Now he's got this young chippie – she's like fifteen years younger than him. One of those drug company sales girls – you know. They hire them for their looks, and they go to the clinics in their short skirts, bat their eyes at the doctors, and get their accounts. I'm sure she looked at George and saw dollar signs."

"Has he been spending money on her?"

"Nope, he wouldn't spend money on anyone. He's the original penny-pincher. He calculates everything down to the cent. He gets a bonus based on how much of a profit he makes for the doctors – so he's on the laptop every day running projections. You should see the shit-fit he throws if I go up to the casino with my girlfriends."

We proceeded to put the case together. I secured the family's tax return for recent years, which showed that George pulled down a healthy six-figure income, and my paralegal put together a marital balance sheet representing their assets and liabilities. It was surprising that, with George earning over two hundred thousand dollars per year, in addition to Shannon's salary from the school district, they had a net worth of less than a million dollars.

We attended a mediation session, as required by court rules, but George's lawyer appeared without his client.

"He had to go out of town," the lawyer said, "but, frankly, it'd be a waste of time to re-schedule. He won't settle for less than two-thirds of the assets. No alimony, either."

"Come on," I said, "that's not gonna fly in court."

Although there are exceptions, the rule of thumb is that marital assets are divided fifty-fifty. Also, in a long-term marriage, with fiscal disparities between the parties, spousal maintenance, or alimony, was appropriate.

"We've got the accounting for it, you'll see. I'll send it to you when it's done."

But we never got the promised information, and the trial date approached quickly. Shannon was our only witness, and I was happy to see that she'd made an effort on her appearance. She'd eschewed the normal stretch pants and sweatshirt for a tasteful, if shapeless, black dress. She'd added earrings and a necklace. Still, she was no comparison to her husband, a handsome guy in a three-piece suit. As we entered the courtroom, they exchanged disdainful glances.

Shannon's testimony went as planned – a recapitulation of the contributions she'd made in the early years, and her dedication to raising the children. We also projected her future needs, to make our case for alimony.

After lunch it was time for George's case.

I noticed three people seated behind George's counsel, an attractive young brunette woman, a middle-aged Native American man in a suit, and another man who appeared, based on his attire and briefcase, to be a lawyer. I leaned over to Shannon, whispering, "Is that his girlfriend?

"No, that's our daughter Sally. She's taking sides with him."

"Why?" I asked.

"Cuz she's just like her father. Their world revolves around money."

"How about those men?"

"No idea," she said.

"Call your first witness, counsel," the judge said to George's lawyer, and the Native American man approached the witness stand to be sworn.

"State your name," the judge said, as he took the witness chair.

"My name is John Thunder," he said.

George's lawyer took over. "What is your job and why are you here?"

"I'm the deputy financial director of the Pokegama Lake Band and Grand Casino, and I'm here because you served me with a subpoena."

"What did that subpoena direct you to do?"

"Produce all records we have relating to the Respondent in this case, Shannon Grandison."

"How do you compile your records?"

"We have a rewards card program. The card gives the customer a discount on hotel rooms, gaming paraphernalia and other products, and is used in lieu of cash. It can be inserted into a slot machine or handed over to a dealer. Our casino has a record of all transactions for the customer, so we can track their activities and offer incentives. So, I have all of Ms. Grandison's reports in this binder." He placed a large folder on the table in front of him.

"What does it say?"

The lawyer behind George's table rose. "Your Honor, I'm James Finnegan, counsel for the Pokegama Lake Band. We maintain strict confidentiality as to our customer records. It's a matter of privacy for our patrons, but it's also proprietary information for our casino. We don't want our competitors to have access to our customer base or their gaming habits. Therefore, we formally object to the disclosure of these records. I'm submitting a memorandum stating our position."

Finnegan approached the bench and handed the judge a legal brief, giving me a copy as well.

"I'm declaring a fifteen-minute recess so I can consider this issue," the judge said. It was fortuitous because I wanted to talk to Shannon.

"There's a conference room right outside," I told Shannon. "We need to get to the bottom of this!"

"Okay," Shannon said, "but first, I want to talk to my daughter."

I went into the room and started to read the memorandum, but I saw nothing of Shannon, and after ten minutes or so I looked for her in the hallway. All I saw was her daughter Sally, who got up from her seat and approached me.

"I considered calling you about my mom," she said, "but it's her business, so I didn't."

"Where is she?"

"Out smoking. Did she tell you about the gambling?"

I gave her a non-committal nod.

"She just about cleaned dad out. They wanted me to testify for him. I won't do that, but I hope she gets her just rewards. She's been out of control for years."

"What do you mean by that?"

"You'll find out shortly," she said, as she abruptly left and walked back into the courtroom.

Shannon appeared at the far end of the hallway. "What's the deal, Shannon?" I said. "Do you have a gambling problem?"

"I told you I go to the casino, with my girlfriends. That's all there is to it." Before I could get more from her, the bailiff emerged and directed us back into the courtroom.

"Parties and counsel," the judge said, "I have considered the issue and hereby direct the witness to answer the question."

"Again, Mr. Thunder," George's lawyer said, "tell us what your records say about Ms. Grandison."

"She's been a customer of ours for a little over nine years. She has achieved a 'Silver Elite' status."

"Define that for us."

"We keep track of the amount of money put in play by the customer over the lifetime of their relationship with us."

"Exactly how much has Ms. Grandison 'put in play' as you call it?"

"A little over 2.2 million dollars."

I hoped the judge wasn't looking at me because I think my jaw dropped.

"Wait a minute," the judge said. "You let this woman lose that much? Don't you ever try to intervene?"

"It's not our decision to gamble the money, your Honor. That's the customer's decision. But maybe I didn't make it clear enough. This is the amount of money she put in play -- she didn't lose all of it."

"How much did she win and how much did she lose?"

"We only track major winnings. Anytime a customer wins more than a thousand dollars, we issue a tax form to them and report it to the IRS. Ms. Grandison is exclusively a slot machine player, so she would typically lose a certain percentage, although she could get really lucky and win a big jackpot. "

"Did she?" the judge asked.

"No."

"If so, what would the result normally be for a customer who played 2.2 million?"

"I'm sorry, your Honor, I have to defer to our lawyer on that," he said.

Mr. Finnegan, the tribe's counsel, stood up and addressed the court.

"Your Honor, we object again. The odds of the house are proprietary information. It would be prejudicial for it to be public or for our competitors to have it."

A lengthy discussion ensued, but at its conclusion, the judge said, "In the interests of justice, I'm directing the witness to answer the question, but I will seal the record.

Proceed, sir," he said to John Thunder.

"For every dollar put in play, the customer recovers approximately eighty-eight cents."

George's lawyer pulled out his calculator. "So, on bets of 2.2 million dollars, Ms. Grandison would have lost $264,000, correct?"

"Only if you follow the average. No one knows for sure."

We were done for the day. More bad news was coming, though.

At 9:00 the next morning, another new face appeared behind George's counsel table. He was a middle-aged man, with thin grayish-red hair, made worse by a combover. He wore jeans and a cheap, ill-fitting plaid sports jacket.

"Your Honor, I call Jason Frederickson," George's lawyer announced.

"What is your profession?" he asked as the witness took his seat.

"I'm a private investigator. I've been licensed in this state for twenty-two years."

"What did we hire you to do?"

"To conduct surveillance on Ms. Grandison at the Grand Casino."

"How did you know when to do this?"

"Mr. Grandison would call me if she was headed that way."

"How many times did this happen?"

"Three times in the past two months, which is consistent with the records that Mr. Thunder presented yesterday in court. Each time, my associate and I surveilled her for twenty to thirty hours."

"Why for so long?"

"Because she'd be in the casino for about that long."

"What did you observe?"

"I have photos and videos, and with the court's permission I'll have my associate bring in a monitor and I'll narrate the video."

The equipment was set up, and a video was projected on the monitor.

"This is from our first operation. Ms. Grandison is stationed at a ten-dollar slot machine. We started monitoring her at 10:00 a.m., just after she arrived at the casino. As you can see, she remains at the machine, leaving only for bathroom breaks, until nine o'clock the next morning."

"For almost twenty-four hours?" George's lawyer asked.

"That's right. The other two visits were the same. She basically sits at the machine, chain smokes and drinks coffee all day and night long. Her endurance is amazing. My associate and I were exhausted by the time it was over, and we were taking shifts."

"Your Honor," I said, "I object to this witness' testimony. How much my client smokes or drinks coffee is irrelevant and immaterial. They're just trying to shame her. "

"I understand, counsel," the judge responded. "However, it lends credibility to the records the casino produced. I'll allow it, but I won't put much weight into it."

Frederickson started the video again. Even though he ran it at top speed, the thirty-hour marathon session seemed to last forever. The quality of the video was excellent.

The next witness was Shannon's husband, George. He brought his laptop and synced it with the monitor next to the witness stand.

"Now Mr. Grandison," the lawyer asked, "have you conducted an analysis of your family's finances, including the effects of your wife's gambling?"

"Yes. As you can see, I have a spreadsheet showing what our net worth is now and what it would have been if she hadn't thrown all that money away up at the casino. If you add her expenses at the casino hotel, her mileage, and the depreciation on our car, together with the losses, our marital estate has been diminished by about $300,000. We would have had $1,200,00, or $600,000 each. But, because of her, we only have $900,000. To be fair I should get $600,000, which leaves $300,000 for her."

He seemed proud of his analysis and shot Shannon an angry sneer.

"And how about your wife's claim for alimony?"

"I did another spreadsheet on that," George said. "Over the course of our twenty-five-year marriage, I earned over three million dollars, but she made only about four hundred thousand. She should be paying me, not the other way around."

"We're at the end of the morning, so now's a good time to stop," the judge said. "I'm sorry folks, but I have another trial starting this afternoon. We're going to have to resume a week from today. Thank you."

We would all have to remember where we were and pick up the following week. After leaving the courtroom, I asked Shannon to come back to my office. When we got there, I told her to wait in the lobby for a minute while I consulted with one of our paralegals.

As you might guess, addiction is a frequent companion in family law cases. Jane Hansen had worked with me for many years, and, after enduring some difficult family issues of her own, had become an expert in addiction and self-help therapy. I explained to her what our case was about and brought Shannon back to meet her.

"Shannon, no matter what happens in your case, we want your life to be better when it's over. Do you agree that your gambling behavior has reached a critical point in your life?"

"Maybe," she said.

After they were introduced, Jane said, "Let's go back to my office and chat. I've got some contacts with a group that could help you."

By the time the trial resumed, Shannon had already been to two meetings of Gambler's Anonymous.

"Jane went with me both times," Shannon told me. "What an eye-opener. Just to know that other people like me are going through this. It means so much."

The week-long furlough in the trial had provided me with an opportunity to prepare for the cross-examination of George. "Mr. Grandison," I said, "you're a numbers man, am I right?"

"I guess so," he answered cautiously.

"I'm going to ask you about your so-called analysis of who put what into this marriage. First, what value do you place on your wife's services as being the primary hands-on parent during the twenty years you had children in your home."

"None. That was her job. I paid the rent and she was the mother."

"I disagree, sir. I submit that if you had had a full-time nanny during those twenty years, it would have cost your family $30,000 a year. For twenty years that amounts to $600,000."

"Your math's correct but I contest the premise," he said.

"And, I further submit to you that the cost of a housekeeping service for the twenty-five years of your marriage would be at least twenty-thousand dollars per year, and that would amount to five-hundred thousand, correct?"

George cleared his throat. "Same answer," he whispered.

"You admit that your wife's efforts helped put you through graduate school when you had almost no income at all. You have earned millions of dollars because of that degree, and will continue earning for the rest of your career, correct?"

"You're right about the graduate school, but you ignore how hard I worked to earn that money."

"The fact is, Mr. Grandison, that you've ignored your wife's financial contribution to this marriage, not to mention the many years of emotional support she has given you. "

"Objection," George's lawyer said, "This entire line of questioning is hypothetical. Totally irrelevant."

"Overruled," said the judge. "You can't stop it just because you don't like it."

At that moment I realized we'd scored – big. There was no need to prolong the trial, and I announced that we were closing our case. The judge said, "I'll give you my decision after a short break." We re-convened a half-hour later.

The judge returned to the podium. "Ladies and gentlemen, in family law, no one walks away happy. Even when someone wins on an issue, the attorney's fees and court costs erode the victory, then there's the emotional trauma of litigating the most personal aspects of your life before complete strangers.

"I understand that Mr. Grandison thinks he is entitled to a dispro-portionate share of the marital estate, but I am unconvinced. As you should know, marriage is a partnership, but there are many more aspects to a marriage than money. You've raised children, you've supported each other and, even though it's over now, each of you has contributed in your own way to this relationship.

"Therefore, I am dividing your assets equally and awarding spousal maintenance in an amount to be determined in a written order which I will mail to you. Thank you and goodbye."

As we walked back to my office, Shannon gave me a squeeze on my arm. "Thanks to you and Jane, my life's turning around. I'm gonna do those twelve steps in the Gamblers Anonymous program, and I'm keeping in touch with you folks – like it or not!" It was the first time I'd seen her smile, and she looked a lot better for it.

The generous alimony order arrived two weeks later and I sent it to Shannon, but I didn't hear from her until months later when a letter arrived.

> *Hello –*
>
> *How are you? I'm doing well. I've got some bad news and some good news. The bad news is that I fell off the wagon. The good news? I hit the jackpot at the slots! I won $40,000!*
>
> *Here's the final payment of my bill, and a little something extra for you and Jane. Don't worry, I'm back in Gambler's Anonymous.*

Enclosed was a check for the attorney's fees, and a smaller envelope with cash. It contained forty-one-hundred-dollar bills and a Post-it – "You and Jane can split this.

Maybe you want to go to Vegas. Ha! Ha!"

CHAPTER 22

A Sip of Sherry

One morning, my receptionist buzzed me, saying, "Your new client is here." She spoke with an inflection that told me something was up, and when I walked out to the lobby, I saw what she meant. My client was decked out in skintight Lycra work-out gear. It left little to the imagination.

"I'm Sherry Maxson," she said.

As I escorted her back to my office, I noticed that the door to the break room was wide open, and two of my partners had posted themselves like sentinels at the coffee table. They must have gotten a heads-up from the receptionist, and their eyes followed us like laser beams as we walked by.

After Sherry took her seat in my office, I excused myself for a moment and walked back to the break room. "You can pick your tongues up off the floor now, guys," I said.

As I left, I heard them giggling like little boys.

Sherry handed me the folder of divorce papers she'd brought from her first lawyer. The Petition said she was forty-seven years old, but she could have passed for less. Her large green eyes were complemented by her curly red hair. She sported what appeared to be genuine diamond studs in her ears. She looked tanned, although it was late winter. As was clearly observable from her skimpy attire, she was in great shape.

"I teach step classes at The Meadows," she said. "It's almost next door to our house."

The Meadows - I'd been there on a guest pass once. It was an exclusive fitness club located in the swankiest corner of the Lake Minnetonka district. Unlike my own gym, which was limited to the usual cardio, weights and fitness studios, The Meadows included a beauty spa, a hair salon, a café complete with a juice and wine bar, and a patio along the lakeshore. The price tag for membership was befitting the luxurious facilities and location.

"The first thing you need to know is that my husband's an asshole. Example? He got me arrested for a DWI. "

"How so?" I asked.

"We were at a party. He'd been flirting with some woman and when we got home we started fighting. I told him I was leaving him. I packed my suitcase and took off. Five minutes later, the cops stopped me. We'd been drinking and he was drunker than me, but I'm the one who got nailed."

"Maybe he was just concerned for your safety," I said.

"Are you shitting me?"

She was probably right about it being a set-up. In the great big bag of dirty tricks that we see in family law, calling the cops on your spouse is right up there with the best of them.

"Now he's got our daughter turned against me."

"Tell me about your daughter," I said.

She pulled out a photo of a pretty girl in a cheerleader's outfit.

"Sandy's a junior in high school. When Asshole moved out, he got an apartment, and she moved in with him. He's never around, so she's over there day and night, fucking her boyfriend. My lawyer hardly mentioned it when we went to court for our first hearing, so Asshole got temporary custody. That's why I switched lawyers."

Not only did Sherry swear like a sailor, but she was always ready to blame others for her problems. As the conversation proceeded, I could smell that she'd been drinking. At the time, there didn't seem to be any reason to bring it up, though, so I let it pass.

"Looking at your court papers, it says that there's a mediation set for next week. Any chance we could settle the case?"

"No fuckin' way. First, he wants custody of Sandy - he's even got the damn custody evaluator recommending it. Second, he's hiding his money so I can't get any. And third, he wants to kick me out of the house. He says Sandy gets to live there with him, so I've gotta go. He's not getting her, right?"

How would I know? I'd just met her. I decided to change the subject.

"Okay," I said. "We'll get back to that. Tell me about the money."

"Asshole has his real estate license, but he's more like an investor. He's got this scam going on with his buddies. One of them, Phil Johnson, is in home construction. Phil builds a house for, say two hundred grand, but he writes up a phony statement, saying it cost four hundred. Then Asshole has a deal with an appraiser who tells the bank the house is worth four hundred grand, and the appraiser gets a kickback, for the inflated appraisal. Then Asshole scrounges up some phony buyer who signs a purchase contract for that price, even if it isn't worth that much, and that guy gets a kickback, too. His buddy at the bank approves a loan for four hundred grand, which is made out to Phil. They split the profit fifty-fifty. The gal at the bank gets a bonus for doing the loan. Everybody's happy." The scheme was news to me, but it was 2006 and, as it turned out, it wasn't that uncommon. Housing prices were bubbling up and people just assumed that everything would be covered by the ever-increasing values.

"Asshole's probably done twenty deals like this in the past year," Sherry continued, "which works out to maybe two million bucks, but it's off the books. His goddamn lawyer says his income is low, so how can he afford to pay me alimony?"

After Sherry left, I started preparing for the upcoming mediation, and as I read through her husband's ocurt submissions, I could see that she was right. Her husband, "Asshole," listed his occupation as real estate/investor. The house was valued at one million dollars, they had about twice that in the stock market, and they each drove a Jaguar. Still, he claimed he only made eighty thousand per year. On an income like that, how did they get to be so well-off?

I also decided to call up the custody evaluator, a veteran psychologist for whom I had a lot of respect.

"I don't like what I see here," she said. "Dad's cooperative, but he's distant. I don't think he has much of a relationship with the girl, but she feels safe with him. Mom cares, but she's self-absorbed, and she's got a temper. You know she had a DWI. When we get a red flag like that we ask that they give us random urinalyses, just to make sure they're maintaining sobriety, but she keeps refusing. I can't recommend her if she doesn't follow through with the program. Could you talk to her?" I promised to and reached Sherry later that day.

"That old bitch!" she said. "I am not going to pee in a cup for that woman." No wonder she was on the outs with the evaluator. We proceeded to discuss the mediation, which was set for the following day.

"Please do me one favor," Sherry asked. "I just got my driver's license suspended for ninety days on account of the DWI. Could you pick me up at home and drive me to the meeting?"

I don't make it a habit to chauffer my clients around, but there didn't seem to be an alternative. The next day I pulled up to her expansive Georgian-style brick home. It was right across the street from the Meadows, convenient for Sherry's fitness job.

"We're ahead of time," she said. "Do you want a quick tour? You'll see why I'm keeping this place."

I stepped into a large atrium, which featured a winding staircase, enhanced by tasteful artwork and well-kept plantings. There were five bedrooms and I lost count of how many bathrooms. She led me out the back door to the boathouse, which held a twenty-nine-foot Bayliner. I had to wonder why their small family had needed such a big place, and why, now with the divorce, Sherry would want it all for herself.

We arrived at the conference on time. It was in a board room in the forty-seventh-floor office of a downtown law firm. Mr. Maxson was already there. I knew from the documents that he was a few years older than Sherry, but the physical difference was striking. His face was puffy, dominated by a bulbous nose. An attempted comb-over only accentuated his baldness. He wore a horizontal striped polo shirt with a bright green sport jacket, a poor choice that drew attention to his expansive belly. Suspenders would have served him better. What a contrast to his fit, athletic wife!

He ignored us as we entered, seemingly absorbed in a phone call that continued until his lawyer asked him to end it. Throughout the meeting, he constantly tapped away on his phone, as if we were a distraction to him.

The lawyer assigned to the mediation began. "This is our only chance to talk directly and honestly about the differences you folks have, so let's cut through the B.S. and try to settle this thing."

He looked at me. "Counselor, tell me how we can get this resolved.."

"First," I said, "as long as we're off the record I want a straight answer on what his income is. They've got a net worth of more than three million. How do you get there from what he puts on the tax returns?"

Mr. Maxson's lawyer whispered briefly to his client, then said, "It is what it is. If you don't believe it – prove it. She's on the returns too, you know."

"Sure, she is," I said. "He shoves a twenty-page financial document in her face and orders her to sign it. What do you expect her to do? Look, if you're gonna stonewall on this thing, it'll come out at the trial. I know about his schemes."

"Oh, so you're threatening us. That's what I call extortion. Maybe I need to call the Ethics Committee."

It went on like that for a half hour, until the mediator suggested we change the subject. "You folks have a sixteen-year-old daughter," the mediator said. According to the information I have from the evaluator, she's a good student at the best public high school in the state. Surely we can reach a parenting agreement that's in her best interests."

I launched into our proposal for joint custody. Sherry would have Sandy at the family home during the week. Her husband would have most of the weekends. During the summer months, her time would be divided equally between the parents.

Mr. Maxson slammed his phone down on the table. "That's not gonna happen. Do you know about your client? Every night she gets tanked. In the morning she goes to the health club and sweats it out in the sauna. Then she works out half the day with her girlfriends, so they can look in the mirror and talk about how beautiful they are, and after that they sit down at the wine bar and drink the rest of the day away. She can hardly see straight by dinnertime. Our daughter hates her. I don't care what – she's not getting Sandy."

As he was talking, I glanced at Sherry. Her face reddened and she shifted in her seat. I was prepared for an angry outburst, but all she said was, "Let's get out of here."

So we did. The mediation was a bust anyway, and the trial was going to start in two weeks.

As we took the elevator down to the parking level, Sherry said, "Look, some of my friends are going to meet me at the Galleria to do some shopping. Do you mind dropping me off there?"

I did mind, but I was stuck with her again. As the name implies, the Galleria is a high-end shopping center not far from her home. I was glad that she'd be with some friends during such a tough day, although I hoped it wouldn't involve drinking.

There was time left in the afternoon, so I returned to the office to get some work off the desk. Just as I was about to leave for home, I got a call.

"Attorney for Sherry Maxson? " A man's voice said.

"Speaking."

"Officer Swenson with the Wayzata Police. This is your client's one permitted phone call. Go ahead, Ma'am."

It was Sherry. "Get me the hell out of here! They've got me in lock-up."

"What happened?" I asked.

"Never mind that. Just get me out!"

I arrived at the reception desk of the sterile suburban police department. As I was signing in and handing over my Lawyer's Registration

Certificate, a young officer approached me. He wasn't especially friendly.

"I'm Officer Swenson," he said. "It'll take a while for your client to process out, so I'm gonna bend your ear for a few minutes about her. "

"Good," I said. "She wouldn't tell me what happened."

"What happened is that she got charged with disorderly conduct. She's goddamn lucky I didn't charge her with assaulting a police officer. We got a call from one of the bars at the Galleria saying that she was causing a disturbance. When I got there, one of the mall cops had her restrained. The bartender told me she was drinking martinis, and she got so drunk that he cut her off. She started screaming obscenities and threw a glass on the floor. There were parents and kids in the vicinity who could see the whole scene. When I got there, she started in on me. She called me a 'cocksucker' and went at my face with her fingernails. Good thing for her she missed. It's all going in my report. See you in court."

I waited in the lobby for another forty-five minutes, wishing I was anywhere else. Finally, Sherry emerged. Considering everything, she didn't look so bad, but she was in a snit.

"Just take me home, and keep your fucking comments to yourself."

As soon as we got in my car, the reek of stale booze, vomit, and unwashed jail cell bodies hit me. I cracked the windows.

"Sherry," I said, "they set up a court date next week for your arraignment, so no funny business when we go there -- you're gonna be cold sober, and appropriately dressed, right?"

"Okay," she said.

"What happened to the friends you were going to meet up with? Maybe they could help us explain what happened when we get to court."

"They didn't show up – I was there by myself."

It occurred to me that her claim of having to meet friends had been just fiction. I had to pick up Sherry again for the arraignment since she still didn't have her license back. As she got in the car, I could see she'd followed my advice. She wore a conservative blue skirt and jacket, although it was form-fitting enough to pique the interest.

"I checked with the Clerk's Office," I said. "We have Judge Goldberg today."

"Yeah," she said, "I did too. He knows me from the club. He comes in for my step classes sometimes."

That figured. Steven Goldberg was known as the "Biking Judge." He'd been featured on television and in the papers for his participation in races, treks and even youth events. He was a flamboyant guy - sort of a publicity hound, and a loose cannon. A couple of years after our case he was reprimanded by the Judicial Board for assaulting a neighborhood kid he thought was being a bully.

"Don't be overconfident," I said. "This is serious. You've got that DWI on your record. He could send you to treatment, or even jail."

We arrived at the courtroom. It was an arraignment day, meaning that we would just enter a plea. The police officer from the jail wouldn't be there – that would come at the trial. I escorted Sherry up to the first row of the courtroom, which was packed with the usual assortment of dirtballs and losers. Just before the judge entered, the bailiff brought in a dozen or so defendants from the jail, attired in their bright orange coveralls, chained to each other. Compared to this crowd, Sherry stuck out like a shining star. That was evident as Judge Goldberg took the bench, because he asked the clerk to call our case before all the others.

As we rose, I whispered in Sherry's ear, "No drama. You are sorry – you are contrite."

Her performance was worthy of an Oscar. As the judge read through the police report, Sherry's eyes filled with tears, and she sagged against me, as if she was drained of strength.

"I'm so ashamed, your honor," she sniffled.

"It looks like you had quite an afternoon," he said with a smile. "Maybe you should have gone to the club instead. Don't you teach on Tuesdays?"

Sherry explained that she'd been at the mediation session. "This divorce has been so hard on me. When my friends didn't show up at the Galleria, I just lost it. Never again, I promise."

"Oh, I don't think we'll be seeing you around here again any time soon," the judge said. "Tell you what. I'm going to put this Complaint in my desk drawer for a year, and I'll tear it up if it doesn't happen again. You're excused. Good luck. See you in step class."

As he said it, I was conscious of the hundred or so pairs of eyes behind me who were watching the proceedings. If those folks thought they'd be getting the same lenient treatment from his honor, they would be sorely mistaken.

The following week we were in a different courtroom, for the beginning of the divorce trial. We were still at loggerheads over the custody and the money. I remained frustrated by Mr. Maxson's hardball strategy on his income. It would have been nice to get Judge Goldberg again, but we'd drawn an officious, sober-looking older man.

The judge told us that he wanted to hear about financial issues first. As to Sandy's custody, all we could do was hope. Sherry had managed to make an enemy of the evaluator, and Mr. Maxson had hired a private investigator who'd discovered what had happened at the Galleria.

I had thought up a strategy. It was risky but the upside was bigger than the downside. I called Mr. Maxson as our first witness. Just before he took the stand two other witnesses I had subpoenaed walked into the courtroom, each with their own lawyer. One was his friend the builder, and the other was the loan officer at the bank who set up his financing for the mortgages. She looked mortified to be there.

"Mr. Maxson," I said, "how many deals have you done this year with your builder friend, Mr. Johnson, who's sitting behind me? "

"Can't remember," he said.

"What if I told you that I've got records from the bank through Ms. Skinner, also seated behind me, that shows over one hundred sales in the past four years?"

"Could be correct," he said.

"Exactly how do you and your partners do these sales?"

"It's all on the up and up," he said.

"I beg to differ, and I'll tell you why." I peppered him with questions about his crooked scheme, including the role his co-horts behind us had played.

"If there were twenty deals in twelve months, at a hundred grand profit per deal, that's two million. How can you claim eighty grand as income on your tax form?" Before Mr. Maxson could answer, the judge interrupted. "I've heard enough. I want both lawyers in chambers, right now. You lawyers in the back – you too."

In chambers, the four of us were seated directly facing the judge, who was at his desk. He was angry. Focusing on me, he said, "What the hell do you think you're doing?"

"It's the only way of getting to the truth, your Honor."

"It's also a way of putting your client behind bars, ever think of that? She signs those tax returns, too."

"I think she has a defense under the 'Innocent Spouse Rule,'" I said.

"That's a pretty weak argument," he said. "The IRS expects you to read before you sign."

Then, facing Mr. Maxson's lawyer, the judge continued, "How can you sit there and let all this get on the record? Don't you know that I'm obligated to report any fraud to the U.S. Attorney? And you two." He turned to the lawyers for the builder and the banker. "Your clients are co-conspirators. What are you gonna do about that?"

There was an extended, pregnant silence. Finally, Mr. Maxson's lawyer said, "Are you really going to call the prosecutor, your honor?"

"Sure will, but if you four can settle the case, I might be persuaded to forget what happened."

The strategy worked. Yes, Sherry could have landed in big trouble. But really, would the Feds care about her, the troubled, clueless aerobics instructor? Not likely. Mr. Maxson and his buddies would be the real targets.

An hour later, Mr. Maxson's lawyer approached me. "I don't care for your tactics, counsel, but we'll agree to let her have the house, and we'll give her five years of alimony. That's it."

"You guys brought it on yourselves with your stupid denials. I've got no regrets," I said. "No deal unless we get the joint custody."

They gave in on that, too. I guess it showed Mr. Maxson's priorities. He, the principled father, so worried about his daughter's welfare, really only cared about the money.

Sherry wasn't happy about the five-year cap on her alimony, but she was ecstatic about getting Sandy back. "It's a new start for us," she said as we left the courthouse.

* * * * * * *

A few years passed by without any word from Sherry. Then one day, out of the blue, the receptionist rang me.

"There's a man out here who wants to talk with you. He says he's from the FBI." My first thought was to wonder what I had done wrong. But after convincing myself he couldn't be there for me, I welcomed the agent back to my office.

"We're investigating a real estate and income tax fraud operation. When we called the suspect's ex-wife, Sherry Maxson, for an interview, she said we should talk to you." Although this was a surprise, it wasn't a shock. Things had changed a lot since Sherry's divorce. The recession had hit. Lehmann Brothers was toast, and Bear, Stearns had disappeared, too. The real estate market had fallen apart like a cheap suitcase, and people were hurting, angry and looking for someone to blame.

"Our focus is on your client's ex-husband, of course, but she signed the tax returns and she's a material witness. Would you be willing to bring her in for an interview with us? Maybe you'd share what you learned during the divorce?"

"Absolutely not," I said. "You should know – that's all privileged."

"You'd be surprised how many lawyers in your position cooperate with us," the agent said.

"And I'd be surprised if that's true," I said, as I led him to the elevator.

As soon as I left, I called Sherry. She was a little shaken by the news, but I told her that she'd be okay. I gave her the name of a lawyer friend of mine who handled white-collar crime, and we talked for a while.

She interrupted the conversation for a moment. "Just a minute, there's someone at the door. I'll be right back."

When she returned, something had changed. I could hear the unmistakable sound of ice cubes clinking in a glass. Had someone really been at the door?

Sherry's speech had started to slur. It was time to end the call. "Before I hang up, I wanted to ask you about your daughter. How are you getting along with her?"

"Oh, her," Sherry said. "We haven't talked in two years."

CHAPTER 23

What Lies Beneath

Do you ever look at people and wonder – what lies beneath the surface? Are these friends - these acquaintances - these strangers around us who they appear to be, or do they conceal deep, dark secrets?

I had a client, Elizabeth. She had an appointment about a divorce, and when the receptionist rang me, I went out to the lobby to meet her. She was there with an older, graying man – obviously her father. Before I could greet her, he rose to shake my hand.

"Drove here all the way from Granite Falls," he said in a friendly manner. It's a county seat in the prairie out west – halfway to South Dakota. He was wearing a brown suit – probably his church outfit. Sometimes people who come to see us are self-conscious about their small-town origins, feeling that they have to dress up to be taken seriously by us "city folks."

He leaned over to me, saying in a confidential manner, "I'm taking care of the financial part of this." He could have spoken more softly, because everyone in the room could hear him.

It all took place in the presence of Elizabeth, who remained seated like an innocent bystander. She wore a plain, pale blue dress. It was buttoned to the neck and trailed to the floor, reminiscent of the pioneer dresses worn by my former assistant, a southern gal who was married to a Pentecostal minister. It seemed to swallow her up, for she was slight, with washed-out brown hair and grayish eyes. She wore no makeup or lipstick. I asked her to come back to the office.

It happens a lot that a client is pressured into legal situations by their families, so I started out by asking Elizabeth directly. "Is this your idea?"

"Oh yes" she said. "After meeting my dad, I understand why you asked. It's coming from me, though. If I don't do something about ending the marriage, my health will just get worse and worse, and then who's going to be there for the kids?"

I asked her to go on.

"After I got out of high school, I just sort of bounced around. I tried going to the community college, but I wasn't ready for that. Then I had one crappy job after the next. The boyfriends I had were in the same boat, and I just wanted to get away from the small-town life, so I moved to the city."

"That must have been a big change."

"We went to Fargo on a class trip once, but I'd never even been in the Cities. Then I met Floyd. He had a respectable job with the school district and he even owned his own house. I was in my late twenties by then, and he was a few years older. He was pretty set in his ways, but I figured that was a sign of stability. For example, he wanted no sex until we were married. After those guys I knew back in Granite Falls, that was sort of nice. So, we got married, I moved into his house and before you knew it, we had a couple of kids – Tommie and Andy."

She was gaining confidence as she spoke.

"Things went downhill from there. He insisted that I join his church. Like about everyone else in my hometown, I was raised as a Lutheran. His church is really fundamental. They believe in purity, so you can't wear revealing clothing or makeup. There's no music except for hymns – no dancing – no fun. They call us Lutherans 'Christianity light,' so I had to leave my church and join his. My parents tried stepping in, without success."

"So that's why your dad was here today," I said.

"Right. It wasn't just religion, Floyd started to cut me off from my family and friends. He only lets me see them a few times a year. I couldn't have any friends outside of the church. Then he harasses me about giving testimony."

"What do you mean by that?" I asked. For me, testimony was what happens in court.

"You're supposed to stand up and tell the congregation about your sins and then ask for forgiveness. It's the only way to purify yourself. Every Sunday someone stands up and goes on about their past or their secrets. It's like some of those TV shows where the audience watches other people air out their dirty linen."

"Why don't you just refuse to do it?" I asked.

"That's easy for you to say. Before we got married, he got me drunk one night and I confessed about things I did with some of my old boyfriends. Now I'm supposed to tell everyone about my premarital sex life. He hounds me about it, and he says if I don't testify about it to the congregation, then he'll do it for me. It's making me a nervous wreck - I've lost twenty pounds. Even worse, he's got our sons riled up about it. Tommie told me that I have to get the devil out of my soul."

I explained to Elizabeth that, if we went ahead with a divorce, her husband would keep the house, since it was his before the marriage.

"That's okay – I figured that," she said. "My best friend from high school said that the boys and me can have her basement until we find somewhere else. Actually, I can't wait to get away from him."

So, she moved out and we went ahead with the case. A few days after the papers were served on Floyd, I got a call from Bonnie Jean Sorenson, his lawyer.

"Before you and your client break up this family, you should have her do some family counseling through their church. I talked to the minister. They've got a program where they get to the bottom of the problem, then they patch it back together through prayer and confession."

Because of my history with Bonnie, I knew that we'd be in for a wild ride on the case. She believed in keeping a high profile and was known for self-aggrandizement. She ran ads with pictures of herself "glammed up." She featured a photo of herself from high school, wearing her cheerleader outfit, complete with pom-poms. The problem was, it was twenty-five years old.

My colleagues and I knew better. She was a small-time operator who could be counted on to turn the simplest case into a fee-generating conflict of wills.

But it was her penchant for free love that made Bonnie infamous among the legal community. This wasn't idle gossip – it was a badge that she chose to wear with pride.

For example, one evening at a retirement reception for a local judge Bonnie approached me for a tete-a-tete. She liked to sidle up close when talking but had a disturbing habit of projecting spittle as she spoke, so I tried to keep my distance.

"You might have heard that I had a relationship with Ray," she said.

She was talking about a friend of mine, whose reputation for lechery was at least equal to Bonnie's.

"That's the last time I have an affair with a married man," she said.

She wasn't telling me anything I didn't already know. To use a legal term, their union had been "open and notorious." It had also been fully digested by the courthouse gossip mill, which had it that each had left with a case of genital herpes, leading to accusations by one against the other which intensified to the extent that a mutual friend had to intervene to cool things down.

My then-law partner Amanda was especially chagrined by Bonnie. Mandy, sharp and savvy and with a proclivity to drop "f-bombs" when deserved, was famous in the firm for keeping her "shit list," an ever-evolving roster of the top ten lawyers, judges and others, who had crossed her path in the wrong way. Other than telling me that Bonnie topped her list, she'd never disclose who else was on it. Perhaps I was on it, too.

Mandy and many of her fellow female lawyers and judges gathered on Friday afternoons to share war stories and imbibe in copious quantities of wine. You could tell when they were at our office from the closed doors and tightly drawn curtains at the conference room and the muffled sounds of clinking bottles and bursts of raucous laughter.

These women, as you might guess, despised Bonnie, since, although they were a growing minority in the community, they were conscious of their image. They perceived Bonnie's conduct as casting a shadow on all of them.

I demurred at Bonnie's proposal that Elizabeth and her client engage in faith-based counseling, telling her that I'd respond after conferring with Elizabeth, but I already knew the answer.

"I'll never step foot in that church again," Elizabeth had told me.

Our initial hearing was before Judge Henderson, a veteran who I highly respected and who, I knew as well, who was a frequent attendee at the women's confabs mentioned above.

It didn't take Bonnie long to launch into her spiel.

"Your Honor, my client's wife, and her lawyer are trying to break up this family. My client's a righteous man, a responsible school administrator, and a deacon in his church, and I've proposed that the parties participate in Christian counseling to stop this tragedy, but they won't respond. So, I'm asking you to order it."

The irony of Bonnie's spirited defense of the sanctity of marriage was not lost on me, or, I suspected, Judge Henderson as well.

"What makes you think I'd do something like that, counselor?" the judge said. "Didn't you study the First Amendment in law school? Freedom *of* religion also means freedom *from* religion.

"Then I'm calling for a deposition," Bonnie said. "We'll show who was the transgressor in this marriage."

"Suit yourself," said the judge, "but I won't put up with a fault-finding expedition. We're past that era."

Days later, we received Bonnie's notice of deposition. It's a procedure typically used for trial preparation, in which the witness, in this case Elizabeth herself, is sworn in by the court reporter, and is asked questions pertinent to the case. The questions can be wide-ranging, sometimes only vaguely bordering on relevancy. It usually happens in lawyer's offices. You might think that would lend itself to a more relaxed atmosphere. But you'd be wrong – it's a high-stress event. Considering

Bonnie's track record, I had taken extra care to prepare Elizabeth for it, but confidence wasn't her strong suit.

Considering Bonnie's efforts to publicize herself as a high-powered, successful lawyer, her office was surprisingly humble. It was located in the lower level (meaning basement) of an aging building along a busy, noisy highway. Elizabeth and I entered the deposition room, which was dark and tile-floored. The conference table was marred by food stains.

I noticed that Elizabeth, for the first time, had eschewed her customary pioneer dress, and was wearing a basic dark skirt and white blouse. She had also added some eyeshadow and red lipstick.

Bonnie, Floyd, and the court reporter had already arrived, so Elizabeth was promptly sworn in and seated next to me. She swallowed.

"Counselor," Bonnie said, "tell your client to cover herself up."

"What?"

"She's displaying her chest. It's humiliating to my client to have his wife expose herself in front of other men."

I hadn't noticed a thing, and, believe me, if there was something to see, I would have. But Elizabeth was so slight and underweight that there really wasn't anything to expose. Before I could react, she'd hastily buttoned her blouse to the neck.

Things went south from there. The questions were intensely personal, inquiring into Bonnie's life before the marriage, including veiled references to her sex life. I objected often, instructing Elizabeth not to answer. Bonnie became more and more agitated, and Elizabeth increasingly panicky. I was about to call for a break when, suddenly, I felt something warm and wet in my crotch. I looked down and was horrified to see a pair of eyes staring up at me.

I leaped from my chair. "What the hell! Godammit, Bonnie, get that dog out of here!"

As startled as I was – everyone else was shocked at my reaction, staring at me with mouths agape. The court reporter was so rattled that he'd knocked his steno paper off its spindle, and it rolled across the room – serpentine style.

I looked down again. There were clumps of long, dirty gray dog hair clinging to my new, silk and cashmere blend navy slacks.

"Son of a bitch!" I shouted.

It took a trip to the restroom and several minutes before things resumed.

Bonnie said, "I want the record to show that counsel just engaged in a profane outburst unbecoming the dignity of these proceedings. Furthermore, my dog, which is a licensed support animal, will be staying."

"No it won't," I said. "If you don't get it out of here, I'm calling Judge Henderson and getting this whole thing moved to the courthouse."

That worked, and she escorted the dog into an adjoining room, although the remainder of the deposition was punctuated by the sounds of it whimpering through the thin walls.

Elizabeth was distraught by the time we were done, so I took her to a nearby coffee shop.

"Don't worry, the worst is over," I said.

I explained that we had an upcoming custody evaluation and that a licensed psychologist would interview the parties separately, observe the children with each party, and conduct testing on Elizabeth and Floyd. I was certain she'd do well and told her so, but she was still shaken.

"I could see him in the deposition," she said. "He was furious, and when he gets like this, he does crazy stuff."

A month passed, and we had gotten notice of the trial. One day, I got a call from our local police chief. He was an old friend of mine, going back to the days when I was a municipal prosecutor and he was a young patrolman.

"We got a report yesterday. It was a guy named Floyd Peterson, and he wants us to arrest you for careless driving. He said you were on the way to your office and you weren't paying attention to your driving – you crossed over the centerline." My stomach did a somersault as I remembered having been distracted by a text, glancing down at my phone, and correcting to get back in my lane.

"Of course, we can't arrest anyone for a misdemeanor that we don't witness," he said.

"Sorry, Ed. I did it, but it bothers me that this guy was following me. He's the husband in a divorce case I have against him."

"Oh, we know that," Ed said. "He said you were having an affair with his wife and he and his lawyer were going to go after you at the trial."

"Not guilty," I said.

I was furious, because, setting aside the immorality of it, having a romantic relationship with a client was a sure-fire way to bring an end to a career. The consequences are severe, as they should be, normally resulting in suspension or, in some egregious cases, disbarment. It seemed that every year some male or female lawyer got caught crossing that line. And, as bad as the consequences were for your career, they could be devastating personally, since the bar association issues a press release about it, ensuring that the public would be fully informed as to who you were and what you'd done.

"Oh, it wouldn't matter to us anyway," the chief said "We have no interest in getting involved in civil litigation, but we worry about these stalker types. We got his license info and I've instructed the squads in your neighborhood to keep an eye out for him. But, do me a favor, will you?"

"Anything," I said.

"Keep your eyes on the road."

"Oh, sure," I said.

"And your rear-view mirror," he chuckled.

Elizabeth and I met for a prep session a week before the trial. This time I noticed even more changes in her. She'd gained some weight, was wearing a stylish green dress, and had tinted her hair. She seemed stronger and self-assured. And, I had good news.

"We've got the custody evaluation, Elizabeth. It says you should get primary custody."

She was pleased, but I could sense something was bothering her.

"I don't know if I should talk about this," she said. "But I don't want to keep anything from you. Last week I stayed with my parents in Granite Falls. Floyd had the kids back here in the city. And, well, I spent the night with an old high school boyfriend."

I don't understand why people feel they have to reveal these things, but they do.

Although I perhaps should have been concerned about how this affected our case, part of me said, good for you, Elizabeth!

"There's no way he'd know since he was up here with the kids. As a matter of fact, he hates my parents so much that he hasn't been down in Granite Falls in years," she said.

That was reassuring, although I couldn't forget about my recent incident with the police.

The trial started off well. I called the psychologist as our first witness. She affirmed her recommendation for custody with Elizabeth, even going further.

"Based on the psychological tests and interviews with Mr. Peterson, I'm endorsing a thorough course of anger management training for him. Furthermore, he shouldn't be permitted to involve the boys in his church. It's causing emotional trauma for them."

Elizabeth did well in her direct testimony also. Then it was time for Bonnie's cross-examination.

"Ms. Peterson," she said. "Isn't it a fact that you spent a night at the Best Western Motel in Granite Falls in the presence of an unrelated male?"

"I object, your Honor," I said. "Relevance and materiality."

Judge Henderson cast an angry frown toward Bonnie.

"Where are you going with this, Ms. Sorenson?"

"We have videotape of her entering the motel in the evening and leaving in the morning. It's obvious that she was having an affair."

"Didn't we cover this ground in our first hearing, counsel? I don't care about this stuff. Unless you can tell me the children were there or someone has a felony on their record, I won't hear it. Objection sustained."

Bonnie paused briefly, leaning over to her client for a word.

"Ms. Peterson, have you had a sexual relationship with anyone else, including your lawyer?"

The judge's face reddened.

"I'm not waiting for counsel to object this time. You're out of line. The question will be stricken from the record."

"I take exception to your ruling," Bonnie said, "and we'll appeal it as soon as possible."

"Appeal away," the judge shot back. "I'll look forward to reading the opinion affirming me. But you'll stop this line of questioning or I'll call the jailer downstairs and have them find a place for you in the women's section."

That finally shut Bonnie up. The trial ended and a month later we received the decision. Elizabeth was awarded custody, child support, and the right to choose the church for the children. Although Floyd was awarded his house, Elizabeth got a fifty-percent share of his state pension and the savings and investments.

A few months later I got a letter from Elizabeth.

"Thanks for everything," it said. "Here's the last payment on my bill. The boys and I have moved down here to Granite Falls. We don't hear much from my ex-husband. He's got another woman – some divorcee he met at the church. I never thought I'd say this again, but - Thank God!"

CHAPTER 24

Hans' Women

Herb and Barb were just the nicest folks you could meet. They were from a small town on the northern fringe of the metro area – the kind of place that started as a stagecoach stop in the nineteenth century but was transformed almost overnight into a sea of McMansions when suburban sprawl finally arrived.

They were in their mid-sixties. I'd guess they were from the stagecoach part of town. Barb was in charge. She was an attractive, gray-haired matronly woman.

"Our granddaughter Annamarie's been living with us for the past three years. Her father, Hans, gave us written permission so we could enroll her in school. He hardly ever sees her. Then last week, he showed up at her school and took off with her. He won't bring her back."

"Did you call the police?"

"We did, but they won't help us because he's the dad, and there's no court order giving us rights."

It was another grandparent custody case. Our society has become one of caretakers – both for the old and the young. Parents, overwhelmed by health or economic crises, often pass the responsibility for their children to their own parents. Yet, when there is a dispute, our Supreme Court has declared the rights of the biological parent paramount, even when it is against the best interests of the child.

Fortunately, Herb and Barb had better standing than most relatives due to having been Annamarie's home for a few years, but to help them I needed to know more.

"What about Annamarie's mother?" I asked.

"Anna passed away three years ago," Barb said. "She had a heart attack while she was taking a shower – she was only thirty-two."

Barb stifled a sob, but she would not lose her composure. She was the embodiment of the overused, but in this case apt expression, "Minnesota nice." Her daughter's death was foremost in her mind, but she would never, ever, force her grief needlessly on another person, especially a stranger. Herb, however, was a little more direct.

"It wasn't a heart attack. He killed her."

"Really? What happened?"

"What healthy woman that age dies like that? Hans is a MedTec – he has access to all kinds of stuff. I'm sure he poisoned her somehow. He wanted to get rid of her so he could enjoy the single life again. That's exactly what he's been doing ever since this happened. It's why he left Annamarie with us."

"Was there an autopsy – an investigation?" I asked.

"Not much of one. The medical examiner said that she'd need more probable cause to justify a detailed analysis. But, let me give you a clue. Hans insisted on an immediate cremation. We found our daughter's will, and she'd asked to be buried at our church cemetery, so he didn't get his way. We've tried to follow up with a county detective. He said we need more evidence."

Barb added, "If we can come up with some proof, the police will get her body exhumed and tested."

I didn't respond, because what could you say? The detective was likely giving them a ray of hope, but the chance of getting a court order for this grisly procedure three years after the fact was about zero. Still, I couldn't begrudge them from hanging on to their hope for justice.

"Hans is the father, and Annamarie will have to stay with him until we've got a court order saying otherwise. Because of the status of the law, we need hard proof to win the case. What can we tell the judge to convince him that there are 'grave circumstances,' which is the standard of proof?"

"The only reason he came and took her was because we just got a state grant for her expenses," said Barb. "Now he wants the money."

Herb jumped in. "Even more important than that - he's never accepted being a parent. He hasn't been to her school. He knows nothing of her life. He's had lots of relationships but won't stick with the same woman for long. I think he's got a screw loose, but then I also think he killed our daughter - so I'm biased."

I had to break them the bad news. Their feelings about Annamarie's best interests were legitimate but lacked the urgency needed to overcome the preference for the biological parent. Considering the paucity of direct evidence against Hans, we'd be lucky to get visitation rights for Herb and Barb.

Despite the grim context, I decided we should give it a try. Maybe some new evidence could come up during the litigation that would help our case, so I served Hans with a petition for grandparent custody. Soon enough, we got a preliminary court order directing mediation, which was to be held at a lawyer's office nearby.

We entered the conference room at the same moment as Hans and his lawyer. What was he like? He was in his mid-thirties and fit, but he had sharp features and unkempt hair. There was something off about him. When he shook my hand, he wouldn't look me in the eye, instead staring down at the floor.

After the mediator gave us the customary spiel about trying to resolve differences without the costs and stress of court, she asked for a picture of Annamarie. "We need to remember that this is about a child – not us," the mediator said.

It's a good tactic to start. I use it myself when I'm the mediator. She looked at Hans first, but he didn't have a photo. Barb did, from Annamarie's Sunday school, which she attended with Herb and Barb regularly. She had a wide, happy face and a pixie-like smile.

"Her Mom would've liked that picture," Hans said. Perhaps he meant it as a friendly ice-breaker, but if so he spoiled it by laughing loudly at his own joke.

How inappropriate, I thought, especially considering the gravity of the moment and the people involved. As the mediator attempted to start a dialogue, Hans asked for a smoke break. Another time, he lurched out of the room, claiming that he had to make a call. His strange behavior led me to wonder if he actally could be a killer.

As the time for trial approached, I asked Barb if she knew of anyone who might be a helpful witness for us.

"I've talked to both of his long-term girlfriends," Barb said. "If you called them, I'm pretty sure they'd vouch for us."

I did. The first woman, Liz, was willing to come to my office. She was surprisingly young, maybe in her early twenties – ten to fifteen years younger than Hans. "He just swept me off my feet," she said. "I'd never had a man dominate me like that. I guess I liked it at the time. I mean, he wined and dined me. He had a nice sports car."

"Did he tell you about Annamarie?"

"It wasn't for months until I found out he had a child. Then, when I asked about her he'd just blow me off. This one time Herb and Barb showed up with Annamarie – she was beautiful and they were so kind, to her and to me, too. That's when I found out that Annemarie's mother was dead. Hans hadn't even told me that, either. It was the beginning of the end of my relationship with him. How can you have a future with someone who hides his past like that?"

Liz promised to help us. She signed an affidavit supporting our case, and we put her on our witness list. The next woman was Kirsten.

As she walked into my office, I was astounded – she was a spitting image of Liz. About the same age, with the same blond hair and blue eyes, and she had the same naïve demeanor.

"I thought he was Prince Charming when we met." She said.

"He was so mature, and he had a good job and his own home. All the guys I'd known before were losers or they still lived with their parents. I moved in two weeks after we met."

The big difference with Kirsten, though, was that she and Hans shared a baby girl. "He wanted me to have an abortion, but I said no. Then I found out about his last girlfriend, Liz. I called her up and she told me about Annamarie. I couldn't believe it. I got Herb and Barb's number from her and I drove over to their house. That's when they told me about Annamarie's mom. I could tell right away that Annamarie loved them. They're good people and I'll help them 100%." I asked when she broke up with Hans.

"It was right after I had the baby. That's the scary part. He didn't even come to the hospital when the baby was born. Then he said something really scary. He said that Annamarie's mom tried to trap him and he dealt with her in his own way, and that's what would happen to any other woman who'd try to trap him again. I think he might have killed her."

"Have you told anyone about this?" I asked.

"No one, but I will now. Put me on your list. Now that I'm a mom myself I couldn't imagine Annamarie being placed in his house."

I mentioned to her that a detective was interested in Anna's death. "Give me his number," she said.

After my initial doubts about our case, I was beginning to have some hope. Herb and Barb would be great witnesses. We had plenty of volunteers from the church and the community who were ready to go to bat for them, and then we had the two girlfriends – especially Kirsten. Things suddenly changed, though.

A week before the trial, I got an emergency call – from Kirsten.

"Take me off the witness list!" She implored me.

"I just found out the government's going after Hans for the child-birth costs they helped me with, and child support, too. He'll take it out on me. I told them to stop it but I think the notices already got sent out. Tell his lawyer I'm off the case. Please!"

She was our best witness and the trial was set to start shortly. Also, she'd raised Herb and Barb's hopes of getting law enforcement back on their daughter's case. Still, we agreed to abide by Kirsten's wishes, so I quickly posted an email to Hans' lawyer, hoping that he'd get it in time to prevent anything from happening.

It wasn't quick enough, though. When I got to work the next morning, there was an urgent call message from Barb.

"There isn't going to be a trial tomorrow," she said, "take a look at today's *Star Tribune*."

HOMICIDE IN SOUTH MINNEAPOLIS

Police reported a homicide in the parking lot of United Methodist Church in south Minneapolis yesterday afternoon. Killed by gunfire was Kirsten Olson, 23, of Minneapolis. Under arrest is Hans Volkman, 39, of Saint Paul. Volkman and Olson had arranged a meeting in a public venue to discuss a private legal matter, police said. Volkman was accompanied by a seven-year-old child, possibly his daughter. Police will not confirm whether the child witnessed the shooting.

I contacted the detective, who told me that Hans was seen at a nearby gas station throwing some bloody towels in a waste can. A witness concerned about Annamarie's safety called 911. Closed circuit video at the church had recorded the incident as well.

A few days later we appeared at the scheduled hearing and Herb and Barb were awarded permanent custody by default - Hans was restrained from further contact with Annamarie. He pled guilty to Murder in the First Degree and got a life sentence, which meant that there was no parole possible for at least thirty-five years.

Was that the end of our case? Actually not.

About a year after Kirsten's death, I got a letter from LAMP – Legal Aid for Minnesota Prisoners. Hans was asking for Annamarie to be brought to the prison periodically for visits with him. The hearing was in two weeks.

My first reaction was that Hans wanted a "field trip". It's what lawyers call it when a prisoner conjures up a special event to get away from the prison for a day or two. It can be a funeral, a wedding or, in this case, a court hearing. Often there's free legal assistance – like LAMP – or it's the notorious "jailhouse lawyers." Although occasionally there's a genuine rationale for the court hearing and even the chance of getting a positive result, more often than not it's just a day out of "the joint." It's hard to blame these guys – you'd do the same, wouldn't you?

The court convened as scheduled and Hans was there with his LAMP lawyer – probably a volunteer from private practice. She and he had been given a jury room, guarded by a deputy, for privacy. The judge called both lawyers into chambers.

"I don't know why we're here," the judge said. "This case was decided a year ago. Why should I change it and force a seven-year-old child to go on a prison visit?"

Hans' lawyer said, "I understand, your honor. I was just assigned to this case. Give me a chance to talk to counsel and we'll see if we can work something out."

She and I were directed to a conference room in the hallway. I wasn't happy about being there and let her know.

"Do you know how much money my clients had to pay me to do this case today? Is he really serious?"

She protested. "Hans really loves Annamarie. Just because he's a prisoner doesn't mean he isn't a dad."

She was surprisingly emotional, and I began to wonder if she actually had been "just assigned" to the case. She was young – maybe thirty, and seemed inexperienced and disorganized, both in her manner but also her appearance. Her dark blue suit was a bit akimbo, and her flushed face begged the question of what had been going on back in the jury room she shared with her client. She looked in her file for something and accidentally knocked the entire satchel and its contents onto the floor. I reached down to help her but she snapped at me. "It's confidential – don't touch it!"

As it turned out, we quickly settled the case. Herb and Barb agreed to allow Hans to send a Christmas card every year to Annamarie. Everything else was dropped. As I suspected, Hans didn't really care about his daughter – it was just a "field trip."

The judge insisted that all parties affirm the agreement on the record in court, so we assembled at our respective counsel tables. As the judge entered the courtroom, I heard laughter from Hans' direction. It was Hans and the lawyer, heads close, sharing something amusing. What a time to be joking, I thought. But then I realized what had happened. Hans had a new woman.

CHAPTER 25

Junkyard Joey and the Prodigal Daughter

Carol was middle-aged, and still a pretty woman. If one could overlook the passage of time, it would be easy to visualize her as a high-school homecoming queen. She wore a bulky but new Green Bay Packers sweatshirt. She was also plain-spoken. "It's over. He's a drunk. He smells. But the last straw is this. He's screwing his own daughter," she said.

"He's a child abuser, too?" I asked.

"Not exactly. When he was a teenager, he knocked up some girl-friend of his. They gave up the child for adoption. Now, she's a 32-year-old woman. She looked him up through the adoption registry last year. I thought it was nice at first, because I never had a daughter, but now they're having an affair."

I've heard some tall tales over the years, and if I'd believed all of them, I would've been laughed out of court many times, so I took this one with a grain of salt. "That's seems pretty outrageous. Do you have any proof?"

"I sure do. He was even too cheap to rent a room. They carried on right in our home while I was gone," she said. "I put a voice-activated tape recorder under our bed, and I caught them in the act." She handed me the tape.

I put it in the machine and, sure enough, the sounds were those of a couple enjoying - as you might say – sexual congress.

"Doesn't that just make you sick?" she asked.

Actually, my reaction was decidedly different as I found myself shifting in my chair.

"You're right – it's awful," I managed. "Did you call the police/"

"Yes, but they said the incest law doesn't apply, because since she's adopted, they aren't legally related."

I should have known that, but I continued with my questions.

Carol had been married for thirty years. Her husband was the owner of Joe's Salvage and Auto Parts. This earned him the nickname "Junkyard Joey" among our staff. "He claims he's a millionaire," she said. "He's always bragging that he operates in cash and barter, so no one will ever know how much money he has, especially the government. He hasn't filed a tax return for twenty-five years. Joey must hoard his money somewhere, cuz he never spends any of it on his family. Me and our two boys lived in the same house for thirty years. Never even took a vacation."

"You mean you haven't filed a tax return either?" I asked. As she nodded her head, I explained to her that we would immediately file "innocent spouse" tax returns on her behalf for all those years. It's a strategy wherein someone like Carol, the "innocent spouse" who knows nothing of the finances, can stay legal. When we didn't have enough information to fill in the amount of her income, we'd enter "unknown."

I wondered how we could prove to the court that Joey actually had the money he bragged about.

It's not an unfamiliar problem for a divorce lawyer. When things are going well, husbands boast to their wives that they're captains of industry -- mountain movers -- but when the divorce happens, suddenly they're paupers, that things just went to hell in the last year.

Typically, we can prove them wrong by digging up their tax returns. If they borrowed from the bank and pumped up their assets in their loan documents, we subpoena their financial statements. Joey, though, had never borrowed a dime and, of course, the government didn't know he existed. For all I knew, he could have buried his money in coffee cans.

"How about his employees?" I asked. "Maybe some of them are in the loop."

"They don't know a thing," Carol said. "Every Friday he takes a wad of cash into the bathroom, sits on the pot and counts out little piles of money for each of the workers. No withholding – no social security – no benefits."

A few weeks later, it was time for our initial court hearing. Joey had hired my friend Doug, who is primarily a criminal defense attorney.

Doug is the fellow you might see on TV standing next to his newly arrested client, saying, "This man is completely innocent and he's looking forward to clearing his name at the trial." We lawyers know that as soon as the prosecutor knocks a couple of years off the client's sentence, Doug will be pleading his man guilty. The TV exposure is great for business, though.

I'd already talked to Doug about my client's accusation of an affair between Joey and his daughter, although I wasn't completely sold on Carol's story or convinced that I could use it in Court.

As the case was called by the clerk, I saw Junkyard Joey for the first time. He was sitting in the back of the courtroom. His jeans were stained with oil and grease. Folds of his hairy gut were hanging below his flannel shirt, available for public viewing. He had the purplish, lumpy nose and rheumy eyes of the committed drinker. When he caught me looking, he sneered at me.

Then, a younger woman walked into the room and sat next to Joey. It had to be the daughter since they looked almost like twins. She, too, was wearing dirty jeans and a flannel shirt, and she grasped his hand, as if in support.

The judge motioned us to follow him into his chambers. "Okay, lawyers, what's really going on here?"

Before I could get a word out, Doug was all over it. "I know what counsel's going to say, your Honor, but he's got no proof and I won't let him poison the well with his outrageous allegations."

I had no intention of going into Joey's disgusting behavior. I only wanted to talk about money. "I don't know what counsel's referring to, your Honor. My concern is that the Respondent is an outlaw. He has no business records. He doesn't even file tax returns. My client's put up with this for thirty years. He's sitting on a gold mine with his junkyard, but we need to be able to prove its value. I'm asking you to order him to pay to get the place appraised. We'll even consult with Doug about who will do the job."

"Anything wrong with that, counsel?" the judge asked Doug. "I can't decide what's fair unless I get the facts."

Doug just shook his head. "You can tell him whatever you want, but I've got no control over him."

"That doesn't please the Court at all," the judge said. "Go out there and tell him to bring $10,000, in cash, within five days. If he doesn't, he'd better keep a toothbrush handy for when I throw him in jail."

We walked back to the courtroom. Doug broke the news to Joey. Then Doug walked away, shaking his head, and Joey walked up to me, pointing with his fat, dirty finger.

"You haven't heard the last of this, numb nuts. I'm getting rid of that guy and hiring me a Jew lawyer!"

"I don't care what you do," I said, "but if you don't pay the money, you be in jail for contempt of court."

My circle of divorce lawyers is heterogenous. By and large, these folks are the hardest working, most competent, and -- believe it or not for a bunch of divorce lawyers -- family-oriented people you could find. Of course, there are a few bad eggs in any group, and the one Joey found happened to be Jewish.

To call Larry Rothenberg a shark would be to demean the animal. He doesn't care about his clients – he lives to create conflict, then pumps up the bill at the rate of $500 per hour until the client runs out of money, at which time he abandons ship. He insults lawyers, judges and court personnel to a degree that many lawyers will not accept a case if he's on the other side. Once he cross-examined some man so brutally during a trial that the poor fellow had a stroke, and had to be carried out from the courtroom on a stretcher. The media ate up the story, and Rothenberg wore it like a badge, proudly displaying a headline from the Minneapolis paper about it in his office lobby.

As the case proceeded, we soldiered through depositions and subpoenas. After a while, our appraisal came back -- the evaluator had given up. "The property certainly has substantial worth," he wrote, "but without access to hard financial data we cannot take a professionally defensible position as to its value."

I was in the process of breaking the bad news to Carol when – out of the blue – a letter arrived from the attorney of the city where the junkyard was located.

"We have decided to clear out all of the salvage yards in our municipality. We're concerned about the environmental damage and want to encourage more residential development. Since your client is on the deed, please pass on our proposal to purchase the property for $1.5 million."

I told Carol. She was as shocked as I was.

The day before the trial, the lawyers were called into a conference with the judge.

Before a word could be said, Rothenberg launched in. "Your Honor, I want Petitioner's counsel disqualified from this case. He ordered a secret recording of my client. That's illegal!"

I had decided not to mention Joey's affair, but now Rothenberg had opened the door for me. "Respondent has been having an illicit affair with his adult daughter. My client had a tape recorder under her own bed, in her own house, which is entirely legal." Larry was livid. "Just by telling you about this, he's prejudicing the case!"

The judge grimaced. "You were the one who brought it up, Mr. Rothenberg. Is it true?"

Larry just shrugged, but I was happy to fill in the blanks for the judge, off the record of course.

The judge was interrupted by another case, and we found ourselves out in the hallway. I was pleased that Rothenberg had screwed up, but was still angry at him for accusing me.

My phone hummed with a text from my assistant. "Mr. Rothenberg is parked on our lot. It's his red Corvette with his name on the plates. Did you give him permission?" I'm an owner of the office building, and the lot abuts the courthouse, so I could see the car from the hallway window. "Larry!" I called to him.

He came over, facing me in a chin-to-chin stance – another intimidation technique of his.

"You're parked in my lot."

"So what. Who are you?" He shot back.

"I own the building and I own the parking lot. The cops are two blocks away, and I'll have you ticketed and towed if you don't move, right now."

He stomped off, and I could tell he didn't believe me, because he was immediately on his phone. Soon enough, though, I could see him pulling on his galoshes and putting on his overcoat.

Some lawyers look back at their careers, cherishing their appearances before the highest courts, or the lofty prose of their appellate briefs. For me, sending this asshole out in the fifteen-below Minnesota winter just to move his car was one of the top highlights. Things didn't improve much for Larry at the trial. His theory was that Carol didn't deserve to share the wealth. Joey Junkyard had built his empire while Carol enjoyed a life of domesticity, he contended.

This life of "domesticity," we countered, included the "privilege" of attending countless truancy meetings, juvenile hearings, and treatment sessions for their two delinquent sons, neither of whom got an ounce of guidance from their absent dad.

I called the city attorney as our witness. He testified that Joe's Salvage and Auto Repair was scheduled for condemnation, and the City would pay the incredible sum of $1.5 million for the land and the business. Yes, he said, the City would issue separate checks directly to each party upon completion if the judge so ordered.

Carol was a great witness, giving Rothenberg as much as he could dish out. Joey's daughter attended the trial daily, sitting directly behind

Joey's counsel table, a constant reminder to the judge of Joey's perfidy. A lawyer with any sense would have refused to allow it.

Carol was awarded half the net worth of the marital estate, and she didn't have to beg Joey to get paid, thanks to the city's separate checks. Larry and Joey appealed it to the higher courts, unsuccessfully. The appellate court made Joey pay our fees, and I'm sure Rothenberg charged him at least six figures.

About a year later, I was walking out of Target one morning and heard a familiar voice,

"Hey, I would've guessed you shopped at Nordstrom's, Mister Lawyer!" It was Carol, walking in with a girlfriend. She'd lost weight and wore stylish clothing.

"I could say the same for you," I answered.

We chatted, catching up with each other and reminiscing about the case. Joey and his daughter had moved up to northern Minnesota and bought another junkyard. Carol was pleased to have him gone.

A few years later, I got an email from Doug, Joey's first lawyer. Joey had died. I decided to check his obituary online and was shocked to see that several women had written glowing memorials. "Joey was the love of my life," one said. But none was quite as flattering as the one by his daughter. "A beautiful and generous man."

I guess you never know.

CHAPTER 26

A Girl on a Horse

He was a block of a man – tall and barrel-chested. He had a generous head of curly brown hair, graying at the temples. I put him in his early forties. The patch on his green work outfit read "Hansen Sod Farms." Although I could tell he'd cleaned up for our meeting, rings of sweat were already encroaching from his armpits.

"Nick Hansen," he said in a *basso profundo* voice. His meaty hand grasped mine in a firm shake.

"I've driven by your place a hundred times," I said. If you want to break the ice with a man, get him to tell you about his job.

"We've been there forever," he said.

Sod farms like Nick's used to be a common sight in the metro area. The peat-based soil was perfect for the crop, and the state government gave the farmers a tax break for agricultural use, calling it "Greenacres" property. At first, the sod farmers prospered when the urban sprawl begat neighborhoods with spacious lawns. Then the municipalities, with their constant need of money for sewer, water, and street projects, gradually stripped the farmers of their tax subsidies.

Nick, whose farm was close enough to the city to provide a view of the urban skyline, was one of the few survivors – a relic in a way. "Gonna stay till the government puts me out of business. The land's so valuable I could sell it tomorrow and retire, but I hope they give me a few more years."

He reached into his shirt pocket, producing a folded-over document entitled *Ex Parte* Order for Protection. *Ex Parte*, which literally means "by the party" is a method by which court orders can be issued without input from the other side. "The deputies knocked on my door and told me I had five minutes to get my things together and then get out. They can't do that, can they? "

"Oh, they can," I told him.

Our current law allows a victim to get a restraining order signed by a judge, barring the alleged perpetrator from his own home, based solely on a sworn statement, or affidavit.

The Domestic Abuse Act has been part of our jurisprudence for some twenty-five years. In the bad old days, it was rare to see a woman in court seeking redress for abuse. The judges – most of them older men – gave little credence to the uncorroborated testimony of a female victim.

The *Ex Parte* process is the greatest benefit of the new law, but also its biggest downside, because a bad-faith party can abuse the very law created to stop abuse.

The order addressed Nick by name. It excluded him from within a ten-block radius of his home and gave temporary custody of the two daughters to his wife.

Violation was punishable by up to ninety days in jail and a fine of $3,000.

The affidavit signed by Janice Hansen, alleged that Nick had pinned her against a wall, and in a fit of rage, threatened her life, saying: "If you don't shut up, it's the last thing you'll say." The affidavit also claimed a past history of domestic assault.

"I didn't do a damn thing – I swear. It says I can't possess a firearm either. Does that mean I can't go deer hunting?"

"For now, yes, Nick, but you have rights. We can get a hearing within ten days."

Nick looked at me incredulously. "You mean it's not permanent?"

"Not necessarily. First, though, what's this about there being a history of prior abuse?"

"Okay. Something happened, but there are two sides to the story. About five years ago, we were coming home from a wedding. We'd both gotten a little too much into the champagne. I made a comment about how one of the bridesmaids had a nice body. Bad move on my part."

"Never a good idea," I said

"Janice blew her stack. She scratched my cheek. Then she grabbed my watchband and twisted it till my arm was bleeding. I was losing control of the car. We could've crashed. To avoid it, I whacked her with the back of my hand."

"How badly was she hurt?" I imagined what a blow from Nick's massive hand would be like.

"I admit it -- she had a bruise," he said. "Someone must have seen our car swerving, because by the time we got home there was a highway patrol behind us. He tagged each of us for domestic abuse since we both had visible injuries."

"What happened then?"

"We went to court and asked the judge to drop the charges, but he was on a crusade about chemical dependency. He made us go to alcohol awareness classes. The whole thing cost us two thousand bucks. It was a waste since neither of us ever drank except now and then, like that wedding. "

"No more incidents?" I asked.

"Nope. We learned our lesson. That's what gets me. I haven't done a thing to her since, never even thought about it."

"Tell me more about your marriage."

"We were high school sweethearts and got married right away. She loved that my family kept horses at the farm." He sighed. "Then the girls came along – Gwen, she's twelve now, and Lily, she's nine."

"I thought we were happy. When the girls got to school age, we decided to move into town. The farmhouse was too old for Janice. She said I smelled like the farm and me and the girls were getting dirt all over the place. We had enough money to build a house in town and, of course, the grass was free, so that's what we did."

Nick asked for a glass of water.

"Things changed after that. Janice turned into a homebody and hardly went out anywhere. She never once went back to the farm. She got to be really close with her sister Sally. That woman's a real ball-crushing man-hater. Sally's tight with some of those women's support groups."

He shuffled his feet. "After a while, it seemed like Janice and the girls didn't want me around. Finally, Janice told me to move to the farm. I was the odd man out back at the house, so I agreed."

"Did you still see your girls?"

"For a while I did. They love the horses, just like their mother used to, and we used to have a great time. You know, until the last year or so, the girls were closer to me than they were to their mom. Janice resented that.

"Look at this," he said as he pulled a creased photo out of his wallet. It was Nick sitting on a horse, with one of the girls behind him and her younger sister in front. They were all smiling and waving at the photographer. "Now I can hardly get them to come, and when they do, Gwen spends the whole day playing games on her phone. Janice calls them constantly. Even Lily acts like she doesn't like me anymore."

Nick shifted uncomfortably in his chair. "There's one other thing. I sort of fell for Dora, my foreman's sister. My wife always puts me down for being out on the farm, but Dora likes me the way I am."

"I can see where this is going," I said.

"Janice got wind about Dora. That's the first time she used the word divorce. I got her to go to marriage counseling with our priest. I said I'd cut it off with Dora and she said she'd let me back in the house."

"How did that go?"

"It didn't really work. She and the girls would hardly talk to me. I even had to sleep in the downstairs. Then all of a sudden, I get these abuse papers handed to me by the deputy."

"Okay, Nick, step out for a few minutes and I'll try reaching her lawyer," I said. The call went right through. I introduced myself and said, "We're going to be asking for a hearing, but do you think Mr. Hansen could see his daughters this weekend? We could set up an exchange at a public spot if your client wants."

"That's not going to happen, counsel. You and your abuser can put your case to the judge, but there's going to be no contact for him if I have anything to say about it."

"Wait a minute," I said. "You'd better be able to prove your case before you start throwing around labels. Furthermore, he's not 'my abuser.' Where's your sense of professional courtesy?"

"You're talking about good manners?" she said with a snort, "I'll put the safety of these children before that any day of the week."

I did my best to end the conversation without further rancor, then called Nick in to break the bad news to him.

"Thanks for trying," he said. "Looks like I'm screwed, right?"

"We'll do fine in court," I said, hoping it wasn't an empty promise. I called the judge's clerk and got a hearing scheduled for the following week.

* * * * * * * *

On the day of court, Nick arrived at my office appropriately attired in slacks and a sweater. We walked over to the courthouse together. When we got to the hallway leading to the courtroom, I saw a group of about ten women and two preadolescent girls in plaid Catholic school uniform dresses.

"Do you know these people?" I asked.

"Some of them," Nick said. "That's Janice and her sister Sally, and those girls are Gwen and Lily. I don't know who the rest are – the lawyer and some women from her sister's support group maybe? She's not supposed to bring our girls to the courthouse, is she?"

"I'll get to the bottom of it." I approached the woman whom I guessed was the lawyer, and introduced myself.

"So, you're the one who demanded this hearing," she said. The lawyer was youngish – perhaps in her early thirties -- she wore a dark business suit, short black hair, and no makeup. "Here are some papers for you and your abuser," she said as she handed me a fistful of documents. One was a Petition for Dissolution of Marriage, and the other was entitled "Affidavit of Gwen and Lily Hansen."

"I thought we had a discussion about calling my client an abuser," I said.

"That's a typical response from a man," she said. "Read the affidavits."

I put the Petition aside for the moment and glanced quickly through the Affidavit. It read in part:

"We are the children of Nick and Janice Hansen. We support our mother's case for domestic abuse against our father. He is abusive to our mother. We feel we have to be vigilant at all times to protect her against his campaign of violence. We feel like caged animals when he is in the house. We don't want to see him again.

I gave it to Nick to review and approached Janice's lawyer. "I hope you're not intending to use this, and you'd better not bring those girls into the courtroom."

"Look who's threatening now!" the lawyer said.

At that moment, Judge Olberg, her clerk, and court reporter walked through the hallway. Typically, this would be a time for a friendly, if formal, greeting, but the judge looked straight ahead. She must have read Janice's papers.

Nick and I sat at our counsel table. Janice and her lawyer were at the other, and their entourage sat in two rows behind them. The women differed in age and ethnicity, but I could sense the anger in their eyes bearing down on the back of my neck.

Janice stuck to the story set out in the Petition and Affidavit, adding her version of what happened the day of the wedding. As you might suspect, the part about twisting Nick's watchband was omitted. Then her lawyer asked if Janice had anything to say in conclusion.

"My husband is abusive to all of us, forcing us to be vigilant at all times against his campaign of violence. We feel like caged animals when he's in the house." The words were almost identical to the girls' affidavit.

Janice's lawyer stood, addressing the court. "Your Honor, we call the two children of the parties, Gwen and Lily Hansen."

I leaped out of my seat. "I object, your Honor! This is highly improper!"

The judge fixed a solemn stare on Janice's lawyer. "Are you talking about the two young ladies who I just saw in the hallway?"

"Yes, your Honor. I realize it is unusual, but they made a special request that you hear what they want to say in this case."

"Counselor, I'm going to defer to what I hope is just your youth and inexperience, because if I didn't, I'd sanction you for this stunt. I looked at the affidavit you filed. Seems like someone has been putting words in the mouths of these girls. Objection sustained!"

I heard a hissing sound behind me. It was some of the women from Janice's support group.

"Bailiff," the judge angrily said, "remove those two women in the second row. To the rest of you, I'll tolerate no more disturbances or I'll clear the courtroom of everyone but the lawyers and parties for the remainder of this case."

I called Nick to the stand. He denied any abuse toward Janice or the girls. I thought he did a good job. I had gotten the police report and court record on the wedding incident, which I felt gave the lie to Janice's one-sided version.

The testimony was complete, and the judge took over.

"In announcing my decision in this case," she said, "I am only making a temporary order. You give me two diametrically opposite versions of what happened. I'm ordering an investigation of this case. I'm also appointing a guardian *ad litem* to represent the interests of the minor children. Until I receive the guardian's report, I will temporarily grant the Petition. But I am not making a finding of abuse, or lack thereof, for now."

Turning to Nick, the judge said, "Mr. Hansen, you are barred from the family home and a ten-block radius thereof. You shall have no contact with Janice Hansen and you will pay family support in conformance with statutory guidelines."

She then turned to Janice, "I am denying your request of no contact between the children and their father. There will be alternating weekend overnight visitation at the farm and you are ordered to deliver the children there.

"Finally, I will say this. Although the children will be part of the investigation, I will not permit anyone to play politics with them. I am deeply disturbed by the attempt to involve them in this trial. And, if I find out this Domestic Abuse case has been conjured up as a subterfuge for someone to get an advantage in the divorce, there are going to be serious consequences."

Nick and I walked back to the office. We took our seats. "You know," he said, "I really loved her. I tried to be a good husband and dad."

Tears welled up in his eyes as he went on. "What really killed me was when I saw the girls in that hallway. When they were younger, they'd come up to me, and each of them would hug one of my legs. They used to call me their 'only boyfriend.' Now they just hate me."

He gasped, trying to continue. "I can't go on with this." The room resonated with his deep sobs, his massive chest heaving as he wept uncontrollably.

I've sat next to clients in court as their dreams went up in smoke after a verdict went against them. I've even been asked to break the news to families of the death of loved ones, and I have. It's part of the job. But, in all my days I've never seen a person so utterly shattered as Nick was that afternoon.

I gave his shoulder a squeeze of my hand and told him I'd wait out in the lobby. As I left, I could see he had the photo of the girls out again.

* * * * * * *

After a couple of weeks, I gave Nick a call. "How's your parenting time going? "

"Maybe I should just give up," he said. "They've been out here twice. Gwen won't hardly look at me. She goes up to her old room and closes the door. When it's time to eat, she just plays video games on her phone. She hardly says anything but yes or no. Her mom constantly calls her.

"I thought we were making some progress with Lily. I got her to take a horse ride, but after a few minutes, she got scared and wanted to come back. Every time she seems to warm up a bit, her mom calls and then she clams up."

"Nick," I said, "would you be willing to shell out a couple of thousand dollars if I can get a child psychologist working for us?"

"By the time we're done with this, I might have to sell the farm, but if you think that's what's best, I'll do it."

I got in touch with an old friend, Dr. Patricia Kaiser, and explained the situation. "I'd prefer interacting with the entire family, including the mother. Do you suppose your opposing counsel would consent to my intervention?" Dr. Kaiser asked.

"Sorry, but we'll get no cooperation from the other side."

"Then I can't make a custody evaluation."

"I'm not looking for that. I need you to help this family reunify – at least the father and the daughters.

The plan was to introduce Dr. Kaiser to the children as an old friend of Nick's. A couple of weeks later, she called me.

"This is one of the worst cases of Parental Alienation Syndrome I've ever seen. These girls have become advocates for their mother in a legal proceeding that's for grown-ups. They need lots of intensive therapy and, frankly, they should be removed from their mother and, maybe, even placed in a relative's home for a while.

"The older girl has completely isolated herself. Lily – I've got some hope for. I've read through the Court papers and I've talked at length to your client. I believe him when he denies the abuse. He introduced me to his girlfriend, but I wish he'd keep her out of sight. Once the girls figure out what's going on with her, it'll set us even further back." A short while later, I got a call from Nick. "I'm so glad we got Dr. Kaiser on the job," he said. "What a change! Maybe it's cuz there's a woman around, but the girls seem so much more relaxed – Lily especially. And, guess what?

"Tell me," I said.

"I think they like Dora, too."

"Your girlfriend? Aren't you getting a little ahead of yourself?" I asked.

"It was just the last time they came. But you can tell they've taken a shine to her," Nick replied. "She took them both on the horses last Sunday, and when it was time for them to go back home, Lily gave her a big hug. She asked if she could stay here at the farm instead of going home. For the first time in a long time, things are getting better."

The following day, I was paged by the front desk. "Counsel, this is Detective Barkuloo of the Major Crimes Unit."

"Oh. Hi Bob," I said. He was an old friend back from my days as a prosecutor, and we'd shared quite a few days in the courtroom, not to mention a fair share of cocktails at the annual reception my firm holds for area police departments.

Why was he being so formal?

"I hate to be the bearer of bad tidings," he said, "but you were identified as the lawyer for Nick Hansen."

"That's right, Bob. What happened?"

"We're preparing charges against your client for child sex abuse."

I was shocked. "What?"

"The victim is a twelve-year-old child – his older daughter. After she comes back tomorrow with her mother and signs her statement, we're asking the County Attorney to file a case against Mr. Hansen for Criminal Sexual Conduct in the First Degree." I couldn't believe for a moment that my client could be guilty of such a thing, but over the years I've been amazed at what some people are capable of doing.

Detective Barkuloo continued. "When he's charged, will you bring him in for booking so we don't have to go out and chase him down?

And, would he be willing to talk to us? Maybe he's got his side of the story to tell."

"Bob, you've got to hear me out on the background to this story." I described the history of the family, including what happened in court, as well as Dr. Kaiser's identification of the Parental Alienation Syndrome.

"I'll talk to the mother about that," he said, "but really the best thing you could do is bring him in so he can tell his side."

As soon as we were done, I dialed Nick's number to break the bad news. His reaction was predictable. "Jesus Christ! It's Janice and those women again. Of course, I didn't do it. Did you tell the cops about her?"

I assured him that I had, and then mentioned what Detective Barkuloo had said about Nick making his own statement.

"You're goddamn right I wanna tell my side."

I told Nick that I'd consider it, and later that day I asked my partner Mike, a criminal law expert, what he thought.

"Talk to the police? Are you fucking crazy? Did you sleep through first-year criminal law? You don't volunteer anything – make them prove their case."

I'm embarrassed to admit that Mike was right. Sometimes even a lawyer can get so involved in a case that he loses his perspective. That's why you should always get an independent opinion.

The next day came and I cringed to think of what it would bring. Shortly after lunch, the phone rang.

"Hi there. Bob Barkuloo here."

Yesterday's formality was gone.

"Since this was such a serious charge, I followed up on what you said. We talked to the mother separately. She denied everything you told us about the court hearing, but I called up the court reporter and got her to read the transcript, and it was consistent with what you said.

"Then I decided I'd talk to the girl alone. After a minute or two she recanted the whole story. Said she'd been trying to help her Mom's case. She was pretty hysterical.

Forget about bringing your man in. We're dropping the case."

"Tell you what, Bob? I'm putting you on my witness list for the custody trial."

"Oh shit," he said. "I hate getting involved in civil matters."

"You and every other cop I know," I said.

As Nick and I got off the elevator for the first day of trial, I wasn't surprised to see Janice's supporters again, but their numbers had multiplied.

Since Janice had instigated the proceedings with the petition and restraining order, she went first. It seemed that her testimony was focused on degrading Nick more than it was on the best interests of the children. No mention was made of the dropped criminal case, but she had plenty to say about the goings on at Nick's home.

"Whenever it was time for the weekend visitation exchanges, they'd beg me not to make them go, but I told them what the judge had ordered. They still want to talk to the judge, by the way. Then they said a woman started showing up on their weekends, and somehow this same person turns up on my husband's witness list. They hated her. They said she ordered them not to take my phone calls. Finally, his little Mexican 'puta' started showing up, too."

"Ms. Hansen, I was a Spanish minor in college, so I know exactly what you just said, and I'm warning you against any further indecent and disparaging comments." Janice's sister and a representative of the women's organization both testified as to Janice's fitness and their belief that she and the girls had been abused by Nick. From time to time, I glanced back at her group of supporters to see if they were behaving, which they were. Eventually, I noticed the appearance of a young, attractive Hispanic woman, who was seated some distance from Janice's people.

I nudged Nick and whispered to him, "Is that who I think it is?"

"Yeah, that's Dora," he said.

I looked back again. It seemed that Dora had caught the attention of many of the women, who were staring at her with jaundiced eyes.

It was now time for our side of the case. I called Dr. Kaiser as our first witness, but immediately after her taking the oath, Janice's attorney jumped to her feet.

"I want this witness disqualified, your Honor. Counsel surreptitiously inserted her into the children's lives, and now he wants to get her opinion on custody. She's never even met my client. How can she make a judgment?"

"Counselor," the judge said, "your point is well taken. I'm granting your motion. The witness is dismissed."

The judge glared at me. "I am expecting a full explanation from you as to why a professional psychologist was inserted into this home without prior knowledge and consent of all parties concerned."

I tried to explain our goal of family reunification, but it fell on deaf ears. It was my mistake to put Dr. Kaiser on the stand, but unexpected setbacks come with trial work.

We had plenty of ammunition left, though. I had read the report of the court-appointed custody evaluator.

"I call Louise Swanson, Licensed Psychologist."

Dr. Swanson took the stand and I submitted a resume of her credentials and asked about her experience with custody evaluations. Dr. Swanson was a veteran of family court and a confidant of many judges, which is why she'd been appointed as the custody evaluator in our case. She'd done interviews of the immediate parties involved, as well as numerous collateral sources. Further, she'd conducted psychological profiles of Nick and Janice through scientific testing, and you can bet that I'd fully informed her of the false criminal allegations against Nick.

"Over the course of my thirty-year professional career, I've conducted more than two hundred evaluations, both on a private and court-appointed basis."

"Have your opinions been validated by reviewing appellate courts?"
"Yes," she said. "Furthermore, my treatise on the methodology of evaluations has been cited several times as authority by our state supreme court."

"Referring to the report you have submitted in this case, Dr. Swanson, is there anything unusual about it?"

"Yes." She put on her glasses and turned to the final page of her report. "In all of the investigations I've conducted over the years, this is the single worst case of Parental Alienation Syndrome I have ever witnessed. I'm aware that this case was started by a petition alleging abuse by the husband. There was an abuse allegation all right, but the abuse was perpetrated on the children through their mother's campaign to turn them against their own father."

"Objection!" Janice's lawyer was on her feet again.

"Yes?" The judge said.

"I request to *voir dire* the witness regarding the use of her so-called diagnosis."

Voir dire is a legal term that describes the questioning of a witness's qualifications.

"Counsel." the judge said. "We all are aware of Dr. Swanson's experience. Where are you going with this?"

"Give me a little leeway and you'll see," she said.

The judge gave her a nod of the head.

"You're familiar with the Diagnostic and Statistical Manual of Personality Disorders, or DSM, aren't you?"

"Certainly," Dr. Swanson said.

"Sometimes psychologists refer to the DSM as 'our Bible', correct?"

"You're right. That's because it identifies all recognized personality disorders," Dr. Swanson said.

"Then explain this to me. Parental Alienation Syndrome isn't recognized as a personality disorder, right?"

Dr. Swanson shifted uncomfortably in her seat, and it looked like the lawyer had scored some more points.

"Thank you. No further questions. I move the Court to disqualify this witness for her baseless characterization of my client."

"Wait a minute," the judge said. "You can't just leave it there with no further questions. I want to know what she has to say. I'll allow her to testify. When she's done, I'll decide if her testimony is pertinent. As long as I'm talking, Dr. Swanson, let me ask you directly to describe this term – Parental Alienation Syndrome."

"Thank you, your Honor," Dr. Swanson said. "Actually, I've published an article on the subject, and with your permission, I'll read part of it now."

She opened her briefcase and pulled out a small binder.

"PAS was coined by American psychiatrist Richard Garner in 1985 when he observed children who emotionally joined one parent in their anger toward the other."

"Under the influence of the alienating parent, the child becomes preoccupied with the denigration of the other parent, which is exaggerated and unjustified.

"One parent perpetuates negative stereotypes of the other. Sometimes the alienating parent more deliberately turns a child through coercive techniques, pressuring the child to withhold affection, even with false allegations of neglect or abuse."

"A typical sign would be the child's parroting of adult language, as we've seen from the affidavits presented by the mother's counsel at the first hearing."

I noticed that the judge was listening intently, as was Janice and her lawyer. I followed up with a question.

"Why would a parent enlist a child in a campaign like this?"

"PAS can be motivated by a combination of personal rage and poor interpersonal boundaries. The alienating parent has a narcissistic personality, which, I might add, is a recognized personality disorder in the DSM."

She pointedly stared at Janice and her attorney as she said it, then went on. "The alienating parent holds on to the failed marriage through hate, blame and relentless attempts at control."

"And, Dr. Swanson, what is the recommended course for dealing with the repair of the damage done to the child and its relationship with the alienated parent?"

"According to a study commissioned by the American Bar Association, success has been achieved by expanding the time the child spends with the alienated parent and limiting the time with the other. In a case as severe as this, it should happen immediately."

The trial went on for the rest of the week. Finally, late on Friday afternoon, the judge indicated that she would announce her decision.

"I find that custody should be awarded to Nick Hansen. On Sunday at 10:00 a.m. he will pick up the girls at their home. From then on, until I am convinced otherwise, Janice Hansen's contact with the children shall be limited to two hours every Saturday at the county visitation center and shall happen only in the presence of a licensed social worker. Furthermore, although I did not allow the testimony of Dr. Kaiser, I find that she would be helpful in repairing the damage that has been visited on these poor children, so she will engage in such therapy with them as she deems appropriate. My written decision will follow in a few days. The court is adjourned."

As Nick reached over with his massive hand to give me a congratulatory squeeze on the shoulder, I heard audible gasps from some of the women behind Janice and her lawyer.

Suddenly, Janice's sister, Sally, rose. "Your Honor, I've been sitting here quietly all week, may I say something?"

"No!" The judge snarled. Instead of engaging further, she rose and strode out of the courtroom. It was the end.

The next morning, my home phone rang. It was Nick. "Sorry about calling you on a weekend, but I'm getting nervous about tomorrow. I already got falsely accused once. Could you come with me when I get the girls, or could you get the police to be there? I promise you'll get combat pay for it," he added with a chuckle.

I thought about it for a moment, then decided it would be a good idea, so I called the police department and asked if an officer could be designated to join us for the exchange. I got a call back a half hour later. "Bob Barkuloo here. I'll come along with you – no problem. After everything that happened with this case, I'd feel better if I see it through to the end."

I thought I was done for the day when the phone rang again. It was Janice's lawyer. Her tone was friendly – almost flirtatious.

"I wonder if we could put off the exchange until Monday," she said. "My client called last night and said Lily has the flu. She even had to take her to urgent care. Would that be all right? On behalf of my client, I'd really appreciate it."

How could I say no? I told her it would be okay.

I called up Nick and Detective Barkuloo and we rescheduled our meeting at Janice's house for Monday morning. The three of us arrived separately, but when we walked up to the door there was a pile of newspapers on the front step, and when I knocked there was no answer.

Calls to Janice's attorney weren't returned, and Judge Olberg agreed to sign an arrest warrant for Janice.

It wasn't until two months later that Janice and the girls were discovered at a women's shelter in Oklahoma. Apparently, Janice had made the connection through some friends of her sister Sally. The girls were returned to Nick. Janice served ninety days at the county workhouse.

* * * * * * *

Several years later, I was at Perkins Restaurant with my family on a Saturday morning, eating pancakes, when, across the crowded room, I saw Nick. He caught my eye right away, smiled, and waved me over.

The girls were with him. They had grown up – a far cry from the Catholic school girls I saw so long ago in the courthouse hallway. Sitting next to them was Dora, and between her and Nick was a toddler in a high chair. She had jet-black hair and beautiful brown eyes. Gwen and Lily were enthralled by her.

"Sold the sod farm last year, but I leased back the stables," Nick said. "I'm rich. I'm retired, and this little one is named Dorita. She just loves going on horse rides with me and her sisters."

CHAPTER 27

The Pine Box Scam

Ottertail County is in the western reaches of Minnesota. Unlike most of the Midwest, through which the Mississippi flows onto the Gulf of Mexico, the rivers here head north, into Canada's wild and woolly Hudson Bay. Although the fields are planted in the familiar corn and soybeans, the westward traveler can sense a change coming, both geographically and culturally.

I don't get out that way often. As a lawyer, there's the risk of getting "hometowned" by the rural judges and juries, who resent the intrusion of arrogant professionals from "the Cities" - that all-encompassing term for Minneapolis-St. Paul. When Eve called from Ottertail, though, I wasn't concerned about the issue. Judge Hjalmar Anderson was assigned to her case. Back when he was still a practicing lawyer, he and I had known each other well and got along even when we were on opposite sides of the table. In addition, I was a small-town guy by birth and knew enough to refrain from the smug slur, "This is the way we do it in Minneapolis."

Eve had married into the Pedersen family, three-generation owners of one of the two funeral businesses in Fergus Falls, the county seat. They were a stolid, Lutheran family, typical of the German-Scandinavian character of the region.

"I actually wanted to get someone from out-of-town to be my lawyer," she said. "My husband knows everyone. Even though I grew up there, I still feel like an outsider compared to him and his family."

"Are you planning to stay in town after the divorce?" I asked.

"Where else would I go? The three kids are going to be living with me, but they love their dad, too. Except for our senior class trip to Winnipeg, I've never been outside of Minnesota. I'd be lost in the Cities."

"Your husband started the divorce?" I asked.

"Yes. He's been telling me for years that it was coming. Kent's a smart guy and a great businessman. He thinks I'm stupid, plus he says I'm ugly because I put on twenty pounds. According to him, I'm just an embarrassment."

An embarrassment? Her husband must be one demanding guy, I thought. She was quite pretty and had a sweet disposition. Who wouldn't have put on some weight after three kids and twenty years of marriage? She was no genius, but she wasn't dumb, either. "Unsophisticated" might best describe her.

"Then he's got Missy -- our receptionist. They've had a thing for a couple of years. She wasn't the first, either. Not that I blame her. She's been a loyal employee for us and she's probably better for him, anyway."

"Why do you say that? I think you're too hard on yourself," I said.

"I've done a terrible thing in our marriage, too," she said, squirming in her seat.

I decided not to pursue this "terrible thing." It was probably a confession of some marital infidelity, but I didn't need to know the gruesome details unless the custody of the kids was at issue, and she'd assured me that was not the case.

"My husband says he'll let me have the house, but that the funeral business belongs to him and his family. He's really worked hard on it, so I suppose that's right."

"Not necessarily," I said, "You'd normally be entitled to one-half of the growth in value of it since your marriage. That could be a lot. How's it doing?"

"Oh, great. We've expanded twice, and four years ago we bought another funeral home over in Kandiyohi County." She fiddled with the strap on her purse for a moment. "But I did something really dumb. I signed a prenup. It says I don't get anything out of the business."

She fished a copy of the prenup out of her purse. Officially referred to as an "antenuptial agreement," it's a contract that is signed before marriage and defines the rights of the parties in the event of death or divorce. Eve was wrong, though. Instead of nothing, she was limited to a settlement of $10,000.

You might wonder why it gave her anything at all. A smart draftsman would always provide a small award to the "unmoneyed party," to ensure that he or she wasn't accidentally overlooked or forgotten. It was like an unhappy diner giving a few pennies to the waitress. If properly done, though, it was legal and binding.

"The agreement states that you had your own lawyer. Is that right?"

"Well, yes, in a way. It was the day before the wedding. I was at the Legion Hall, with a bunch of friends decorating for the reception, and Kent showed up and said I should come with him to his lawyer's office to sign something important."

She sighed. "Kent said that he was sorry, but his parents insisted on it and there wasn't going to be a wedding if I didn't cooperate. I couldn't believe it – we'd never talked about such a thing. Then he introduced me to this guy who said he was going to be my lawyer. They gave us a room and he asked if I had any questions, but I just wanted to get back to helping with the wedding preparations and have everything go smoothly, so I signed it. Now, my lawyer is a partner in Kent's lawyer's firm.

She gave me a pleading look. "I guess there's no way out of it, is there?"

Probably not, I thought. The scenario wasn't new to me. Her husband's last-minute legal ambush was not unprecedented. It is typically the wealthy husband who wants the deal. The bride, who just wants the wedding to come off without a hitch, is defenseless. Kent and his lawyer had been savvy enough to come up with separate legal counsel for Eve, even though it seemed phony, to overcome any coercion claim. Several years before I'd had a similar case, and our challenge to the prenup had been dismissed because of this strategy.

I had a few ideas, though, and there was always a chance that Judge Anderson would see it our way.

"It's a long shot, but we'll do our best," I said.

"Considering that I did a terrible thing in the marriage I probably deserve to lose," she said.

There was that "terrible thing" again. She clearly wanted to talk about it.

"I guess you should tell me what happened."

"I had a job at the hospital a while ago, and we gals liked to go out after work on Fridays. One night, these guys showed up and joined us. I had too much to drink. Well, anyway, I spent the night with one of them."

"Ah," I said, "did your husband find out?"

"I told Kent about it myself. He'd forgiven me, but every time I screw up he reminds me of it. He told his parents, too, and they've never acted the same to me – especially his mom."

"How long ago was it, and how long did it last?"

"It was eleven or twelve years ago, but it was just the one night."

"Eve," I said, "stop beating yourself up about this. You've been a good wife to him. You raised three kids together. How about his affairs, and forcing you to sign the prenup? He's the one who should be apologizing."

"He just has this way of putting me on the defensive," she said.

It seemed there was no way of improving her low self-esteem, but we could try to help her financial fortunes. We had subpoenaed the tax returns and supporting data for the funeral home business. Within a couple of weeks, our forensic accountant gave us her report, show-ing that the value of the business had increased three-fold, almost two million dollars over the course of the twenty-year marriage. If it hadn't been for the prenup, Eve would have been entitled to half of it.

I had her in to discuss the report. "It doesn't surprise me that we did so well," she said. "Kent does such a good job at drumming up business. About fifteen years ago there was a terrible car accident that killed four students from the high school. He was really angry because our competitor got three of the four funerals. He said – never again."

I guess dead bodies are the stock-in-trade of the funeral business. Is that wrong? To put it in perspective, I've had physicians complain to me when they didn't have enough new cancer patients. And, what keeps personal injury lawyers in business?

"Kent started paying kickbacks to ambulance drivers and med techs – even cops – if they refer a death to us. Then he came up with a plan to make a better profit off our funerals."

"How so?"

"By making a big profit off the caskets. Kent's really good at convincing the customers that they need to go first class. He keeps the selection room stocked with a dozen or so Batesville caskets. It's the gold-standard brand. The bereaved can choose from several different styles and prices."

"How much do they go for?"

The most popular casket runs about twenty-five hundred bucks. Our wholesale price on that one is twelve hundred or so. We already profit from the markup, but Kent figured we could do better."

"How?"

"There are these Chinese companies that make cheap imitations of the Batesville models. They sell at wholesale for just four hundred. It almost doubles the profit."

"Can the customer tell the difference?"

"Someone who is in the business can see it. For example, the handles on the premium models are rated for up to six hundred pounds, but the knockoffs are fragile. If you know to look, you can tell. But, you know how vulnerable people are when they lose a loved one."

"Doesn't word get out?"

"He's got that covered, too. He rents warehouse space up in Perham, an hour north of here. The Chinese models arrive in a shipping container and get delivered up there. He drives a hearse up there after hours to do the switch. The only people who know about it are his parents, our secretary, and me."

Wow! I thought. That's fraud! No wonder our accountant's report made mention of the extraordinary margin of their profits over COGS (costs of goods sold).

"Do we have to tell the judge about it?" she asked. "I don't want to cause him any more grief."

I would have been happy to, but that would lead to what we lawyers call Mutually Assured Destruction, or MAD. An expression that dates back to the Cold War, it refers to what would happen if either of the two superpowers had used nuclear weapons. They'd both be destroyed. In Eve's case, the exposure of Kent's fraudulent behavior could put him out of business, or worse. If Judge Anderson heard the truth, he would be required to report it to the Attorney General, where the white-collar crime division would have a field day with Kent. What good would that do Eve? She needed support for the children, and if she got a settlement, he had to be able to pay it.

As the day of trial approached, I did a Google search of "casket scams." Although there wasn't anything directly bearing on Kent's scheme, there was plenty of material under the general subject. I printed several articles, enlarging the font to ensure they could be seen from the opposing counsel table.

Eve and I met the day before the trial to rehearse her testimony. It took a little longer than normal because she was so nervous about being a witness.

"What should I wear tomorrow?" she asked.

"Dress like you're going to church," I said. It's what I tell all of my clients, and it would especially apply in a small town like Fergus Falls, where the judges tend to be conservative about appearances.

I arrived early the next morning for the trial and was unloading our trial exhibits out of my car when Eve drove up next to me. I was shocked by what I saw. She was wearing what might be called a "sundress," which provided maximum exposure. I tried without success to avert my eyes from her ample bosom. Eve noticed my discomfort. "I'm sorry, I forgot about what you said about the church clothes." She looked anything but sorry as she smoothed the already clinging dress.

I asked her if she had a sweater. She didn't.

We walked into the stately but timeworn courtroom. Her husband and his lawyer were already seated at their counsel table. Kent was wearing an appropriate conservative pinstripe suit. As a funeral director, he probably had several. His parents were seated in the row behind him. A mean smirk appeared on Kent's face when he noticed Eve's display of skin, and he glanced back at his parents. His mother slowly shook her head, although his father appeared somewhat appreciative.

As Judge Anderson entered, I slid the stack of casket scam articles to the edge of our table, just a foot away from Kent and his lawyer.

It drew immediate attention. "What's this stuff?" the lawyer angrily whispered. "It's not on the exhibit list. I'll get sanctions against you and your client if you try to use it."

I responded with a gesture that said, "You'll just have to wait and see."

Eve began her testimony about the details of the prenup signing. She sobbed as she identified her signature on the agreement. It looked like Judge Anderson was moved by her version of being set up by Kent and his lawyer the day before the wedding. I wondered if his unimpeded view of Eve's cleavage had softened up Judge Anderson. Maybe she deserved more credit than I'd thought.

I forged ahead with Eve. "Mrs. Pedersen, did you review the accountant's observations about the profit margin of your husband's business?"

"I did."

"How much money does your husband make through the marketing of caskets?" Kent was becoming agitated. He'd seen the Google articles. He turned back to his father, who leaned forward. After a few moments of *sotto voce* discussion, Kent turned back to his lawyer, grabbing his sleeve and whispering to him.

"Your honor, my client's feeling ill," the lawyer said. "Could we take a ten-minute break?"

The judge granted it, and I suppressed a grin as Kent, his parents and the lawyer went to a nearby conference room. It lasted far beyond the requested ten minutes. Finally, the court reporter knocked on the door to inform them that the judge was anxious to resume the proceedings.

The lawyer stuck his head out. "Bear with us," he said. He seemed less sure of himself than when the trial had started. "We're going to make an offer."

An hour later, the case was settled. Eve got the house, child support and alimony, and a handsome settlement for the business. I assumed Kent would continue with his scam, but I didn't worry about it. I'd scored with a scam of my own – and so had Eve.

Blunt Talking

I've had all kinds of cases, but never thought I'd become immersed in the world of punk rock.

It started when two perfectly normal-looking women presented themselves to me. They were mother and daughter, and they shared the same attractive features – blue eyes, blond hair and slim, athletic builds. Katherine looked to be about sixty, and Bridgid was half her age. Katherine was a librarian at the university and her husband a successful real estate developer. They lived in the high-rent district of the city.

"Bridgid was always an achiever," Katherine said. "She was good in academics – in fact, she was the valedictorian at her high school." Katherine mentioned one of the best public high schools in the state, both admired and envied. "She really excelled in athletics and because of her tennis, she got a full scholarship to the University of Southern California. Then she met Ricky." Katherine's lips tightened into a straight line as she looked sternly at her daughter.

Bridgid quickly came to her own defense. "Once Odin was born three years ago, I grew up quickly. Ricky's out of the picture for me now, but he wants custody of Odin. That's why we're here. I don't really think he wants to be a full-time dad. He just wants to get back at me for dumping him."

"Not up to it?" Katherine said. "He's unfit. He's crazy. He's a drug addict. I don't want him anywhere near our grandson. I don't care what it costs."

"Thanks for your commitment, Katherine," I said. "We'll employ the resources necessary to put on a strong case, including expert witnesses. First, though, I'm going to need some private time with your daughter. She's my client, after all."

After Katherine had excused herself, Bridgid got straight to the real story. "Mom thinks everyone should be perfect like she is. I was the good girl all the way through school, but once I got two thousand miles away from here, I realized how sheltered my life had been. I made some friends who were into the music scene in LA, and well, it wasn't long before my life was all sex, drugs and rock and roll. My parents don't know the half of it. I dropped out of college, and after a couple of months, I moved in with Ricky. He was eighteen years older than me and I'd never met anyone like him before.

Would you like to see his picture?"

"Sure," I said. Bridgid pulled a chair next to me so we could both look at her iPad.

"His real name is Ricky Isaacson," she said as she pulled up Google, "but his stage name is Ricky Blunt – you know, like a marijuana blunt? That's good for his fan base. His music's all about drugs and the wild life."

"Is your son's legal name Isaacson or Blunt?" I asked.

"Blunt, I'm sorry to say. Ricky went to court and had his name legally changed. "Ricky had Odin on his Facebook page, too. They were both dressed up in black leather, sitting on his motorcycle.

"It's sort of cute, see?" Bridgid pointed to the computer screen. It didn't look so cute to me.

Bridgid then had me hit the prompt that started Ricky's live performance on the screen. It was from some punk rock club in LA. Ricky strutted around the stage, barechested in his skin-tight, studded jeans, pointing his phallic guitar in every which direction. He had unnaturally black hair, a wrinkled face, and a bit of a paunch.

My tastes run to Mozart and Dvorak, though I try to be open-minded. To me, Ricky's sound defied the definition of music. He was quite the showman, but I had no trouble understanding how a young woman like Bridgid – who even if she was tired of her white-bread, upper-class upbringing -- could fall under his spell.

"You like this music? Seriously?" I asked.

"The drugs helped," Bridgid said.

"How did you end up back here in Minnesota?" I asked.

"When my folks found out I wasn't in school anymore they cut off the money. Ricky wasn't getting anywhere with his music, so they offered to let us come back and live with them. My Dad got him a job in a hardware store and I started working as a coach at our tennis club."

"Quite a difference from the music scene," I remarked.

Bridgid smiled. "After I got pregnant with Odin, my world changed. I sobered up and went to some AA meetings. Ricky -- he was too independent to live with my parents. Then he got fired from his job for insubordination. That was it for me. We split."

"If I hired a chemical dependency expert and you were drug-tested today, would you be clean?" I asked.

Bridgid hesitated. "I did some 'X' with my new boyfriend last weekend." She must have seen the puzzled look on my face, because she quickly added, "You know, ecstasy."

"Bridgid, I'm no prude, and I try not to be judgmental because I've heard about everything in my business. But when you're in a custody case, drugs are not, repeat not, a good idea."

"Not even pot?"

"No drugs."

"Come on, marijuana isn't really a drug. Haven't you tried it?"

I had a flashback to early in my career when I'd been hired by one of our wealthy clients to defend his son on a charge of selling marijuana to high school students.

He was a typical spoiled rich kid. The day before court, I had him in to prepare.

"You know, man," he said in his whiney voice, "the older generation doesn't get it. We all do drugs." Referring to one of the local judges, he said, "Just last night I smoked a joint with his son."

"Keep it to yourself," I said.

"Have you ever smoked marijuana, man?" he said.

Without thinking I responded, "Look, I grew up in the sixties. Who didn't?" I immediately wanted to retract this ill-advised response, but then I thought – why not make a teaching moment out of this?

"Look, there was a time when I knew I had to grow up," I said, "and that was the end of it for me. Now's the time for you too – you're damn lucky you're not in jail right now. Next time, you're going to prison."

We talked for quite a while, and he seemed to be impressed with my honesty. The next morning we stood before the judge, a crusty old humorless guy, and I was ready for the big *mea culpa*.

"I've talked at great length with my client about his mistake, your honor. He understands that actions cause reactions, and he realizes it's time for him to take responsibility."

I went on from there, and if I must say, it was a pretty good speech.

Then the judge turned to my client. "Do you have anything to say before the Court imposes sentence?"

"Yeah, man," my client said, "you people don't know what's going on with kids today. You know, the only adult in this courtroom who's smoked marijuana is my lawyer."

I wanted to slap him in the face. I looked up at the judge, expecting the worst, but he just gave me a shake of the head and a rueful chuckle. I could hear snickers in the courtroom behind me.

It was a relief to escape the sanction of the judge, but the courthouse rumor mill immediately sprang into action. By the end of the day, it seemed like every one of the fifteen hundred employees, together with all of the judges and visiting lawyers had heard what the little puke said. I was the butt of jokes for quite a while.

My client got a great deal – a misdemeanor plea, probation, and no jail. I was lucky to learn this lesson so early in my career – never tell a client anything about your personal life unless you want to hear it again somewhere.

* * * * * * *

"My past isn't relevant," I responded to Bridgid.

"No more ecstasy and no more boyfriend until our trial's over. I'll hire a chemical dependency evaluator to do a report on you and a psychologist to do a custody evaluation."

It didn't seem like she understood the seriousness of her situation. "Then it shouldn't matter what I do, right? If we're paying these people, they're going to be on our side."

"Wrong again," I said. "If we're going to have credibility with the court, our witnesses have to be absolutely neutral. That means you are going to have to be a sober spinster whose life revolves around one thing – your three-year-old son."

Things went pretty well thereafter. I got positive reports from our experts about Bridgid as well as the predictable negative feedback about Ricky. Then I got a call from Bridgid's mother, Katherine.

"Ricky's been crowd-sourcing the case," she said.

What did this mean? I wondered.

"Look at Ricky's Facebook page," said Katherine.

I scrolled through dozens of cute pictures of Odin and his Dad, and found a narrative about our case.

"Men's rights matter!" it said. There was a description of how Odin was being taken away from Ricky by Bridgid's lawyer and how the "crooked system" was biased against men. There was a link that the reader could click on and donate to the "Ricky Blunt Defense Fund for Dads."

Perhaps you've seen the billboards for "Men's Rights" law firms – they usually depict a handsome young father with his adorable son biking along with their loyal dog. But here's the truth. For every genuine client, there's a guy trying to weasel out of his financial commitments.

Or, it's a second wife pushing her man into court because she's tired of chipping in for the child support they're sending to her predecessor.

In addition to having to deal with the online funding campaign, we'd drawn the short straw on the judge. The Honorable Patrick Flaherty had been assigned to our case. I didn't care for him. Judge Flaherty was new to the bench, but by no means was he a young guy. He was known for constantly reminding his captive audiences of lawyers and court personnel that he came from the "big, downtown firm" that had represented the state in its landmark anti-tobacco lawsuit. He condescendingly allowed that he'd have to learn the ropes "out here in the suburbs," but that should be easy after the high-stakes world of his vast experience.

The consensus among we lawyers was that Flaherty had a serious case of "Black Robe Disease" – an expression we use to describe how some judges let their egos run wild.

On the first day of the trial, our team was ready. Bridgid had behaved as directed and the evaluations were favorable. We'd also carefully rehearsed what she and her mom would say about Ricky – that despite everything he said and did on his Facebook rants, we respected his role as father. He could have liberal rights with Odin, as long as he was drug and alcohol free.

Katherine didn't care for this strategy, but I thought it was a winner, and eventually she agreed. What we hadn't prepared for, however, was the scene at the courthouse.

As we got off the elevator outside the courtroom, we found that Ricky had assembled a small army of supporters. Although the men and women were of varying ages and origins, they were uniform in their black leather, tattoos and sour dispositions. They had enough rings and body piercings to start a scrap drive.

I noticed, in particular, a young woman who would have been attractive but for a large safety pin pierced through her cheek.

I had to enlist some bailiffs to clear a path through the throng for Bridgid, Katherine, our two experts and myself.

"Men's rights!" they shouted as we passed. "Mister big-time lawyer, you're gonna lose today, man."

It wasn't the first time something like this had happened to me, but for Bridgid and Katherine it was terrifying. Finally, we were seated and the trial was ready to start. Ricky's people took their seats as well, although many had to be coaxed by the bailiffs into removing their hats. Ricky made a grand entrance to spirited applause.

Judge Flaherty gaveled the room to order, and we started. First up was our custody evaluator. Her testimony went well, and I motioned to Ricky's counsel to proceed with cross-examination.

Before opposing counsel could speak, the judge laid into our expert witness. He demanded to know how many times she'd recommended custody for a father. Who had paid her fee? Was she prejudiced against Ricky because he was a punk rocker?

Fortunately, the custody evaluator was a courtroom veteran, and she respectfully but directly pushed back. It was no contest. Our vaunted "downtown lawyer" of a judge clearly didn't understand the first rule of cross-examination. Never ask a witness, especially an expert, a question unless you already know what the answer's going to be. He tried the same approach with our chemical dependency evaluator, with the same results.

When Ricky took the stand, it appeared that the judge had done some Wikipedia research about punk rock. "Before we start, Mr. Blunt," he said, deferentially, "I'm curious as to how you define your musical style in comparison to the Sex Pistols."

Ricky appeared surprised but quickly grasped that he could turn the moment into a success. "Not so much them, your Honor. More so along the lines of Ronny Thunder and the Heartbreakers."

Judge Flaherty then looked at his notes, and said, "Well, what about 'Green Day?'"

This went on for a while, until the judge turned to me, and said, with a smile, "I don't think counsel for the Petitioner is enjoying our conversation."

Ricky's supporters got a laugh out of this. I could have played along with a good-natured, self-deprecating smile, but instead, I shot back a steely glare at the judge.

You fat, bald, pompous ass! I thought. What do you think you're doing, sucking up to this weirdo and his menagerie of misfits? No one's taking you seriously. They aren't laughing with you – they're laughing at you! And, another thing, you don't know jackshit about trial practice. I bet you never got anywhere close to a meaningful part of that tobacco case. They probably had you stuck in some corner of the law library, racking up billable hours for the big guys. And, speaking of the big guys, if you were any good you would've made partner and you'd be downtown banking five or six times more than your little judicial paycheck. On top of that, Patrick Flaherty, you're an insult to my Irish heritage!

As I said before, I didn't care for this guy.

After a day and a half, the trial concluded. I was sure the judge would have to rule in our favor or the Court of Appeals would reverse him faster than you can say "marijuana."

"The Court has been presented with compelling evidence on both sides," Flaherty said. "This is a close case."

You fool, you're just playing the crowd, I thought.

"I will take the case under advisement and make my decision after I have considered it fully."

I was sure he had already made his decision, but he didn't want to announce it in front of a crowd of angry Ricky Blunt supporters. True to form, a week later we got the result we wanted – a clean sweep for us on Odin's custody.

A couple of days after the trial my intercom rang. "There's a woman out here who wants to see you," the receptionist said.

I walked out to the client waiting area. The receptionist gave me an exaggerated eye roll, pointing to the corner where a strange young woman attired in black clothing sat. Something about the safety pin piercing her cheek looked familiar.

"Sir," she said, "You did such a good job in Ricky's trial. I'm wondering if you'd take my case."

CHAPTER 29

School for Scandal

Wainwright and Evans, LLC, was a ten-lawyer firm located in a Colonial-style three-story building next to our large, ugly suburban courthouse. I'd worked there for about a year. One day, I was asked to report to Mr. Wainwright's office. Another young lawyer had been fired the previous week for lack of income production, so I wondered if I was next.

He was one of the senior partners. He was prominent in state politics, highly intelligent, and had an engaging personality. In my brief tenure, he'd gone out of his way to show me the ropes. To me, he was a mentor.

"You know who Senator Hansen is, don't you?" he said. "He's a friend of mine." I did indeed know of the Senator. He was a liberal icon in our state, and was a regular face on the evening news. He was often mentioned as a possible future governor.

It didn't surprise me that he was a friend of my boss. Mr. Wainwright was a moderate Republican, anathema in today's GOP. He was widely respected for his propensity to reach across the aisle, effect compromise, and pass bills.

"Axel helped with some of my legislation, and I'd like to return the favor. He just got served with divorce papers and he's pretty down about it. How about taking his case?"

I was thrilled by the opportunity. Like the Senator, I was a Democrat. A job well done could be a launching pad for a young lawyer with a bent toward politics.

"He'll be here this afternoon," the boss said, "I'll introduce you."

Two hours later Senator Hansen was sitting in front of me. He was every bit as impressive as he was on TV. Unlike my boss - a button-down Brooks Brothers type – Senator Hansen was dressed modishly, his blonde hair longish in the style of the day. He was a tall, handsome man, and his presence made my modest office seem even smaller. In his early forties, he had the chiseled face and piercing Scandinavian blue eyes that Minnesotans are known for, and one could see why he was so popular with women voters.

He leaned forward, his knees almost touching my desk. "This is awful for me. Kirsten's the love of my life, but now she wants to destroy my reputation and clean me out financially. And our kids, Bjorn and Erik, are just turning into men. They'll be devastated. Doesn't she care about them?" He pulled out a handkerchief to dry his eyes. "On top of that, she wants to clean me out financially."

I'd handled exactly one divorce case in my career, and it was an easy no-money affair. Otherwise, I'd been assigned to bottom-rung cases, like drunk driving defenses.

How should I respond to this high-profile, emotionally distraught client?

"I know it's hard, but get you through it. We're on your side."

"Well, that's White of you." He responded with a wry smile.

I winced at the racist expression and struggled to square it with the advocate for equality that I knew from the news. "How did this get started?"

"I had an idea something was going on six months ago because she was gone a lot," he said. "I put my legislative aide on it. He's a retired cop, and he knows how to sniff things out. He set up a phone tap on her, and, sure enough, she was seeing her old college boyfriend on the sly. Bill tracked them down to the guy's boat on Lake Minnetonka and staked it out. He made a key, got into the boat slip, set up a camera, and, you know what? We've got 'em on video, going at it like rabbits."

"You can get her for this, can't you?"

"I'd like to," I said. "But we can't use the tapes. In the first, your man trespassed by getting into the boat. On top of that, phone taps are illegal without a Court order. "

"You bet it's illegal," he said with a wink and a nod. "I wrote the law on it. But you can still get this stuff to the judge, if you know what I mean."

"What do you mean by that?" I had a sinking feeling about the direction of the conversation.

"Oh, grow up," he said. "Just leave an envelope with the tapes and a couple of thousand bucks on the judge's desk. He'll see things from a different perspective, as they say. I personally know of two cases right here in this county where it happened."

He reached into his briefcase and handed me a wad of one-hundred-dollar bills. "Here you go. If you're nervous about the cash, just buy a couple of plane tickets to Las Vegas for the judge and his wife."

"I could go to jail for this," I said, trying to figure a way out. "I'm going to have to talk to my boss."

"No, you aren't," he said, raising his voice. "This is confidential. You know the ethics code. Repeat this to anyone and I'll report you to the Board of Professional Responsibility. As a matter of fact, I'll tell them it was your idea."

My hands were sweating, and my heart even skipped a beat or two, but he was ready to end the conversation.

"Here, take her divorce papers and get back to me after you've talked to her lawyer. Do a good job for me and I'll make sure your boss hears about it." He abruptly left.

I took a look at his wife's Petition, noticing that her lawyer was from one of the top Twin Cities firms. He was a Fellow of the Academy of Matrimonial Lawyers – a prestigious group of experienced lawyers and judges. Coincidentally, I was buzzed by the front desk. It was the lawyer.

"Greetings, counsel. I understand you're representing the Senator. Welcome to the case. Shall we meet over lunch? I can get us in at the Minneapolis Club on Friday." The Minneapolis Club was a refuge of the rich and powerful. It would be exciting to be there.

When I pulled into the ramp on Friday, a receptionist had my name on a list of invited guests and summoned a white-gloved valet to park my car. Rosewood paneling covered the walls of the dining room and waiters clad in tuxedos wove through the tables. The aromas of the gourmet cuisine permeated. Still, the scenario was intimidating. The wife's lawyer recognized me and rose from his table to introduce himself. I'm sure it was easy for him to pick me out since I was years younger than everybody but the help. My off-the-rack clothes contrasted sharply with others in the room, and I wondered if there was a dress code. The lawyer was fiftyish and taller than me, and he had a confident, and somewhat aristocratic, demeanor. "Can we go by first names?" he said. "I was a little surprised to learn you were on the case, but I suppose there's a connection with your boss, am I right?"

I couldn't think of how to respond to this backhanded compliment, so I let it slide. I had the same anxious feeling I'd had with the Senator. Did I belong here?

"Let's get down to brass tacks," he said. "Your client wants to be governor. Sure, the divorce may set him back a little, but he's got lots of friends with lots of money and he'll bounce back. His wife is entitled to a generous settlement. She's been the charming wife whenever the cameras are on, and she's carefully guarded the family secrets. If he treats her right, it can stay that way."

What did he mean by that? He didn't volunteer, though, and spent the rest of the lunch laying out his client's financial demands and regaling me with war stories about his notable victories in court. The walleye was terrific, the martinis were dry and he paid the bill, but I was relieved when it was over.

On the way out, he put his hand on my shoulder, and said, "This is sort of unusual, but I took the liberty of reserving a room so you could meet my client." He led me down a corridor covered by fading portraits of past club presidents.

He opened a door and there she stood. She was stunning –a Nordic siren from a Wagner opera. Strikingly blonde, she was shapely, too – wearing a tight blue suit that revealed just enough. Unfortunately, her angry countenance belied her beauty.

As soon as the lawyer introduced me, she said, "My asshole husband forced this divorce on me. I know exactly what he's up to. A friend of mine saw his tin badge ex-cop hanging around the yacht club and we hired our own detective. We found the hidden mikes and the cameras."

The lawyer asked her to step outside for a minute. "Neither of our clients are angels, but if what she says is true, she's got a point. Your man has to come clean with it, and if you're in on it somehow, then you'd better too."

I wanted to defend myself but was without recourse to respond, hemmed in by the parameters of confidentiality.

We were interrupted by a hard knock on the door as Mrs. Hansen stormed in. "He may think he's got me in a spot, but you just tell him this. My son Erik? He is not his kid. If he'd been around the house back then he would've noticed something was going on, but all he cared about was getting his pretty face in the paper. He doesn't have a clue, but maybe you should break the news to him."

Was it true what she said about their ten-year-old son? My God, I thought. My client's not perfect, but he doesn't deserve this.

* * * * * * * *

The Senator came to my office the next morning to prepare for the pretrial conference, which was the next day. I told him about the discovery of the microphones. It didn't go over well. Then came the hard part.

"I've got something to tell you, and you aren't going to like it. Your wife tells me that she can prove Erik isn't your real son. She claims she was having an affair back then. She'll keep it quiet if you pay her the alimony she's asking for." He was upset, all right. The blood rushed to his face.

"Oh yeah? Tell her she can fuck herself. Truth be told, that kid's always been a loser."

I gasped, but he went on. "She can have him. Tell you what, I'll pull him out of school this afternoon and break the news myself!"

I persuaded him to hold off until we met for court, but his eyes narrowed as he said, "Remember our discussion before. You need to get to the judge. I expect it to be a done deal by tomorrow morning. He'll see things from a new perspective."

I didn't care if some lawyers operated that way, although I doubted that they did. I cared more about my future than his.

I could feel the stress kick in as I took the file out on the back porch that night to prepare for court. I poured a gin and tonic and watched the boats float down the river. It was delicious. I poured another to keep it company. The anxiety faded away and for the first time in weeks, I started to relax.

Before too long, though, the bottle was empty and I stumbled into bed.

The alarm rang at 6:30 – I'd set it early so I could be ready for court – and as I stood up a crushing headache hit. I was nauseous and nicked my neck shaving. It took three tries just to knot my tie. Despite the early alarm, I was still twenty minutes late. Thank God the judge had another case, but my condition must have been obvious.

"What the hell happened to you?" the Senator demanded. I hoped he hadn't noticed my bloodshot eyes. "You okay?"

The other lawyer approached. "Counsel," --no more friendly first names for him— "we have to talk. This is dead serious." He got the law clerk to find us a room, and I took a seat.

"The Senator told my client that the judge knows about her and the boyfriend. He says you had the tapes and played them, and the judge already decided the case. Tell me this isn't true, because if it is, I'm headed right downstairs to the Sheriff's Office you'll both end up in jail!"

It wasn't even nine o'clock and it was already becoming the worst day of my life. I didn't respond to the lawyer, instead went back into the courtroom, took my client by the sleeve and led him down to the end of the hallway."

I was livid.

"I don't care who you are – we're done. I'm asking the judge to remove me as your counsel. By the way, your money and the plane tickets are sitting in my desk, where they're going to stay. What made you think I'd ever get involved in a bribe?"

"Okay," he said. "It was a mistake. Just ask her lawyer if she'll talk to me one-on-one for ten minutes. I think I can work it out with her."

It seemed like a futile gesture, but I passed on his request to the lawyer, and he came back a minute later. "I talked to her. Even though I'm completely against it, she's willing to have it out with him in private."

As soon as everyone was gone, I dashed down to the restroom, then over to the courthouse cafeteria for coffee, returning in ten minutes. I was surprised to see the three of them waiting for me.

"They've decided to put off the case for a few months." the lawyer said. "Maybe a cooling-off period would be best for everyone."

Considering where things had been before the break, I could hardly object.

That was the last time I saw Senator Hansen in person. The next day a courier was at the front desk to pick up the file – he'd hired another lawyer. I had to break the news to my boss, but, actually, it was a relief. I wondered if I was cut out for divorce law, or was I better back with the drunk drivers?

* * * * * * * *

A few weeks later I arrived at work to find a copy of the Minneapolis Tribune on my desk. On the front page, there was a large color picture of my client, his beautiful wife (in the same blue suit), and two good-looking boys.

AXEL HANSEN ANNOUNCES CANDIDACY FOR ATTORNEY GENERAL

the headline said. In bold print below:

SETS OUT PLATFORM OF LAW & ORDER -- FAMILY VALUES.

CHAPTER 30

Secrets and Lies

She handed me a sheet of notebook paper. Scores of small scraps – maybe a hundred of them – were meticulously taped on it in legible order. It was a love note.

"I knew he was up to something, especially when he rolled in at four in the morning," Bianca said. "Then the next day I found this in the trashcan in his den."

The message, in a woman's handwriting, was intimate, if not explicit. It referenced a rendezvous, hinting at the pleasure that would follow.

I was impressed by the time that must have gone into assembling the incriminating note.

"You confronted him on it?"

"Oh yes. But he just got mad. Said I was stupid for not figuring it out sooner."

"That's pretty harsh."

"It's the way he treats me. It's my own fault for putting on weight and sitting around the house feeling sorry for myself. If I try to divorce him, I'll come out with nothing, because he's the one who made all the money."

"You've decided to go ahead with a divorce?"

"Definitely. Maybe I'm not the smartest person in the world, but I've got my self-respect. I'm not going to be his housekeeper while he runs around with this woman." She told me about her marriage. Boutros Khoury, her husband, had been a young intern when they met twenty-five years ago. A recent immigrant from the Middle East, he was saddled with debt, working around the clock. She was a young nurse – also an immigrant, from Panama.

"We'd make a good team, he told me. I'd help with the debts, while he finished his training. Then we could settle down and start a family."

Now, two children and thirty pounds later, Bianca was, literally and figuratively, excess baggage. On the other hand, her husband, Dr. Khoury, was a highly respected anathesiolologist, a million-dollar-a-year man.

Bianca was selling herself short. It was true that, even after three decades in the U.S., her English was sketchy. As we chatted, I learned that her interests ran to celebrity news and daytime TV dramas. Her clothes looked like they had arrived with her from Panama.

Still, as the primary caretaker of their two teenage daughters, she'd helped her family to be successful. She was a good-hearted person and wasn't deserving of the shabby treatment she got from her husband.

It would have been helpful to get Bianca's insight into the family finances, since the balance sheet I had received from the husband's lawyer looked suspicious. Dr. Khoury's high income was evident from his tax returns. According to his sworn statement filed with the court, however, the bottom line was surprisingly modest.

"What happened to the money?" I asked.

"I don't know. He always handled everything." She shook her head. "Now he's blocked the checking account. I can't even pay you." She wiped away a tear.

With a sigh, I turned back to the file. Another long wait for the fees, I thought. "His lawyer claims your family had an extravagant lifestyle, but your net worth isn't anything special. What's the story?"

"His family was really rich when he grew up in Syria. He wanted a big house on Lake Minnetonka. He bought a huge boat – a 35-foot lake cruiser. Our daughters go to the Breck School. He pays for a car service to take them every day, and we hired a French tutor who comes to our home three days a week.

"My family was poor. I was happy just to be in the States, married, and a mother. I didn't need all of this. All these extras. This show-off stuff. "

"How about the girls?" I asked.

"Boutros told them what's going on. His girlfriend's young and pretty, just like I was when I met him. He introduced her to them and they think she's great. He was hardly ever home all those years, but when he was, he spoiled them. Now they say they want to live with him, not me." She stifled a sob.

I had sent a demand letter, setting out a settlement proposal that highlighted Bianca's contributions to the family. His lawyer, a woman I didn't know, called me the same day I faxed it to her.

"Your client's had an easy life, especially since she quit working after the children came," she said, angrily. "I don't think the judge is going to care for some lazy, middle-aged woman asking for a free ride."

I was non-plussed. "If that's your attitude, we're wasting our breath. See you in court."

Soon enough it was time for the trial. Despite the negative vibes from the other side, we worked on our trial prep with high hopes.

On trial day I arrived at court early. Opposing counsel was there as well. She was a younger woman, wearing a severe black suit and an arrogant expression. Instead of offering a handshake, she said to me, "So I finally meet you, counsel. I must say that your reputation has preceded you." It wasn't meant as a compliment.

While it was true that I was known for going to bat for my clients, I always tried to keep it civil with opposing counsel.

At this point, Bianca entered the courtroom. She wore a silk shift, but it had been made for a younger woman. Sweat stains showed up under her armpits. The hem of her dress rode up as she walked, and her shoes were scuffed and discolored.

Dr. Khoury entered in an expensive-looking Italian suit. He was with two women.

"Who are they?" I whispered to Bianca.

"It's his sister and his girlfriend," she said.

The sister was tall, thin, and dressed in a fashionable business suit. Her striking Mediterranean features mirrored those of Bianca's husband. The girlfriend, also tall and thin, was a tall blond stunner. At least a decade younger than Dr. Khoury, she wore an ice-blue runway-style dress with a thigh-high slit on the side, and high, spiked heels. The contrast between these three and Bianca could not have been more striking.

It was not the first time I've seen a man bring his girlfriend to court. I usually object, but when I asked Bianca if she wanted to make an issue of it, she shook her head. After conferring with her client for a minute, the lawyer said, "This is our final settlement offer," and handed me a spreadsheet. The husband would get the home and custody of the children – Bianca was to get about 20% of the savings, which had been diminished greatly in the preceding months.

"What makes you think we'd take a low-ball deal like that?"

"Considering what she deserves, she should be happy. Plus, we'll give her some support for a year so she can get her nurse's license back and become a productive member of society again."

Raising her voice enough for everyone to hear, the lawyer added, "The deal's off the moment the judge walks in. You'd better take it." She pointed at Bianca with contempt, "Just look at her."

Bianca lowered her head and crossed her legs, pulling down the hem of her dress. Maybe she realized that the clothes she'd chosen weren't appropriate, but she didn't deserve the humiliation. It made me mad, and I felt like lashing out. After all, how could she afford anything better when she'd been cut off from the checking account?

I went over to her and gently took her hand. I was going to come through for Bianca in the trial, I thought. "No," I responded to the insulting proposal.

The trial started. The Boutros' counsel announced it would start with the testimony of his sister.

"Why don't you start with your client?" asked the judge, a veteran of family law.

"The family background is fundamental to our case," the lawyer said.

The sister, Teresa Khoury, was CFO of a notable investment firm in the Twin Cities. She had come to the U.S. at the same time as her brother. They were well-established, wealthy Arab Christians in Syria, and their town of origin had borne the family name, but the factional conflicts in their country had decimated their prospects. She spoke of the hard work it had taken them to get to the top of their professions in their adopted country.

Perhaps she was trying to impress the judge with this, but it all seemed self-congratulatory to me. I glanced up at the judge to get a read on how it was being received. To my astonishment, she seemed entranced, even star-struck by this glamorous, successful woman. As the sister went on, she and the judge would catch each other's eyes, smiling like sorority sisters.

Finally, my frustration got the better of me. "I object to this, your Honor. How is this possibly relevant?"

The response was curt and direct. "Objection noted. Now sit down, counsel." The judge turned back to the witness. "Sorry about that," she said.

"I was just finishing up, anyway. It seems so unfair that someone would want to profit from all of our hard work." She glared at Bianca. "We've had to overcome so much prejudice in this country."

It was about as much as I could take. You're having such a terrible life? I thought. I bet it sucks when you're sitting in your penthouse office in the Wells Fargo Tower, or when your brother cruises around the lake while his wife takes care of the kids.

Time was up, and the judge scheduled the second day of trial for late the following month. She explained that the delay was the fault of the heavy court calendar, but it seemed like her apology was directed at our opponents.

* * * * * * * *

A couple of weeks later, Bianca called and asked to see me. "I found something. Can I bring it in?"

Thirty minutes later she was sitting across from my desk.

"I have to move out of the house," she said, "but I refuse to leave it in a mess. So, I was cleaning under the bed, and this book was there."

The book was entitled, *Managing your Offshore Investments*. Dog-eared and worn, it was a compendium of strategies for hiding money, evading the IRS, creditors, and "greedy" relatives.

"I assume this is his handwriting," I said, referring to numerous notes in the margin.

She nodded with a smile. She knew this was important.

There was a chapter entitled "Where Your Money is Safe," which listed several international tax havens. Some were circled in blue ink: Cayman Islands, Luxembourg, and, of course, Switzerland. I noted that inside the back flap of the book, Dr. Khoury had scrawled, "Standard Bank of the Isle of Man?"

Maybe this is why the balance sheet was so underwhelming.

"Bianca, I've got a plan," I said. "I know a forensic accountant. He's like a financial private detective."

Bianca perked up, sitting straight in her chair.

"He's expensive -- $500 an hour, but he's sharp as a tack."

"How can I pay for that?" She asked.

"We'll have to swing a loan from one of those litigation-investment firms. It's high interest and they'll make us both sign for it." The thought excited me. "But I think this guy will be worth it," I said.

She agreed. Even though the ethics rules required that she was the principal debtor, I'd be the one repaying the loan if things didn't pan out. I made the arrangements and soon the investigation was underway.

A month later, it was day two of the trial. This time, thanks to the substantial loan we'd secured, Bianca was attired in a tasteful suit that fit perfectly.

Dr. Khoury's crew arrived in full force, exuding confidence. His girlfriend was wearing another gaudy dress, and, I thought, Bianca's understated, modest clothes outclassed her.

Dr. Khoury took the stand, and his lawyer led him through a lengthy description of the family finances, his position on the custody of the girls and his various complaints about Bianca and her request for alimony. After a half-day, it was my turn for cross-examination.

I was ready. A lot of work and money had gone into the pursuit of the clues we were given from the hidden book. Our financial man, Bill Cord, had tracked down Dr. Khoury's account with the Standard Bank of the Isle of Man. Armed with this information, I approached Dr. Khoury. "You've described your assets on the sworn statement that your lawyer has provided the Court, is that right, Dr. Khoury? ALL of the assets, correct?" I asked.

"Of course," he responded.

"If something was missing, that would mean you'd lied to us?"

"I don't lie," he said.

"Good." I handed him the book, "*Managing Your Offshore Investments.*"

"This is yours, isn't it?" He paged through the book as if he were looking at it for the first time. He maintained his arrogant demeanor, but I was directly in front of him and could see a tremor in his fingers.

"Well, Dr. Khoury?" the judge asked, after minutes of silence.

"This is just something another doctor gave me to look at. I never took it seriously."

"Are these your notes in the margin?"

He looked at the book again. "So, I may have made a few notes, but it doesn't mean anything."

"What's this?" I continued, handing him a document from the Standard Bank of the Isle of Man, entitled "Deposit Registration." "That's your signature, isn't it? The same signature that's on the Sworn Statement of Assets that's in front of you."

He flinched at the question. He craned his head, trying to catch the eyes of his lawyer, but I was standing between them, intentionally blocking his view.

"It seems to be," he said.

"Finally, what's this?" I asked again, tendering another document from the bank. It was a current monthly statement. "It says you have a balance of $660,000, right? I don't see that on your Sworn Statement."

"Where did you get that?" Dr. Khoury demanded.

The judge fixed her gaze on the doctor and then his lawyer. "Explain, counsel!" she demanded.

"I need to approach the witness stand to discuss this with my client," the lawyer said.

After a brief whispered conversation with Dr. Khoury, the lawyer said. "I'm sorry, your Honor, but I have to plead the attorney-client privilege – it's confidential. "

"That's your right," the judge said, "but it's the Court's right to hold you both responsible for filing a false Statement of Assets, and I will."

The judge nodded her head toward Bianca. It was clear she'd had a change of heart about Dr. Khoury.

There wasn't much more to the trial after that. A month later, the decision arrived in the mail. Although Dr. Khoury was awarded custody of the daughters, the house, and the boat, Bianca received permanent spousal maintenance (or alimony), a cash settlement equal to half the value of the Isle of Man account, the marital estate and the medical practice, as well as all of my fees. Dr. Khoury, and his lawyer, were ordered to pay the cost of Bianca's forensic accountant.

Why didn't Bianca's husband go to jail for perjury, you might ask? There are actually two reasons. First, if every lie in family court was referred to the criminal process, the prosecutors wouldn't have time for anything else. Second, what good would it do Bianca and her children to have Dr. Khoury in prison, when he was the sole source of financial support for the family?

* * * * * * *

A couple of years later I got a phone call from Bianca. She had gotten her nurse's license back and was working at a clinic on the Caribbean island of St. Barts – about as far from her ex-husband as possible. Her oldest daughter was thinking about law school, and she asked me to consult with her about it. I gladly agreed.

"What's your relationship with the girls now?" I asked.

"Way better. They came to see me here, after their father threw out his girlfriend for another one. Just like he did to me, of course.

"I've got a fiancé. He's just a shop owner, but at least he's not an arrogant, lying jerk like my ex-husband. I'm done with the secrets and lies."

CHAPTER 31

The Cutlass Supreme

The receptionist tapped on my door. "Your new client is here." Her name was Azra Kartal, according to the intake form. Azra?

I rose to greet her, and she took my hand firmly. There was a vague familiarity.

"Azra," I said. "That's a lovely name."

"It's Turkish for virgin," she replied, with a deep, bawdy laugh.

Azra was a contrast from the austere, Nordic women to whom I had become accustomed in Minnesota. Her long, dark, curly hair cascaded below her shoulders. Rings and necklaces added to the exotic aura, and her bracelets jangled as she opened her folio. Azra was short and curvy, with wide hips, a narrow waist, and a generous bosom, partially concealed by a loose-fitting top.

"You will get me through this divorce, yes? My first lawyer, she is a sissy."

As she spoke, it dawned on me why Azra was familiar. Back then, my office was in a bank building. The most direct route to the courthouse was to walk through the bank itself. I enjoyed this, watching the people on the bank floor, greeting those I knew. That's where I'd first seen Azra, I now remembered. There was a commotion in the teller line, and it was Azra, arguing loudly with one of the loan officers. He was getting an earful from her.

"I did not make overdraft. My husband did. Give me refund!" She was advancing; the loan officer was retreating.

"What's wrong with your case?" I asked. "Your lawyer is well-known and respected."

"She says nothing to the judge when my husband's lawyer talks. My daughter Berna. Why isn't she with me? A twelve-year-old girl should live with her mother. Look at this. Read."

She handed me an affidavit from her file. It was signed by her husband, Ralph Brunson.

"Thirteen years ago," Ralph testified, "Azra informed me that she was pregnant with my child. Of course I married her, and our beautiful daughter Berna was born. Only two years later, Azra told me that she had gotten pregnant on purpose to trick me into getting U.S. citizenship for her. I loved her, even after I learned that she had an unsavory background in Turkey. She worked as a nightclub singer and had multiple male lovers, some of whom have kept in touch with her. When we were dating, she was insatiable, but we have not had intimate relations for years. She says she's had it with men."

Azra was ready when I looked up from the page. "He is number one liar. I am not a lesbian. I like men. He is disgusting. Unclean."

"The affidavit says you are separated. Where is Berna?"

"She is with her father. He has poisoned her mind. He told her his lies about Turkey."

I was pressed for time, and her file was large. I told Azra that we could meet in a few days after I had read through everything.

As she left the office, she turned back for a minute, smiling.

"You are married?"

"Yes. I am."

* * * * * * * *

Later the same day, I met another new client, Jamie Pratt. He was twenty-two, according to his questionnaire.

Jamie was agitated as he took his seat. "Wish I wasn't here," he said. He handed me a legal document. *State of Minnesota v. James J. Pratt.* It was a paternity case. Jamie was a tall, athletic young man. He had a narrow face, and bright, blue eyes. A shock of whitish-blonde hair fell to one side of his forehead, and he had a pronounced dimple on his chin. He was wearing a sweatshirt with the name of our local community college on the front. I started to ask Jamie about himself, but he interrupted me.

"Hey, would you mind if my mom comes in? She knows more about this stuff than me."

That was surprising. Who wants his mother involved in a personal matter like paternity? I told him it was okay with me if that's what he wanted.

"I'm Alice," she said.

She was Jamie's mother, for sure. An attractive forty-ish woman, she had the same shock of blond hair, blue eyes, and a dimple on her chin.

"Genetics must run strong in your family." I meant it as a compliment, but she was ready to get down to business.

"I bet you see this a lot," she said to me. "These girls are on the make all the time. I told him to stay away from that place. They see this handsome young guy and his hot car and think it's a ticket to Easy Street. Show the lawyer that letter, Jamie."

He handed the envelope to me. The letter was one page long.

Jamie –

This is Sally Johnston. The girl from White Bear Lake. I don't know if you remember me. We met at The Mermaid last fall. The thing is, I got pregnant after that, and you're the father. Now I have a baby boy, and I named him Jamie.

I didn't want to bother you about it, but when I started getting AFDC the social worker said the county would have to go after you for support. I'm sorry.

Sincerely,

Sally

P.S. Here's a picture of Jamie. Isn't he cute?

"See what I mean?" Alice said. "She's trying to entrap him into marrying her." She turned her head toward Jamie. "You aren't thinking of doing that, are you?"

Jamie meekly shook his head.

She turned back to me. "I'm going home now. We took separate cars. I'll pay Jamie's attorney's fees. Please look after him for me."

Now that Alice had gone, it was my chance to learn more about my client. "Jamie, what's your biggest concern? Do you want to talk about your rights as a father, or is it the money?"

"I don't care about the baby. I mean, I hope Sally does well, but everything in my life is going to hell. I don't have time for a child."

"What do you mean by that?"

"I graduated from high school two years ago. I was the center on the basketball team, and we took the state class 5A. The U. of M. recruited me and said they'd give me a big scholarship. Then, just before the signing date, this kid from Georgia shows up. He's taller and better than me, and all of a sudden, no scholarship. Now I play for ARCC. They pay for my tuition, but it's nothing compared to the U."

ARCC is Anoka-Ramsey Community College, derisively referred to by some as "Almost Real College."

I tried some positivity with Jamie. "I know some of the faculty at Anoka-Ramsey. They're fine people, and lots of folks get a good education there."

"That may be, but I made some mistakes. When I thought I was getting the scholarship, I got a couple of credit cards. Made a down payment on a '77 Cutlass and signed a lease on a fancy apartment. Now I'm living back at home, and I'm behind on the car payments. Then Sally comes along with this lawsuit. I don't even know her. "

"Jamie, you knew her well enough to bring a new life into the world. I know you've made some bad decisions, but this is one you must bear for a lifetime."

Jamie sunk into his chair. "My mom says she wants to meet Sally and the baby. Is that okay?"

"I don't object. It's up to you and your mom. But I also want DNA testing. The county will pay for it, and then you'll know for sure if Baby Jamie is yours."

It was the end of the day, so after Jamie left, I headed to the parking ramp. On my way, however, I bumped into him. He was outside of the building, smoking. When he saw me, his face lit up.

"Hey, wanna see my Cutlass?"

Why not? I followed him to the car.

It was black, with red trim. A 70's version of a sixties muscle car. V-8 engine, bucket seats, a moon roof. Jamie could see I liked it. "I'll take you for a spin."

I always try to have a degree of separation from my clients. But this I couldn't resist. Jamie had one of those air freshener pine cones hanging from the rear-view mirror and the smell saturated the inside. As he drove us around, he opened up about himself.

"I was really crushed when the U dropped me. All I ever wanted to do was play big-time basketball. At the junior college, we get like a couple hundred fans at a game.

My teammates are nice guys, but the ones I had in high school were better players."

"How do you like it at ARCC?"

"It's okay. I actually like the business course I'm in. I was thinking I could use the A.A. degree to get a decent job. But now," he shook his head and swallowed, "looks like I'll have to drop out. There's another year of payments on this car, and then there's Sally."

It was depressing to hear it, but he was probably right.

"I bet this Cutlass really goes," I said, hoping to lighten the atmosphere.

"Hey! You wanna drive it?" Jamie smiled.

This was way past my attorney-client boundary line, but I thought, what the hell?

As the poker saying goes, "In for a dime. In for a dollar."

"Sure, I'd love to."

In seconds I had the Cutlass in the fast lane, and before I realized it, the speedometer was at eighty. The powerful V-8 purred as it accelerated, and I thought of my boring Ford station wagon back in the parking ramp. After a few pleasurable miles, I pulled over. Jamie was beaming, proud that his car had impressed me.

* * * * * * *

A few weeks passed without a word from either of my new clients until I got a call from Alice.

"I met Sally and her baby yesterday. This is my grandson, for sure. He even has a family dimple on his chin. He's just the most beautiful baby. Call off the DNA tests. I asked Sally if she'd marry Jamie. That way, we'd have her and little Jamie in our home where he could be safe. I told Jamie to see you tomorrow. Maybe you could talk him into proposing. He respects you."

"Sure, Alice. I'll see him, but he's my client – not you. It's his choice whether to waive the DNA test, and it's definitely his choice what to do with his life."

"I'm the one paying for this!"

"I understand, but my ethical responsibility is clear."

* * * * * * *

The next day, Jamie was sitting in my office.

"I know what my mom told you. She means well, but she doesn't know the whole story."

"What do I need to know?"

"That I can't marry Sally. That I'm in love with another woman. Someone you know."

"Who's that?"

"Azra Kartal. She's actually the person who sent me to you."

I'm used to surprises in my job, but this was a bolt from the blue. Azra? She was twenty years older than Jamie.

"How serious is it, Jamie?"

"Azra's a special woman. She's been all over the world. There's something else. I hate to admit it, but I never knew much about sex. I sure have learned from her. I've been staying overnight at her home, except for when her daughter's there. Azra says that we'll be together for good when her divorce is over. That's why it'd never work with Sally."

Representing paramours can be an untenable position for a lawyer. It was always a problem in fault divorce, where the judge can actually penalize a party for adultery. But even in no-fault divorce, it often creates an unresolvable conflict of interest. For example, what if the lawyer for Azra's husband had discovered the affair? A twenty-two-year-old man in the home with a pre-teen girl? What if Jamie were called to the witness stand to testify about it in Azra's trial? He could be asked about anything – drug or alcohol use in Azra's home, interactions between Azra and her daughter, confessions made to him by Azra about her past. A lawyer couldn't be representing both persons in that courtroom.

I explained the dilemma to Jamie. His response?

"If you have to drop someone, I suppose it has to be me. I love her."

That wasn't surprising. The problem was, though, that Jamie needed my help more than Azra. Frankly, I liked him better, anyway. It was time for a talk with Azra.

"Young Jamie?' She replied. "He is such a boy. He says he loves me, but he knows nothing about love. I can't have a friend? We never had sex, anyway." I found this hard to believe, but whether they had sex was beside the point. "Regardless, Azra, I can't represent you both, so why don't the two of you talk it over and get back to me with a plan."

* * * * * * * *

A week later, Alice called the office to make an appointment. She was in the next day.

I could tell something was wrong the moment she walked in. Her eyes were puffy. Her gait unsteady.

"Jamie's dead," she said. "He was in his car in our garage. We found him in the morning. The motor was still running."

I gasped. "I'm so sorry. What a shock."

"It's all that Turkish woman's fault. He told us about her the night before he died. He loved her and she dumped him. She said they couldn't be together because you were going to drop her, so it was over between them. He never told us about it before." The tears descended down her cheeks, smearing her mascara and making a mess of her face.

Because of me? My heart dropped. She wasn't done, though.

"We're not blaming you. You were just doing your job. I hate to sound cruel, but isn't suicide a coward's way out? Of course, I loved Jamie with all my heart, but his last few years have been one failure after the next."

It was all I could do to keep my mouth shut. I just stared out the window, thinking of the young man whom I had grown to like so much.

Alice brightened up. "Sally still wants to live with us. The problem is, I don't trust her. Don't know if I can count on her. Could you could get me custody of little Jamie?" I wasn't in the mood to embark on a disquisition of the law of third-party custody, but I had to respond.

"The problem, Alice, is that you don't have any standing to start a custody case. You just have to keep Sally happy for at least a year to have any rights."

"Then you could be our lawyer?"

"I guess so."

Alice reached into her purse. "Here's your last bill. I'm sure it's more now. Jamie always talked about how much you liked his Cutlass. I'm wondering if you'd take the car and forget about the bill? There's only a year of payments left, and it's worth a lot more."

The car Jamie died in? But, still . . .

"Okay, Alice, I'll do it."

* * * * * * *

After Alice left, I started dictating instructions to my staff to close Jamie's file and clear his account. Then it occurred to me. What about Azra?

It didn't take me long to decide. I asked my secretary to type up a form and bring it in. It was entitled Notice of Withdrawal of Counsel.

Two days later, Azra was on the phone. "I pay my bill. How can you do this?"

"As far as I'm concerned, we're done."

"I will report you. You will be in trouble."

"Go ahead, Azra. I won't do you any good. I'm within my rights."

* * * * * * *

That 1977 Cutlass Supreme. What a sweet ride. Although Jamie's air freshener was long gone, it still smelled like a pine forest. That made me remember him.

CHAPTER 32

Show Me the Money

At two miles wide and two-and-a-half long, Square Lake is accurately described. Historically, it was Squaw Lake, but years ago the government rebranded many offensively-named geographical landmarks. Some would derisively call this political correctness, but to the residents of the nearby Mille Lacs Indian Reservation, it was overdue.

Idyllic is a good word for Square Lake. It is emblematic of the outdoor splendor of Minnesota. The water is clear, fed by a pure, cold spring entering from the west side. The lake is populated by walleyes, northern, bass, and muskies. What makes it unique is that there is only a single gravel access road, veering off the highway. The road divides into two privately-owned sections (the rest is part of the reservation). One section is owned by the Gustafsons, the other by the Smithfields.

John Gustafson was a court reporter friend of mine. After repeated invitations, he coaxed me into a visit to the family compound. On arrival, I got a sense of why it was so important to him.

There were eight cabins spread across several acres of cleared forest land. "Cabin" is really a misnomer. They were houses, occupied by various generations of the family. A dozen young cousins were at play on the beach, or swimming out to the raft, or being pulled by a motorboat on water skis. A picnic had been organized. Burgers and beer, and more beer. Someone brought a small watermelon, infused by a hypodermic needle with vodka. What fun!

* * * * * * *

Years later on a cold winter day, a young man named Curt Gustafson made an appointment to consult with me about a divorce. I recognized him the moment he walked into the office. He was one of the cousins from Square Lake, a nephew of my now-retired friend John.

Curt was in his early thirties, wearing slacks and a long-sleeved shirt. There was a patch on the shirt with his name, also identifying his business – North Star Movers. In the modish, fashion-conscious days of the eighties, Curt, with his clean-shaven pasty face, crew-cut and upright-bearing, was a throwback.

"My Uncle John sent me here. He said it's going to be a messy case and you've been around the block."

"Tell me more, Curt."

"Back ten years or so, my buddies and I would head over to Wisconsin for weekends. One guy's folks had a cabin, and they let him have it when they weren't there. We told everyone that we were fishing, but, actually, our principal activity was barhopping."

That rang true to me. Midwesterners often refer to Wisconsin as "the party-state." The Wisconsin Department of Health Services reported in 2019 that 64.8% of state residents had used alcohol within the preceding month, versus the national average of 55.1%. The state leads the country in the number of taverns per resident, and, historically, it had a lower legal drinking age than neighboring jurisdictions.

"One weekend, we went to a strip bar in Turtle Lake. Mindy was on the stage. She was hot and flirty. We went out a few times. She was having trouble with an abusive boyfriend, and before I knew it, she moved in with me."

He paused. "I was having my own problems, and things were sort of rocky between us."

"What problems?"

"I was an alcoholic. It's my family culture, I guess. Up at the lake, we saw our parents constantly drinking. Even when I was fifteen years old, my cousins and I would sneak over to the Blue Goose and get served."

"The Blue Goose?" I think I'd heard of it, but couldn't remember for sure.

"It's the main bar over on Mille Lacs. Sort of a nice place, but we mainly hung out in the parking lot, drinking and smoking. Sometimes we'd get into it with the local Indian kids." Curt pointed to his eyebrow. "This scar? Got it in a fight."

"Curt, you spoke of being an alcoholic in the past tense. Is that accurate? "

"I quit seven years ago. It wasn't easy, and I had some relapses, but it's been over five years now that I've been completely sober. Mindy, too. She was hooked on booze and drugs back in Wisconsin. We were quite a pair when we first met, but when I quit, she did, too."

"You have two kids?"

"Angela's five and Bonnie's three."

"If you're getting divorced, what's the best for them?"

"Staying with their mom. I work fifty hours a week. People move on the weekends, so when most dads are with their families, I'm out there supervising my teams. Mindy's good with the girls, although she has her limitations."

"Such as?"

Curt closed his eyes for a moment, composing his thoughts.

"Mindy's never grown up. That's her big problem. She's still the teenager that I met at the strip bar. The truth is meaningless to her. When she gets caught in a lie, she acts like she never said anything in the first place."

I noticed his fingers trembling as he went on. "A perfect day for Mindy is when she's the only woman around a group of guys. She likes them looking her over, and she's always been a flirt. Now, she's taken up with someone. I've got proof."

"What kind of proof?"

"Absolute proof." Curt reached into his briefcase and pulled out a mini-cassette. "I bought a spyware kit and set it up on our home phone. She was in the bathtub last week, and was talking to her boyfriend on the extension. You gotta listen, it's pretty hot." I was upset that he had done this. "Curt! It's illegal to record a phone call between two people if neither has consented to it."

"It's my name on the account."

"Only if you were a participant in the call."

"At least will you listen to it? I want you to understand what I've been going through."

"I'll think about it." I slipped the tape into my file. It would be legal and within the attorney-client privilege as long as I didn't use it, but the whole idea left a sour taste.

* * * * * * *

Two weeks later, it was time for our first court appearance. The Initial Case Management Conference is a proceeding instituted in recent years. The parties appear in front of the judge who will preside over the case from beginning to end. The judge typically orders them into mediation and encourages them to confer after the hearing. It was my first opportunity to meet Mindy and her lawyer.

The lawyer was Ben Hall. I knew him from a previous case. He was barely thirty years old, well-dressed, and friendly. He worked for a large, respected firm, and sported the navy suit and blood-red Oxfords that one would expect from a young associate attorney.

After the judge excused us, I suggested that we convene at my office, which was across the street from the courthouse. We all took the elevator up to my boardroom. It was impossible to ignore Mindy. She was easily five-foot-ten, inches taller than Curt, her lawyer, and myself. She was slender but well-proportioned, with long permed hazel hair. She wore a tight, short cornflower-blue dress. It worked for her.

I caught Curt's eye as he stared at Ben and me. He'd picked up on our interest in his wife and was chagrined at the attention she was getting. In hopes of changing the negative tone, I called the meeting to order.

"I think it would be good for each side to set out their goals in this case. Maybe we have more in common than we realize. Curt, why don't you start."

Curt unfolded a sheet of notepaper from his vest pocket. We'd rehearsed this. "Mindy betrayed me and her marriage vows. But, that's her way. Lying and cheating."

Ben reacted immediately. "We won't put up with this. Mindy, let's get out of here." He started to gather his documents and get up.

"Sit down, Ben," I said. "We'll stick to the format. No disrespect. Right, Curt?" Curt sheepishly lowered his eyes and nodded his head. "I'm sorry. No matter what happened, Mindy's a good mom to our girls. I love them, but they're better off with her. I'll see them on my days off, and I'll pay child support. She can stay in the house for a couple of years, then she either sells it or refinances it so I can get my share. But if some guy moves in with her, then it gets sold right away."

"What about the cabin up at Square Lake, Ben?" I asked.

His face reddened. "It's mine, of course! I owned it when I married her and it was a gift from my parents."

Ben looked up. "Let's take a break. Leave us for a minute."

Curt and I stepped out. He went downstairs to smoke while I sat in the reception area and picked up a magazine. I could overhear muffled conversation between Ben and Mindy. After a few minutes, their voices grew louder, leading to raucous laughter. Unfortunately, at that very moment, the elevator doors opened and Curt walked in. Before he could react, I knocked on the boardroom door. "Ready?"

As we entered, I saw that Ben and Mindy had moved closer. Mindy was leaning toward Ben, whispering in his ear. It was obvious that Ben was entranced by her. He might have been smart and ambitious, but he had a lot to learn about being a lawyer.

"We're okay with what your client proposes," Ben said, "not for the part about a boyfriend in the house, though. They'll both be divorced. Why shouldn't she have the same freedom as him?"

"Except for the fact that he owns half the house," I responded.

"Okay, we can talk about that, but the big issue for us is the cabin. We'll get it appraised, but your client told Mindy it's worth five hundred grand. She's entitled to half. Either he pays her for it, or she gets one-half ownership and the right to use it equally."

Curt angrily interrupted. "No way! That place stays with me and my family! This meeting's over."

Curt's complexion progressed from red to purple, and I was worried about what would happen next.

Ben leaned over to Curt, rubbing his thumb with his fingers. "Show me the money." Mindy giggled as he said it.

"Curt," I said, "go back to my office while I wrap this up." After he left, I turned to Ben. "That was uncalled for. You knew how upset he was. How do you think we'll ever settle this if you act that way? "

"It's just deserts for his insults."

* * * * * * *

I stopped for coffee before going back to my office, hoping that Curt would have settled down. It seemed to have worked.

"Can I get you some coffee, Curt?"

"Despite my sobriety, I think I'd prefer a Manhattan," he said with a chuckle. "Seriously, though, she can't have my cabin, can she?"

"Sit back, Curt, and listen. Your cabin is non-marital property, which means you owned it before the marriage. There are two kinds of non-marital property. See this painting behind my desk?" It was an abstract piece, admired by me but reviled by my law partners.

"Let's say my parents gave it to me before I was married. I hung it on this wall and it's stayed here ever since. After I got married, the artist suffered a tragic death and his work became famous. My parents paid a hundred dollars for it, but now it's worth a hundred thousand. When I get divorced, it's all mine. Why? Because I never changed a thing about it. The increase in value is what we call 'passive appreciation.' "

"Makes sense," Curt said.

I'd given this speech hundreds of times and knew that the hard part was coming.

"Let's say that instead of the painting, my parents gave me a hundred dollars cash. Instead of spending it, I gave it to a smart stockbroker. I got married. Once a month the broker would call me to discuss his strategy, but I just followed his advice. After a few years, that hundred dollars was worth a hundred thousand. When I get divorced, do I get it all?"

"Of course, you didn't do anything. Just like the painting."

"Sounds good, but the law says otherwise. I participated in the decisions about the money. Sure, I followed the broker's advice, but I didn't have to. It's what we call 'active appreciation.'"

"What does that have to do with my cabin? That's real estate. Real estate doesn't change."

"You're wrong, Curt. After you got married, you took out a loan and added a bedroom for the girls. That increased the value. Even without that, you kept the place up. Mowed the lawn, painted it, and did the fix-it projects. All the things homeowners do. "

"You're damn right I did! She didn't raise a finger. I was up there every day I had off while she was down here in the Cities living it up."

"You mean taking care of the children, keeping the house, being your wife. No, Curt. Mindy gets part of the increase in value, and part of the equity you got in paying off the loan."

He was starting to get red again. "How much?'

"I'll let you know after the appraisal."

Actually, the state supreme court has established a format for cases like this, called the *Schmitz* doctrine, an algebraic formula that divides the shared portion of an asset from its non-marital component. In the shorthand that lawyers use, one might ask the other, "Have you Schmitzed it yet?"

Things were getting tense, and I didn't need to make it worse by trying to explain this to Curt.

Curt stood up, gathering his papers. "Thanks for your help, but as far as I'm concerned, this is all bullshit!" He rushed out of the office, slamming the door.

* * * * * * * *

A week later, I got a call.

"This is Ann Gustafson. I'm Curt's mother. Can my husband and I meet with you as soon as possible?'

"Come in this afternoon."

They remembered me from the cookout with the watermelon. Roger and Ann were in their fifties. He was wearing a gray sports jacket with an open-collar shirt. It went well with jeans. I saw Curt in his mother. Ann was pert and athletic. You could picture them at the golf course.

"Thanks for seeing us so quickly," Ann said. "We've got two issues, both of which require your discretion."

"Discretion comes with the job."

She clutched her purse. "We're sad to say that Curt started drinking again. It happened right after that meeting with Mindy and her lawyer. What's worse, he got a DWI."

It was Roger's turn. "He was at the Blue Goose with his cousin Alan. That place is Curt's Achilles heel, especially when he's with his cousin Alan. Goes all the way back to when they were kids."

Ann shook her head. "Anyway, they were there for a couple of hours, then they took off for the casino. The tribal cops stopped them at the entrance. So, this is our first issue. Is Mindy going to find out about this through the divorce case? If she does, she'll make it hard for Curt, and us, to see the kids."

"No, it wouldn't normally come up. She hasn't been at the cabin lately, I'd guess.

She doesn't read the local paper, does she?"

Roger chuckled. "I don't think Mindy reads much of anything."

"What's the other issue?"

Ann spoke. "Just that we'll stand behind Curt. You know, financially."

"What do you mean by that?"

"Meaning we'll pay whatever it takes to get rid of that wife of his. We don't want to see her up at the lake ever again. Just don't tell Curt about this. He thinks we're meddlers."

"That's great of you, folks, but you really need to hash this out with your son. My primary allegiance is to him."

Roger and Ann seemed disappointed, but there wasn't any other way out of it.

* * * * * * *

That Saturday was the coldest day of the winter. Thank God for the YMCA.

My routine was to sit in the sauna before working out. Get the numbness out of the toes and start a sweat. The pool is visible through the sauna window. The usual weekend crowd was there. Lots of kids jumping and splashing, their overweight parents and grandparents lounging in the chairs surrounding the water, and there, in the water with the kids, was Mindy.

As you might suspect, she was dressed for the occasion in a skimpy bikini. I had to laugh, watching the men sitting with their wives, pretending not to be looking at Mindy. I was struck by how much fun she was having with the kids. Not just her own, but the rest of them. If they splashed her, she splashed back. When they ran up the steps to the slide, she did, too. She was in her element.

* * * * * * *

A few weeks later, it was time for the trial, Judge Fitzmaurice presiding. He had not been at our first appearance, but I knew him well. Although he was courteous, he was a "meat and potatoes" guy. He suffered no fools, and it was right down to business.

Ben must have gotten the message because when Mindy walked into the courtroom with him, she was in a shapeless, patterned shift. Her hair was up and she wore glasses. I wondered if they were real. They were going for the schoolmarm look, I suppose. Knowing what I knew, it was hard to buy into it.

Curt looked good in a navy blazer. He'd shown me a red wristband. "Two weeks sober. It stays on me for a year." He kept his cool when Ben walked by, paused in front of him, rubbed his fingers, and said, "Show me the money."

The highlight of the trial was the expert testimony regarding the cabin value and the application of the *Schmitz* formula. Our man, Patrick Schwartz, was a CPA and licensed appraiser. He came up with an indexed report and presented it in PowerPoint. "The martial portion is $80,000, meaning that a party maintaining ownership should compensate the other with a payment of $40,000."

Curt winced, nudging me and whispering, "Forty grand? Seriously?" I'd seen what was coming from Ben, so evaded a response.

Ben's expert was George Bigham, who I knew from previous litigation. How did Ben, with his big firm resources, come up with such a whacky guy? George had a tic. When he got nervous, he'd blink his eyes. Not a normal blink, but instead one that contorted his whole face. It was distracting. Worse, it gave the impression that he might be lying.

"Based on your professional qualifications, Mr. Brigham, was is your opinion as to the value of the marital portion of the cabin property?" Ben asked.

George shuffled through his report until he found the right page. He blinked twice.

"Two-hundred-thousand."

"So, if my client is to be made whole, she should receive a payment of half that?"

"Correct."

Judge Fitzmaurice leaned in. "Did I hear that right, sir? A hundred thousand? On what basis?"

Three blinks. "It's all in my report, your Honor."

* * * * * * * *

A month later, the decision arrived. As I suspected, Patrick Schwartz's report controlled. Curt owed Mindy forty-thousand dollars. He'd made peace with his parents, and we sent their check to Ben.

A few weeks later, Curt called for an appointment. He walked in with Roger and Ann. As they were seated, Curt pulled out an envelope. The return address read: United States District Court.

It was already opened. A Chapter Seven notice of the personal bankruptcy of Mindy Gustafson.

"Why'd I get this?" Curt asked.

"You're listed as a possible creditor, Curt. The bankruptcy lawyer just wanted to cover all bases. She doesn't owe you any money, does she?"

"I guess not, although she put us all through a lot of pain."

"How can she file bankruptcy when we just sent her forty grand?" Roger asked. I looked through the pages of the petition until I found the answer. "Take a look at page ten. It lists 'exempt assets.' These are what you can keep even after a bankruptcy. It says here, 'Retirement IRA, Wells Fargo Bank - $40,000.' That qualifies."

Ann looked at the entry. "What a crook!"

"Well, if it makes you feel any better, look at page thirteen, where it lists nonexempt debts. Those are the ones that are eliminated through the bankruptcy." At the top of the list was: Benjamin Hall, Esquire - $29,750.

For the first time since I'd known him, Curt laughed.

"Can I tear off the first page?"

"Why not," I said.

Curt took a red ink pen off my desk and wrote:

"Dear Ben,

Show me the money.

Sincerely, Curt Gustafson."

"Can I send this?"
"I'm not stopping you."

CHAPTER 33

Alyce

Alyce's right arm was in a cast, supported by a sling. It was the first thing I noticed about her. To stand up and greet me, she had to push herself up with the other arm. The polite thing would have been to ignore it. Still, after decades of experience with people in the worst moments of their lives, my suspicions were aroused.

"This is my friend Myrtle."

A heavy, matronly woman looked up. She smiled but kept her lips closed.

I shook hands with both women. "Do you want Myrtle to come back with you?"

"You can do this on your own, my dear," Myrtle said. She tilted her head toward Alyce. "She just doesn't like driving in the city, and then there's that broken arm."

As Alyce sank into one of my well-upholstered office chairs, I realized how pretty she was. Wavy red hair, green eyes, and a nice figure. She wore a conservative navy pantsuit.

"My friends said I had to see you about my husband." She reached into her sling and fished out a Kleenex, clutching it.

"Is that what *you* want?"

"I guess so. Things have never gotten this far before." She used her good hand to point to the cast.

"What happened?"

Her voice lowered to a whisper. "Brendan pushed me down the stairs."

"My goodness. Why?"

"I wanted to go to his company's Christmas party. I used to every year. He and his partners started together twenty years ago, and we wives were close back then. Now, the company's grown by leaps and bounds, and the only time I get to see the other gals is at the Christmas party. Brendan says I only go because I like to flirt with his partners." She reddened, raising her voice. "And that's not true!"

"At what point did it turn violent?"

"We were in the kitchen, standing in front of the basement door. It was open. All of a sudden, he pushed me. I went down head first. It's a wonder I didn't break my neck."

"Did he apologize?"

"No. He did drive me to the doctor, and he stayed with me the whole time, but I think he just wanted to make sure I didn't tell on him, and I didn't. I told the nurse that I tripped."

"Has anything like this ever happened before?"

Alyce raised her left hand and lifted a curl that covered her temple. "This was last year." It was a diagonal scar, two inches of discolored skin. "He never wanted kids. He told me I'd look ugly if I got pregnant, so I said, 'Why don't we adopt a child?' He took the shovel from our fireplace and hit me with it."

"We've got to stop this, Alyce."

"I know I should do something, but does it have to be a divorce? How about a separation?"

"A legal separation is counterproductive. It takes as long and costs as much as a divorce, but if you decide later that you want a divorce, you have to start all over again. Instead, I'd recommend an Order for Protection. With an OFP, you can get a restraining order, have him removed from the home, arrange financial support, and get an order that he attend the Domestic Abuse Project, which could teach him something about himself."

* * * * * * * *

In less than a week, we were in court. An advantage of the OFP process is that it is given priority on the court calendar. Alyce had been staying with her friend Myrtle since the papers were served.

When I entered the courtroom, I noticed that her husband and his lawyer were already there. I recognized his lawyer. George Ryan was a courthouse veteran. He was smart but had a tendency to unnecessarily dramatize his cases. We shook hands.

"This is Brendan Ritter III," George said, referring to his client, a well-dressed middle-aged man. Mr. Ritter ignored my extended hand. He looked down, then raised his eyes to mine. "Your client's a drunk, but you're probably too stupid to know that."

At that moment, the judge entered and told the parties to take their seats. "Now folks, this is your first appearance. I've read the petition, so I need to know from Mr. Ritter's counsel whether he will be admitting the allegations or demanding an evidentiary hearing. Counsel?" He looked to Ritter's lawyer.

"We deny, and demand an immediate hearing."

"Very good. That's your right. Unfortunately, there isn't a date available until two weeks from today. Counsel for the Petitioner, do you have any requests for relief in the interlude between now and then?"

I stood. "Your honor, my client is in danger if she has to reside with Respondent. You've seen the photos we attached to her petition. The abuse has been repetitive. We want to see Respondent removed from the home until further order of the court." Opposing counsel rose immediately. "That's an outrage, your honor. We have due process. A person can't be denied his property without being heard in court."

The judge motioned for the lawyer to sit down. "You know that the Domestic Abuse Act permits this procedure. It's been upheld by the Supreme Court. In light of the seriousness of these allegations, and in the interests of both parties, Respondent will vacate the homestead at 5:00 p.m. today, taking with him his personal belongings. Both parties are restrained from any contact with the other until the evidentiary hearing." He banged his gavel and left the courtroom.

I glanced to my right. George was shaking his head, and his client's angry stare was fixated on Alyce and me. "Let's go, Alyce," I said.

Myrtle joined us as we walked back to my office. When we arrived, I selected a couple of brochures from a display we kept in the lobby.

"Alyce, we have a women's support group on the first floor of this building. They're funded by the county, and offer services to victims of abuse. I know these folks, and they do good work."

I handed her another brochure, lowering my voice. "I don't know whether there's anything to what your husband said in court, but the government also offers chemical dependency counseling, free of charge." I noticed Myrtle nodding her head.

"I never had a drink before I married Brendan. He always keeps the liquor cabinet full." She looked up. "I've usually had my first glass of wine by lunchtime. I must admit, it gets me through the day."

"He does it to manipulate you," Myrtle said. "Now that he'll be out of the picture, you can try cutting down, or even quitting."

* * * * * * *

A week later, I got a call from Alyce. She sounded like she'd been crying. "I'm frightened. He says he called the judge about me."

"Wait a minute, Alyce. There's a restraining order. He's not supposed to have any contact with you."

"That doesn't stop him. He calls every day."

"Then you should block the number."

"Maybe I will, but he says that you and I have been out for drinks, and he's reporting it to the judge. The ethics committee, too."

"You know that's not true, so ignore it."

"It's not that easy. He's used to getting his way, and nothing will stop him."

* * * * * * *

Another couple of weeks passed. As I suspected, nothing had come of Brendan's false accusations. One day, the law firm's bookkeeper knocked on the office door. "This came in today's mail." Inside the envelope was our bill for Alyce, along with her check. Scrawled on the bill was this:

"Thanks for your help. Here's your payment in full. Brendan and I have decided to reconcile. Stop the proceedings."

Abuse cases are often dropped by victims. Sometimes, it's because of economics, or because the abuser has enlisted the victim's children or family as allies, or he pretends to change. In Alyce's case, though, there was no family, and money wasn't an issue, either. Did she have some secret agenda? Was it all about making her husband jealous?

Why did Alyce do it?

* * * * * * * *

A year later, Alyce was in my office again. As before, she was with another woman. "This is Ruth Deschayes. She wants to talk to you first."

Ruth was nothing like Myrtle, Alyce's friend from the previous year. As a matter of fact, Ruth looked like a fifteen-years-younger version of Alyce. She was dressed in a business suit. Although she didn't have Alyce's green eyes, Ruth had the same red hair and pleasant figure.

"Is that right, Ruth? You want to talk to me?"

"Yeah, I promised." Her eyes darted from side to side, and beads of sweat had formed on her upper lip. However, she followed me back to my office. "I really don't want to be here, but I promised Alyce that I'd help her."

"How do you know each other?"

"Well, this is the hard part. She found out that I was having an affair with her husband."

"Really?"

"I guess Brendan forgot to throw away a personal letter I'd sent him. He's one of the bosses at my company. She put two and two together, and called me up."

"Is it still going on?"

"No, it's over. I'm ashamed of myself for getting involved with him. Here I was, an MBA from Penn State. An independent woman with a responsible job. Just got promoted, too."

"How'd it happen?"

"He began stopping by my office to talk. I could tell he was interested." She shifted, re-crossing her legs. "He's good-looking and a smooth-talker. I told him about the big break-up I'd had with my fiancé. Never should have opened up about that."

"Did he take advantage because he was your boss?"

"That would be an easy excuse for it. Actually, I'm just as much to blame. I was at the Christmas party, having a good time, drinking wine with some of the secretaries. Well, maybe too much wine. He stopped by and asked me to come to his office – he'd just had it remodeled. In five minutes, we were making out, and an hour later checking into a motel."

"So, Alyce reached out to you?"

"Yeah. I about had a heart attack when she told me who she was. I figured he was married, but it never occurred to me that his wife would track me down. My first reaction was to hang up, but she sounded nice. I was curious to meet her. She said we should have lunch -- no drinks and no tears. Believe it or not, we hit it off."

"Why did you come here today?"

"Sort of a long story. She asked me what she should do. Go to counseling or divorce him? I said it was up to her, but as far as I was concerned nothing is too rotten for him."

Ruth's hand trembled as she reached into her purse. "See this?"

It was a photo of Ruth. Specifically, the front of her neck, which was marked by ugly purple bruises. "I had to call in sick for a week till these faded away."

"What happened?"

"The same that happened the last time I fell for a married man. It was wonderful at the beginning, but then I was expected to be at his beck and call whenever he could get away. I've got my own life and I wasn't going to give up my friends and interests." I was impressed with her candor. She continued.

"I got up my courage and told him it was over. He was furious, choking me and saying my career was history if I left him. I managed to dial 911 on my cell, then he stopped. Can you believe it, the next day, this was delivered to my front door, with a bouquet of roses."

It was an expensive "I'm sorry" card. Ruth had also taken a photo of the bouquet. "Keep these, and feel free to use them in court. As a matter of fact, I'll be a witness for Alyce."

"Are you still at the same job?"

"For now. I've got some resumes out. I feel pretty secure for the time being. After the choking and the card, I went to his partner, Mr. Boswell. I told him the whole story, and that I'd met with an employment lawyer. He felt terrible about it, he said. He promised that I could stay with the company as long as I wanted and that he'd protect me from Brendan."

"Do you trust him?"

"Yes, because I made him call my lawyer and repeat it all to her."

I thanked Ruth for her courage and willingness to help. She was relieved to end the conversation. I asked Alyce to come back in.

"You shouldn't have to go through this alone, Alyce. I remember your friend Myrtle. Can you count on her for support?"

"That's another battle to be fought," she said. "Myrtle has terminal cancer. I'm taking her to chemo tomorrow."

"Would you consider therapy? Maybe going to an AA meeting?"

"Actually, I've been to some group sessions at Rays of Hope." She pointed down. Rays of Hope was a first-floor tenant in our building. "What a relief to be able to share my experience with other women – all kinds of women."

"I'm so happy to hear that."

"Still, I'm wondering. Can we use Ruth in our case?"

"It's a good question, Alyce. As I've told you, we have no-fault divorce. That prohibits us from bringing up marital misconduct. But ..."

Alyce interrupted. "You mean all this abuse is irrelevant? All this adultery? He just walks?" Her face flushed and her lip quivered. A second later she broke into tears. I gently pushed the Kleenex across my desk. "We won't let that happen. First, you have been abused and traumatized. This cries out for long-term rehabilitation. We need to get a forensic psychologist to set up a recovery plan for you. Second, we will get an economist to address your financial needs."

"What's that for? An economist?"

"In my years of doing this work, I've observed how much women can get shortchanged in divorce. It's not enough that you get an equal share of the assets, or even enough alimony to meet your needs. Your husband has a good job, and a good education. Even if you go for a degree, he will increase his income exponentially, while you'll be just getting established. In ten years, the difference in your prospects versus his will be like night and day. He's not responsible for you forever, but in a long-term marriage it should be for a long time."

Alyce wiped away the last of her tears and looked me in the eye. "What about Ruth, though?"

"I have an idea. We can use her as a secret witness."

"What does that mean?"

"Normally, we have to submit a detailed witness list to Brendan and his lawyer ten days before the trial. However, that doesn't apply to a witness we use to impeach false testimony. I am certain that once we bring up your need for therapy, Brendan will deny the abuse. That would give us the opportunity to bring in Ruth to tell her story. That would blow the case wide open. All we have to say on our witness list is 'Rebuttal witnesses, if any.' He'll never know what hit him!"

"That's wonderful. Because you know what? I want you to get him. Get him good."

* * * * * * * *

Two months later, we were ready for trial. Brendan had stonewalled the mediation. Even his own lawyer apologized for his conduct. Meanwhile, I'd interviewed the professionals we would use as witnesses at the trial. In addition to the psychologist and economist, we would have Dax Bakken, CPA, to outline the property settlement and provide an analysis of Brendan's retirement package and his executive stock option plan. My staff had written up Alyce and Ruth's testimony in outline form so they could be prepared to testify. The two of them came in together the day before the trial.

"Is this the first time either of you has been a witness?"

"First time."

"It's easier if you treat it like a conversation between the two of us. Keep eye contact with me, or the judge if he asks something. Don't even look at Brendan. He'd just try to intimidate you."

They shared another look. Alyce spoke. "Actually, we went through all of this Tuesday night, at the group session. We're ready."

"You too, Ruth?"

"Yes. I've been there the last two weeks, with Alyce. I don't think we'll ever be close friends, but we share a common experience – being victims. Listening to those other women, and evaluating my own life, I've learned something about how I've gotten into these messes."

* * * * * * * *

The day before the trial, I got a call from George Ryan, Brendan's lawyer. "Let's meet a half hour ahead of time and see if we can settle this case." Sounded like a good idea to me, so I talked to Alyce and conjured up a proposal.

George was waiting in the courthouse hallway at 8:30 the next morning. "I'm set up in a conference room. C'mon in. The only thing is, my client's insisting he be in on the discussion."

It's easier if it's just the lawyers. That way, the meeting can be more candid, but it seemed that George's client didn't trust him to be alone with me.

Brendan was dressed in a three-piece navy pinstripe suit. He greeted me with a scowl. I laid out our demand. Admittedly, it was on the high side, but that's the way negotiations get started. After I set out a proposal, including property division and alimony, I added, "If you could make a contribution of $5,000 to Rays of Hope, the women's support group that has helped your wife so much, we'd have a deal."

Brendan slammed his palm on the table, "And you could suck my dick."

* * * * * * *

The first day of the trial was consumed by the testimony of the various professional witnesses, whom we had scheduled at intervals. With what they charge for their time, we couldn't have them sitting in the courthouse hallway all day. It went well. The next morning, Alyce was to testify. We'd rehearsed this. In addition to normal financial issues, she would be describing the marital abuse in detail. As we walked across the parking lot to the courthouse, I picked up on her nervousness. Other than saying hello, she was wordless. I harbored a fear that, despite her recent progress, she might have fortified herself for the upcoming ordeal.

On entering the courtroom, I saw a familiar person sitting in the gallery. She smiled and nodded to me, but I couldn't initially place her. Alyce noticed this. "You remember Myrtle."

Myrtle, the overweight friend from last year, looked like a ghost. She'd easily lost a hundred pounds. A turban was wrapped around her head, and she had the pallid coloring of someone with a terminal illness.

Alyce leaned over and gave Myrtle a hug. Alyce perked up at the physical contact. "I'm ready for anything now," she said with a smile.

It's always easier to precede the dramatic with the mundane, so the first hour of Alyce's testimony was centered on her monetary needs. Yes, she admitted, she fit the stereotype of a displaced homemaker, someone who had set aside the completion of her education in exchange for her commitment to the marriage. Now was the time to finish the last two years of college. Anticipating the coming cross-examination, we described her growing dependency on alcohol, as well as her progress in confronting the addiction.

You might as well admit the weakness in your case before the other side seizes on it.

Finally, it was time to focus on the abuse.

I had the clerk mark the photos that the clinic had taken when Alyce came in with her broken arm. As I was passing copies to Brendan's lawyer, I noticed, for the first time, how serious this injury was. It wasn't just a broken arm. It was a compound fracture. Alyce's forearm was askew, and there was a nasty lesion where the bone had broken her skin.

As soon as he saw the photos, Brendan's lawyer rose. "Your Honor, it's obvious that counsel is pursuing Petitioner's false claims of abuse. I object. We have had no-fault divorce for decades. It's irrelevant and immaterial."

I was ready for that. "Yesterday, we presented the testimony of a forensic psychologist who established my client's need for long-term therapy. This inquiry sets forth the foundation for that claim."

The judge didn't hesitate to respond. "Objection overruled. It's pertinent to her future needs. If you want to contest what she says, you have the right of cross-examination."

Alyce did well in describing the incident in which her husband threw her down the stairs. Then I asked her to show the judge the scar on her forehead.

"Can you tell us what led to this injury?"

"I asked him if I could have a baby, then . . ." Tears rolled down her cheeks.

"We'd better take a fifteen-minute break," the judge said.

I supported Alyce as she stepped down from the witness stand. Myrtle took over for me, as they made their way to the women's room.

By the time we resumed, Alyce had regained her composure, as she described other examples of the verbal and physical abuse she had suffered at the hands of her husband.

Her testimony must have been effective because when it was time for George's cross-examination, he stood. "Your Honor, we would like to reserve our questioning until after my own client takes the stand."

"Permission granted," said the judge.

* * * * * * *

After lunch, Brendan assumed the witness chair. Another hour was devoted to financial matters. Then George moved to the abuse issue.

"Mr. Ritter, you heard your wife tell us about several events of alleged assaults.

How do you respond to that?"

"It's totally false. I've never touched her."

"Then, what really happened?"

"She's a raging alcoholic. She gets drunk every day. That incident where she fell down the stairs? I didn't touch her. She lost her balance. I helped her get back up. Took her to the doctor's office. Stuck with her the whole time. That scar on her forehead? She woke up in the middle of the night. Fell down on her way to the bathroom and hit her head on the dresser."

"How about her other claims of verbal abuse?"

"It's all a lie. Do you know what it's like to be married to an alcoholic?"

"So, you are not an abuser?"

"Never. Not to her or any other woman."

The judge turned to me. "Counsel, are you ready for your cross?"

"Your Honor, just as Mr. Ryan did when it was his turn, I have a special request. I would like to call a rebuttal witness at this time."

"I guess turnabout is fair play. Granted."

I turned to the bailiff. "Please call Ruth Deschayes."

Ruth wore a conservative, black pantsuit, and carried a manila file. As she took the oath and sat on the witness stand, I glanced over at George and his client. Brendan was a bright red. He leaned over to

George and whispered to him, at the same time gesticulating and pointing at Ruth.

George rose. "Your Honor, counsel's behavior is outrageous. This person isn't on his witness list. It's an illegal ambush!"

The judge snapped back. "You know the rules, counsel. She's a rebuttal witness. Proceed."

I asked Ruth some foundational questions. Where did she live? Where did she work? Did she know either of the parties?

"I am acquainted with Mr. Ritter."

"How so?"

"We worked together, and we had an intimate sexual relationship."

"When was that?"

"It started last Christmas, and ended a couple of months ago."

George stood again. "Irrelevant and immaterial. This has nothing to do with the issues in this case." I stifled a chuckle, because George was just about to learn how relevant it was."

"Overruled again," said the judge. "You'll get your chance when she's done."

I continued. "Ms. Deschayes, if I told you that thirty minutes ago Mr. Ritter was in your very chair, and stated that he had never abused any woman, how would you respond to that?"

"If that's what he said, he was lying."

"What do you have in your folder?"

"Photos."

I handed copies to George and the judge. Brendan blanched when he saw the ugly bruises on Ruth's neck.

I had Ruth describe the incident leading to the injury. That ended my questions. The judge fixed his gaze on Brendan, then turned to George. "Your turn," he said with a frown.

"Fifteen minutes recess, please," George asked.

* * * * * * *

"Now, Ms. Deschayes," George said when we resumed, "you knew that my client was a married man. Correct?"

Ruth seemed perplexed by the question. "I wasn't sure at first. I found out later."

"Didn't you have any concern about the morality of what you were doing?"

I shot up to object, but the judge beat me to it. He took his glasses off and stared at George and Brendan. "Really? Is this the best you can do, counsel? You and your client are on shaky ground. If I were you, I'd go out in the hallway and settle this case with opposing counsel. Otherwise, you're not going to be happy with what I decide." He stood up and promptly exited the courtroom.

I leaned over to George, and whispered, "Same terms as I told you when we started. Take it or leave it."

Alyce, Ruth, Myrtle and I walked down the hallway to the vending machines and sat at a table. A full hour later, George tapped my shoulder. "Come back and talk to me." Once we were out of range from the ladies, George said, "All right. He's really pissed, but we'll do your deal. Not the five thousand bucks to the women's shelter, though."

"Tough nuts, George," I said. "You want to go back in and start the trial again?" Before he could respond, the bailiff walked over. "The judge wants everyone in the courtroom now."

Once we were assembled, the judge asked if we had a settlement. "We do," I said, and recited the terms. "Finally, your Honor, Respondent agrees to make a contribution of five thousand dollars to Rays of Hope women's shelter."

The judge nodded and turned to George and Brendan. "Do you accept this agreement?"

"Yes," George said.

The judge looked at Brendan. "That question was addressed to both of you. Do you accept it, Mr. Ritter?"

Brendan stared at the table and began shaking his head. A pregnant pause ensued. Finally, he softly said, "Yes."

* * * * * * *

Two days later I was at my desk, dictating the final decree, when Alyce called. She was upset.

"Myrtle died last night. I was with her to the end. I feel like it's my fault because I dragged her to the trial."

"It's not your fault, Alyce. She wanted to be there, and it was obvious she was at death's door."

"Her funeral is Saturday, and it would mean a lot to me if you came."

Not something I'd normally do. It's important to keep a professional distance from your family law clients. It mattered a lot to Alyce, though, so I made an exception.

The ceremony was in a small, evangelical church in the suburbs. It was an open casket. Myrtle was laid out in a black dress, heavily made up, and wearing a gray wig. Despite the best efforts of the funeral director, the ravages of the cancer were obvious. As I sat in the pew, I saw Alyce in the same row, across the aisle. She nodded to me, and then I noticed that Ruth was sitting next to her. As the preacher led a prayer, I realized that she and Alyce were holding hands.

CHAPTER 34

Pumpkin

In recent years, millions of people have chosen to live together without marriage. What happens when things don't work out? An explosion of cohabitation litigation. Sometimes referred to inaccurately as "palimony" lawsuits, these cases arise between unmarried people who seek redress for conflicts about money or property or financial support.

Unfortunately, the law hasn't caught up with this societal change. The governing statute says that, "If sexual relations between the parties are contemplated between a man and a woman . . . out of wedlock," a contract concerning property and financial relations is enforceable only "if it is written and signed by the parties."

If this language seems strange, rest assured that it's not just you. Lawyers are mystified as well. Really, how many romantic relationships begin with a man and woman sitting down to discuss a contract?

* * * * * * * *

Brant made a good first impression. Middle-aged, with gray-blonde hair and brown eyes, he wore a conservative suit and polished ox-blood shoes. I caught a whiff of liquor, but, after all, it was the afternoon. Maybe he'd been with friends or, like many clients, was nervous about meeting a new lawyer and had needed some "Dutch courage."

"My lawyer quit on me," he said. "He did a good job on my divorce, but then when this woman, Olivia, sued me, he said it wasn't his expertise and that I should see you." Actually, his lawyer had already tipped me off. I'd handled a couple of complex "palimony" suits.

"Brant, your lawyer did right by you. He'd never had one of these cases, and he knew I had. If you'd come in to see me about a corporate matter, I would've referred you somewhere else."

"Okay. I guess. It's just that I paid him fifty grand for the divorce, and I ended up losing half of everything I own, then this other gal wants half of the rest."

I asked him to show me the pleadings on the lawsuit. It was entitled *Rasmussen v. Erickson* and claimed that the Plaintiff, Olivia, had maintained a romantic relationship with Brant Erickson for three years, while he was married to his former wife. Olivia had contributed money from her 401K plan – to the tune of forty-five thousand dollars – and "countless" hours of labor toward the improvement of Brant's lake cabin north of the Twin Cities, which she described as their "love nest." Brant and Olivia had the same employer – a major med-tech corporation. When their love affair had been exposed, Olivia was transferred to another department, at a lower-paying position.

According to Olivia's complaint, Brant had promised her that, as soon as his divorce was finalized, they would elope, and he'd sign one-half of the cabin over to her.

Instead, he announced that he was done with Olivia, was going to become a "permanent bachelor" and left her like "an abandoned pet shooed out of the car door in the middle of the country." She demanded compensation for her money and labor and lost earnings at the company, and continuing support for the "loss of consortium and emotional impact of her distress."

As I read through the allegations, I noticed Brant becoming increasingly agitated. "Did you want to say something?" I asked him.

"She tricked me into this deal. Once she got me involved with her, she threw herself into it. She just went crazy about my lake cabin. She camped out there on the weekends. Then she hired a contractor to put in a new screened-in porch and upgrade the bathroom without even asking me. I was able to convince my wife that it was my project, but when Pumpkin, I mean Olivia, changed the wall hangings and put in flowers out front, it was obvious that it was a woman's touch. That's how the divorce got started."

"You're not saying you're completely innocent, are you, Brant?"

"Oh, I'm not. She was sexy and available. When she came on to me, I wasn't thinking with my head, if you know what I mean. But she wasn't the only one to suffer. I got into hot water at work, too."

"They demoted you, too?"

"The boss put me on private probation, but eventually I worked through it. I just got bumped up to department manager, but it took a hell of a lot of ass-kissing." I noticed in Brant's paperwork that there was a mediation set between the parties and lawyers in a couple of weeks. I asked Brant if he had noticed this.

"Can you fill in it for me on that? I don't want to be around her. She's gonna make a scene."

"You have to be there, Brant. It's all confidential. Also, it'll be a good chance for me to meet Olivia and find out more about her case." Brant looked unconvinced.

The mediator, who had been selected by Olivia's lawyer and my predecessor, convened the session in the walnut-paneled boardroom of his upper-floor downtown office. He would not have been my choice. The best mediators are those who provide direction and suggestions on how to settle a case, but this fellow was too passive. He was more like a referee, allotting each side a specified interval to state their case, hoping that a productive dialogue would follow. Olivia went first.

She was several years younger than Brant. Dressed in light blue denim jeans and a matching jacket, she was weighed down with two or three chunky necklaces, heavy earrings, and numerous rings on her fingers. She wore high, cowgirl-style boots and had bright red, curly hair.

Her lawyer was a bald, overweight gentleman in an ill-fitting suit. The two of them seemed out of place in the sophisticated environs of the downtown law office.

"Olivia," he said, "tell these folks about how you and Brant got started on this relationship." This was a common strategy in litigation. Lawyers use the mediation process to lay out their client's case, but also as a rehearsal for the testimony that will come at the trial.

"It was an affair, plain and simple," she said with a shrug. I think she was trying to appear confident, but it came off as superficial. As she smiled, she fidgeted with the beads on her bracelet.

"We worked together. Brant was my boss' boss and I was a secretary. One Friday night, everyone went out for happy hour. After a while, Brant and I were the only ones left, and that's when it started. Well, we didn't 'do it' that time, but there was some kissing and hugging."

"Tell us about your relationship."

"He called me 'Pumpkin'."

"Why?" the lawyer asked. It was obvious they had rehearsed this.

"Actually, it's kind of a funny story. The next week I left a note on his desk, inviting him to my apartment for a drink. I'd read an article in *Cosmo* that a surefire way to get a man excited about you is by baking a fresh pumpkin pie. It's something about the spices, it said. Well, I did it and it worked. Afterward, I fessed up to him about it, and from there on out he called me Pumpkin. It was our little private joke."

I saw her trying to catch Brant's eye as she told the story, but he refused to look at her, fixing his gaze on the downtown skyline.

The lawyer led Olivia through some financial documents detailing the withdrawals of the $45,000 from her retirement account. Olivia had also done a summation of her hours of labor contributed to the lake cabin. For example, there was an entry for: week of November 5 – forty hours stripping wallpaper @ $25/hr = $1,000. It looked like she had conjured up these numbers for the lawsuit, instead of having kept a contemporaneous record. We could dispute this after-the-fact record keeping, I thought, but she'd counter by saying that she never expected to have Brant walk out on her at the time she was doing the work.

Finally, the mediator asked a question.

"Ma'am, you knew at some point that Mr. Erickson was married, didn't you?"

"That's so, and I sorta felt bad about it. But he told me he wasn't happy, and she was a compulsive spender and they'd be getting divorced, and then we could get married. I loved him and I believed him." Tears welled in her eyes.

I stole another glance at Brant as she said it. He still looked out the window, but his hands were trembling.

The mediator called a ten-minute break, and when we returned, he told Brant to tell his version of the story.

"Mr. Erickson," the mediator said, "these proceedings are confidential, so you should feel free to speak. Let's start where Ms. Rasmussen left off. Was it right what she said about your marriage?"

Brant evaded the gaze of the mediator as he spoke, and said nothing. A pregnant silence ensued until, after a minute or so, he said, "I'd rather not answer that question. "

"You have to respond, Mr. Erickson," the mediator said. "That's why we all went to the trouble of coming here. Do you need to consult with your lawyer?"

"Yes," Brant said. The mediator found an anteroom for us. When the door closed, Brant said, "Get me out of here. I can't stand being in the same room with her." He was in a state. His hands trembled, and his face was flushed. Although he'd seemed fine when the meeting had started, I could smell booze on him now. He must have had a flask in the briefcase and imbibed during the break.

My efforts to encourage Brant to proceed were in vain, and I had to go back into the room by myself to announce that we would not be continuing. It didn't go over well. "I can't stop your client from walking out of here," the mediator said, "but I can and will order him to pay my fee and those of Ms. Rasmussen's attorney. I will also report this development to the presiding judge."

It cost Brant five thousand dollars, but he reluctantly paid it. "I thought I was going to have a stroke."

****

The trial was now imminent, so we began discussing our strategy. I reminded Brant of the law about the requirement of a written contract, and asked him if there was anything in writing between Olivia and him.

"Nope. Nothing. That means we win, right?"

"Not necessarily," I said. "I've had a some of these cases before. Those times I represented the woman."

"What?" Brant seemed upset by this. "I thought you were on my side."

"I'm on the side of my client, whoever that is."

"So, you must have lost, then."

"No. Actually, we won both times."

"How can that be?"

"For every rule, there's an exception. The problem, Brant, is that this law can produce harsh results, and judges find ways around it to do justice."

"Then why even have the law?"

"All I can tell you is what I know. In one of my cases, the judge decided that, even though there was nothing in writing, the parties had an 'implied contract,' because they opened a joint bank account. Another time, my client quit her job to take care of her boyfriend's two sons, and the judge gave her financial support from him until she could get back on her feet. He called it 'restitution.'"

"That can't happen here, can it? Why don't we say that she should've been paying rent to me for all the times she stayed at the cabin? Or how about this – she enjoyed the sex, too. Can't we deduct that from her claim she made for 'loss of consortium?'"

As he said it, I pictured myself being in court, quantifying the value of Brant's "services." Instead, I promised Brant that, even though it was a long shot, I'd try for a dismissal based on the literal meaning of the "written contract" requirement.

The trial was set before a newly-appointed judge. Her legal experience was as a commercial lawyer in a major downtown firm.

Olivia was attired in the same denim pantsuit and had a coterie of supporters, all women. Before she stepped up to the counsel table, she hugged each one of them.

Brant had met me at the office. He was unaccompanied, and it looked like sleep had evaded him the night before. As I began to lay my files out on the counsel table, a clerk appeared. "The judge wants the lawyers in her chambers in five minutes."

Judge Swanson was a wisp of a woman. She was engulfed by her black robe. "I don't know why they assigned this case to me. When I interviewed with the selection committee, I told them that I didn't know anything about family law."

She was obviously unhappy, but I stifled the urge to remind her that the taxpayers were paying her salary. She sought the job, a position that many lawyers lusted for, and had used political pull to get it. Judges are not allowed to select which cases they get. "So, you brought this case. Tell me what it's about," she asked Olivia's lawyer. He launched into a description of Olivia's complaint and how unfairly Brant had treated her. Judge Swanson seemed unmoved.

She turned to me. "Why didn't you settle this case already? You went to mediation. Now you dump this all on me? I'm busy."

I brought up the cohabitation statute, pointing out the absence of a written contract. It wasn't my job to point out the exceptions that had been made in my other cases. That was for Olivia's lawyer to do.

"All right, counsel," the judge said. "I'm not familiar with this law. Wait in the courtroom while I review it, then when I'm ready we'll start the trial."

We all sat in the courtroom, expecting the judge to appear any minute, but time dragged on. In the quiet of the courtroom, we could overhear muffled laughter from inside the judge's chambers. I guess we were excluded from the frivolity.

After about an hour, Judge Swanson made her entrance. "I apologize but I had an important call," she said, and motioned for Olivia's lawyer to proceed.

Olivia took the stand, and her lawyer began with some simple foundational questions about her background and how she had met Brant. No more than ten minutes had elapsed before Judge Swanson interrupted.

"Ms. Rasmussen, let's cut to the quick. You engaged in a sexual relationship with Defendant, correct?"

"Yes, your Honor," Olivia answered.

"Now you want money because of that?"

"Money, yes. But justice, also."

"What were you thinking of, then?" Judge Swanson said. "You had no written agreement with him?"

"No, your Honor, that never occurred to me."

"Well, I'm sorry, ma'am, but ignorance of the law is no excuse. You could have consulted with a lawyer, or you could've exercised some common sense. You did neither."

The judge looked at the lawyers, and said, "Is there a motion?"

I was so shocked by the events that, at first, I didn't realize that the question was directed at me. I stood. "Your Honor, Defendant moves for a directed verdict, dismissing Plaintiff's cause of action."

"Granted," Judge Swanson said. She picked up her file and walked out of the courtroom without saying another word.

Olivia looked pleadingly at her lawyer, asking him what had just occurred. He whispered the news to her, and she began to sob. One of her friends approached to lend her emotional support, while the others stared daggers at Brant and me.

"Let's get out of here, right now," I said to Brant. A credo of mine is that when things go your way, clear the scene before anything changes. We quickly exited the courthouse, and when we got to the parking lot, Brant asked what had happened.

"It's over, Brant. You're a free man."

"Well, isn't that great?" he said. "Let's go somewhere and I'll buy you a drink." I declined. Some lawyers will have a drink, and even social-ize, with corporate customers. Not a good idea with family law clients, unless you enjoy listening to confessions, self-pity, and grievances, all enhanced by alcohol. Instead, I returned to the office and sat at my desk, trying to absorb what had happened so quickly.

It was nice to win, I thought, but there's such a thing as winning "too big." Olivia had asked for her money back, to be paid for her labor, and to receive compensation for her emotional losses. What did she get? Nothing. Not even the opportunity to present her case. I suspected that Judge Swanson was searching for a quick way out of sitting through a messy trial. Olivia would file an appeal, for sure.

Another problem about winning "too big" has to do with your client. It's like what happens when a sports team gets off to a better-than-expected start. The fans may be thrilled at first, but they quickly get used to the idea, so when the season slides back to mediocrity, they won't accept it. Pretty soon, the manager gets fired.

I explained to Brant that Olivia would probably appeal, and that it would serve us well to make an offer to her in hopes of settling. He was incredulous. "The judge ruled for us, didn't she? Now, you're telling me to give Olivia money? I have enough trouble paying you."

I was right about Olivia's appeal. A year later, I walked into the State Capitol building, where the Supreme Court was scheduled to hear our case.

Olivia had first filed with the Court of Appeals, which had denied her appeal. However, the Supreme Court agreed to take the case, along with a similar but unrelated one. The "Supremes," as we lawyers call the high court, rarely touch family law proceedings, concentrating instead on criminal appeals and lawyer discipline matters. Because of the appeal, Brant had spent more money on his legal fees than it would have taken to resolve it out of court. I had continued to urge Brant to settle, but he wouldn't offer a dime.

The scene at the Capitol was bizarre. It was the morning after the 1998 election, and Jesse Ventura, a professional wrestler, had "shocked the world" (his words) by upsetting the Republican and DFL candidates in the gubernatorial race. National network reporters were conducting interviews of politicians in the hallways. It would have been fun to listen in, but the first concern was our case.

There are seven justices in the Supreme Court. The hearings are in a dark, cavernous room. As I entered, another case was concluding. I was relieved to see that the gallery was empty, except for Olivia and her lawyer, as well as a couple of young lawyers who were clerks for the justices.

There was nothing remarkable about the justices, except for Alan Page. A former defensive tackle for the Minnesota Vikings, he had been one of the fabled "Purple People-Eaters" defense. Page had earned my respect, not only for being the Most Valuable Player in the NFL but for demanding to be traded when the coaches pressured him to "beef up" by taking steroids to enhance his size and strength. When his playing career was over, he went to law school and eventually was elected to the Supreme Court. A six-foot-five Black man, he stood out easily from his brethren.

While waiting for the preceding case to end, I searched the room in vain for Brant. He was supposed to meet me in the courtroom. Even though only lawyers and judges are allowed to speak in appellate proceedings, clients are permitted to sit behind their lawyers. Their presence is important so the justices can see the faces that are behind all of the technical legal issues.

Olivia had made her presence notable. She had eschewed the denim look, perhaps on the advice of a friend. Instead, she was in a bright orange suit, with long, ruffled sleeves and a snug-fitting skirt, complemented by matching jewelry. Looking at her, I couldn't avoid thinking of her nickname, "Pumpkin." Her lawyer, however, had kept the same ill-fitting, timeworn gray suit from the mediation.

When our case was called, I took my seat at the counsel table. By that time, it was obvious that Brant was a no-show. It was disappointing, but not totally unsurprising. I couldn't blame him for being frustrated by the never-ending saga of our case. We had only spoken by phone in recent months, and he had been increasingly brusque and remote.

The chief justice rapped his gavel, and we were underway. As he did so, I heard the shuffle of feet behind me. Thinking it might be Brant, I turned my head, only to see thirty or so young Asian men and women seating themselves in the galley.

"I'd like to welcome our friends from the Shanghai Bar Association to our court," the chief justice said. "I hope you find our case interesting and educational."

I inwardly cringed. My performance would now be scrutinized by all these young lawyers as well as the seven justices.

The Chief Justice directed his attention to me. "Counsel, I do not see your client with you. Is it your intention to proceed without him?"

It was a rhetorical question. What were they going to do, wait for Brant to show up? It was just to put me on record as waiving his right to be present.

"Yes, your Honor," was all I could say.

Olivia was the Appellant, so her lawyer spoke first. He went through the elements of her claim, something I had listened to countless times by this point. As he spoke of Brant's faithless promise of marriage, I noticed Olivia reaching for a handkerchief, then dabbing her eyes. Was it real, or an act? A few of the justices were watching, though.

Lawyers expect to be interrupted in appellate cases where there are multiple judges. Their questions are often about arcane legal points, prompting lengthy dialogues that seem incomprehensible to laymen. However, Olivia's lawyer spoke without a single interruption.

When my turn came, I had hardly started before Justice Page spoke. "Counsel, your argument implies that litigants, such as this lady, should be able to see into the future when a relationship begins. They're supposed to call their lawyer, if they even have one, to start drafting a contract?"

I wasn't shocked that this point came up, but that it was so early on, and from Justice Page as well, was unsettling. I noticed that he had glanced at Olivia as he said it, and then the empty chair behind me. I decided to be honest in my answer.

"Perhaps the law is harsh in certain cases, your Honor, but that was the intention when it was enacted. Maybe this court could suggest, in affirming my client's position, that the legislature revisit the issue with an eye to alleviate these hardships."

I was hoping to encourage the justices to pass the buck to the politicians, but it didn't seem to impress Justice Page. "Uh-hum," he said noncommittedly, "proceed with your argument." As I did so, several other justices chimed in, many of them with challenging questions. It was a relief when it was over.

Sixty days later, the decision arrived in the mail. I called Brant.

"The directed verdict was reversed," I said. "The court ruled that Judge Swanson was wrong to stop the trial before Olivia could finish her side of the case. Furthermore, they directed her to retry the case and consider all claims of hardship. I expect to get a new trial date shortly, so we need to meet."

Brant's angry reaction was predictable. When he appeared for our office conference the following week, I was shaken by his appearance. He still wore a nice suit, but his eyes were rheumy, his face flushed. Where there had been a whiff of alcohol in our first meeting, my office was now permeated with it.

"How can this be happening?" Brant said, his eyes darting one way, then another.

"I thought we won a year ago."

"That's what happens sometimes. Let's see how Judge Swanson handles it now." A month later we were in court to find out. We had waited in the gallery most of the morning while some other cases were resolved. Olivia was back in her denim jeans and jacket and seemed upset. Brant, on the other hand, was "pickled." I'd asked him to be sober but to no avail. In fact, I sat in another pew to avoid being nauseated by his breath. Eventually, the room cleared and the judge called us up to our respective tables. She had a sour expression on her face.

"Here we are again, it seems," she said, with a shake of her head. "I had hoped the defendant's counsel had done a better job in the higher courts defending my decision." What an outrageous thing to say, I thought. In the first place, I wasn't her minion – I had my own client. She was the one who cut Olivia's case off before it had hardly started.

Secondly, it smacked of bias against Olivia. Was she setting up another appeal? Then she turned to Olivia and her lawyer. "If you think my mind has changed about your behavior, ma'am, you're sorely mistaken. You expect me to correct your own mistakes, which were entirely foreseeable. I have a lot of discretion in this case, and I'll use it as I see fit."

Olivia's lawyer rose. "With all due respect, your Honor, you seem to have prejudged my client's case from the very beginning. I am compelled to ask you to recuse yourself from these proceedings."

"Your motion is denied," Judge Swanson said emphatically. "You'll get your trial this afternoon. Court is adjourned until then."

Olivia and her lawyer left the courtroom with their heads down, while Brant tugged my arm. "Maybe this judge is on our side, but I can't take another day in court. Can we settle with Olivia?"

Finally, I thought. After a year of hardball, you want to kiss and make up? Still, based on Judge Swanson's attitude, Olivia might be vulnerable. Keeping in mind that she had cashed in $45,000 from her IRA, I had an idea.

"Brant, I know you bank at Wells Fargo across the street. Go over there right now and get a cashier's check made out to Olivia for twenty-five thousand dollars, then meet me here ten minutes before starting time this afternoon.

He did, and when I spotted Olivia and her lawyer in the hallway, I approached them and made the offer. The lawyer's response was immediate. "No! You and your client can go to hell. We're seeing this through until we get some justice." I turned and started walking away, but then I heard Olivia's voice, "Stop. Give me a minute to talk with my lawyer."

Without returning to Brant, who was sitting in a conference room, I waited at the far end of the hallway. Ten minutes later, Olivia's lawyer walked over.

"This is against my advice, but if your man sweetens the pot by five grand, we'll make it go away. What a miscarriage of justice. After paying me, she'll still be in the red."

I passed the proposal along to Brant, and in twenty minutes he was back with $30,000 in one-hundred dollar bills. "Would you do me a favor?" he asked. "When you give them the money, please tell Olivia that it wasn't personal. She'll always be Pumpkin to me. "

"Tell her yourself," I said.

CHAPTER 35

The Hard Stuff

They were big people.

"Alan," he said, introducing himself and reaching across my desk.

As we shook, I felt the strength of his grasp. He could have crushed every bone in my hand. Easily six-three or four - probably three-hundred pounds. He had a round face and a fringe of brown hair. The glasses softened his imposing image, but his smile seemed forced. I'd put him in his early forties.

"And I'm Pam." She had a solid frame but a friendly demeanor. A bleach blonde with encroaching dark roots. Only a few inches shorter, she was at least five years younger than her husband.

I detected the unmistakable odor of an alcoholic beverage. It wasn't that unpleasant, though. Sort of fruity. Had they been at a bar?

"Just did a twelve-hour shift," Alan said.

"Where do you work?"

"At the Hamm's brewery."

"He smells like beer. Always does." Pam added. "It's better than when we lived on the Range. He'd be a thousand feet underground all day long. You hadda mop up after him when he got home."

She was talking about the Iron Range, a unique string of communities that follow the seam of low-grade ore running from west of Duluth up to the Canadian border.

"We're Rangers, and proud of it," Pam said. "Unfortunately, we couldn't make a go of it up there. The economy up there is feast or famine. Don't have no job security. I'm an EMT, but I was working in a bowling alley."

She was right about the Range. The mining industry is dependent on the international market. The unions are strong, and wages are good, but it makes our steel less competitive.

"We got a family now. Five-year-old twins – a boy and a girl. Alan's son Sam's in the Cities with his mom. That's the short version of why we're here."

"That crazy ex got me in this mess," Alan snapped. He took a piece of paper out of his pocket and shoved it in front of me.

I took a look. It was a citation, charging Defendant Alan Severson with Assault in the Fifth Degree against his son, Samuel. Typically called "simple assault," it is a misdemeanor, carrying a maximum penalty of ninety days in jail, but Alan's case was charged out as a gross misdemeanor, which carried a maximum sentence of a year in jail. It was alleged that Samuel had been a prior victim of Alan's violence.

The room was quiet as I finished reading the citation. Pam broke the silence. "Sam, he had it coming. He's a good kid, but his mom lets him run wild. When he gets in trouble, she always takes his side. If it was up to me, there'd be consequences."

"She means it," Alan said with a chuckle. "Pam played defense on the Hibbing women's hockey team that won Class AAA at State. "

"They called me 'The Enforcer,' "Pam said, laughing.

I showed them the statute I had been reading. "This is no joking matter, folks. I don't see a police report. What happened, Alan?"

"Like she said, Sam's got himself in trouble again. He got caught with marijuana on the school grounds. Suzie, that's my ex, told me about it when I picked him up for the weekend, so I let him know how I felt about it."

"If that's all it is, why are you charged with assault?" I asked.

"I didn't assault him! At the most, it was a shove, but he pretended like it was a lot worse and did a flop on the floor. Then he got up and took a run at me, so I just stepped out of the way and he crashed into the kitchen cabinet, face first. You know, that kid's already five foot ten, and he's pretty clumsy. Of course, Suzie was all over it and dialed 911. Same deal as last year. She likes to see me stew."

"Tell him what else Sam did," Pam said to Alan.

"For one thing, he spit in my face. And for another, he called me a motherfucker. A fourteen-year-old kid to his own father! He's the one who should be going to court." Alan's face reddened as he raised his voice.

"Okay," I said. "What happened last year?"

"I didn't touch him. Suzie had some scum-bag ex-con staying over at the house. We were out in the driveway, discussing it. All I did was take a golf club out of my car, then the kid jumps in front of her -- like I was gonna hurt her," he snorted. "After I left, she called the cops and said I threatened him."

"I'm sure you know by now that a threat is the same as assault, whether or not you hit him."

"That's what they said in court," Alan said. "But I don't see it that way. I was just trying to protect him from his slut mother and her dirtball boyfriend."

I glanced again at the summons and realized that the first court appearance was to be later in the week. "When we go to court, I need you both to be there, and you need to be calm. If you're this upset, it will be easy for the judge to picture you being violent with Samuel."

"We can get the case dismissed then, right?" Pam asked.

"We'll see. Sometimes the prosecutor wants to make a plea bargain."

* * * * * * * *

The day arrived, but, despite my request, I still hadn't gotten any documents from the prosecutor. Alan and Pam were waiting outside the courtroom. They were cleaned up, wearing sweaters and slacks. I could still smell the beer on Alan. It probably gets into your pores if you work at a brewery every day.

The scene in the courtroom was typical for a Monday – chaotic. The room was full of defendants and their friends and families. The bailiffs brought in a dozen orange pajama-clad jail inmates, chained together and handcuffed, and seated them in the jury box. The prosecutor sat at his table with a stack of files, facing the judge. A group of defense attorneys had lined up, waiting to get a moment of his time. The judge convened the proceeding and read the defendants their constitutional rights, encouraging the resolution of their cases, then left for his chambers.

Just as I rose to approach the prosecutor, Pam grabbed my sleeve and whispered to me, "She's here! Alan's ex, Suzie." She motioned to a heavily made-up middle-aged woman in the back row. "Can you ask her why she came? I hope she's not going to make trouble for us."

I decided to give it a try and went over to introduce myself. She wore a mini-skirt and an abbreviated green blouse, both of which exposed too much. It's like she bought the clothes in hopes of losing a lot of weight, but the plan failed. There were silver rings on her ears, nose, and lips. Someone moved over to give us space.

She started in on me right away. "You're the lawyer, right? Well, sit down and get an earful from me." I was overwhelmed by her sickly sweet perfume.

"Did your client tell you about his years of abuse, or did you fall for that crap he told the cop about how he was the victim?"

I didn't know anything about the case other than what Alan told me, so I asked her to go on.

"You know, we've done this court deal before, a year ago. Just look at the pictures from last time."

She handed me a half dozen photos. "This is what Sam looked like when we got back from the ER."

Both eyes were swollen almost shut. Some of his hair had been shaved off, and there were stitches on his bare scalp.

"I covered for Alan Severson for years, but I gave up a long time ago. Shoulda taken Sam and moved out of the state, but he loves his dad too much. Now I'm afraid he'll turn out just like him."

"Can I have these pictures for a minute?" I asked. "I need to discuss this with my client. Promise I'll bring them back."

I called for Alan and Pam, indicating that I wanted to talk to them out in the hallway. We found a quiet corner and I displayed the photos.

"What is this, Alan? He didn't do this to himself! Why'd you lie to me? Maybe you should find a different lawyer."

"Now, hold on," Alan said. "It looks worse than it was. Maybe I hit him once, but doesn't a father have rights to discipline his own son? His mother lets him walk all over her."

I noticed Pam was shaking her head at Alan. "Pictures don't lie, my dear. It's obvious. You lost it. Let our lawyer try to get you a deal."

I went back into the courtroom and noticed that the prosecutor was in a lull, so I asked him to talk to me about the case. "Oh, you mean that Severson file? Look, I know it's not your fault, but this guy's doing time if I have anything to say about it." He noticed that I still had the photos in my hand. "You've seen the pictures. The judge will be available in a minute. Let's go talk to him."

The judge was in chambers, talking on his phone and drinking coffee. He gestured to us to sit down, and quickly ended his call.

"That was the court administrator," he said. "People think I'm in charge because I'm the judge, but it's more like I work for her. She just set me up for a week-long jury trial starting tomorrow morning. See all these files I've got? We need to settle cases or we'll be stacked up for months. Which one do you have?"

The prosecutor briefed the judge on our case, showed him the pictures and pointed out Alan's prior history. "I'm asking for six months for this guy, your Honor. How else is he going to get the message?"

The judge was nodding his head. "I can understand that. Domestic abuse has been swept under the rug for too long. I'm glad we're finally waking up about it."

I was shaken by his readiness to throw the book at my client.

"What do you say, counsel?" The judge asked me.

"Well, your Honor, if that's what he's facing, then we've got nothing to lose by going to trial. My client's got a defense. He was enforcing reasonable discipline --"

I was interrupted by the prosecutor. "With all due respect to counsel, his 'defense' is a crock of shit. If he takes it through a jury trial, my demand goes from six months to a year."

"Settle down," said the judge. "It's not your job to impose a sentence. It's mine. But a warning to you, defense counsel. Push too hard, and you'll be sorry."

Summoning up some courage, I tried a different tack. "Here's a proposal. The Domestic Abuse Project has an intense program of treatment for abusers. And it's not some easy 'chalk talk' deal. Ten weeks of hard therapy, four hours per night. The participants have to pay their own way."

"I've heard of it," said the judge. "But if you're thinking your client's going to get the charges dropped, forget about it. He's got to plead guilty. I impose a sentence. If and only if he completes it, I'll suspend it. If he screws up, he's off to the workhouse for a year."

It was time for some brave talk on my part. "I'm confident he can do it, your Honor. I've already discussed this with him and his wife. They're both anxious to get things turned around. He knows it's hard stuff to get through. We'll be back in a little while, ready to put in the plea."

Alan and Pam looked nervous. "Let's get a conference room," I said.

I explained the seriousness of the situation, and what could be gained by taking the deal. "I went out on a limb for you, Alan. I know you don't think you did anything wrong, but you're a minority of one. Go to the workhouse for a year and you're out your job. Maybe worse."

He agreed, and we went before the judge. One of the difficult moments in making a plea is when the defendant has to acknowledge his guilt, and I've seen hard-earned deals fall through when someone had a last-minute change of heart. Even though I doubted his sincerity, Alan went through with it.

After it was over, a probation officer took him to an office to enroll for the program. Suzie approached Pam and I. "I hope this works," she said. She put her had on Pam's shoulder. "It would've crushed Sam to think he put his dad in prison."

Three months later we were back in court for a review hearing, to see if Alan had complied with the requirements of the program. Failure on his part would surely have resulted in a term at the county workhouse. I'd gotten a heads-up from Pam that good news was in store, but I still wanted to hear it from Alan, so I'd reserved a conference room for us to prepare for the proceeding.

Once again, Alan and Pam were appropriately attired for court, but as we settled in, I sensed that something had changed, although I couldn't immediately put my finger on it.

"So, folks," I started, "are you ready for this?"

"Sure, we are," Pam said, with a big smile. She gently took Alan's hand. "Tell him, honey."

"Did the whole program," Alan said. "What an eye-opener. You start out thinking it's just about you, but then you meet so many other people, from all walks of life. All races and all places. I'm telling you, this abuse thing is big." A tear trickled down his cheek. "I learned about myself, too. I quit my job at the brewery. "

"Oh, that's what's different," I said. "I don't smell the beer on you."

"True confessions," Alan said. "It wasn't just on me. It was in me, too. I was drinking all day long. Honestly, about a third of the guys I worked with are drunk by the end of their shift."

Tears started to well up in his eyes. Pam noticed it and gave his muscular arm a hug.

"All my life, I've thought I was in control, but, really, the booze was. I was weak, and I took it out on the family. I'm ninety days sober. You won't see me back here again." I inwardly cringed. How many times had I heard "never again" from a client?

When we appeared before the judge, the probation officer was called as a witness. "The Domestic Abuse Project reports to us that Mr. Severson completed all of the requirements of their program. In fact, he was the number one student in his group. We recommend that he be discharged from the remainder of his obligation to the court."

For myself, it was a deeply satisfying moment. What had started as an ugly, disturbing case had ended with what promised to be a lasting success.

* * * * * * * *

Three years later, I saw Alan's name on my appointment calendar. There was no indication of what it was about, but when I went out to the lobby to greet Alan, it was clear that something was wrong. He had a wide white bandage over his nose and something like a plastic cast underneath it. His right ear was swollen and discolored, and there were stitch marks on it.

"My gosh, Alan," I said, "Were you in an accident? Is Pam okay?"

He shook his head, sheepishly, and handed me a yellow envelope with the emblem of the Hennepin District Court printed on it. I opened it and found what cops and lawyers call a DANCO – Domestic Abuse No-Contact Order.

"The cops showed up yesterday afternoon and handed this to me and told me I had five minutes to get my stuff together and get out of the house," Alan said. "They said I was lucky that Pam wasn't pressing criminal charges against me, or I'd be in jail. I guess I should be grateful for that, but how come I'm the one who has to leave? Look what she did to me. She doesn't have a scratch on her."

I remembered that Pam was proud of being "The Enforcer" on her hockey team.

"I'm sure there's an explanation," I said. "Let me read the order."

Pam was named as the Petitioner, meaning that she'd started the case, and her supporting affidavit was stapled to the order. It described an incident which had occurred the previous weekend at the family home. The eight-year-old twins of Alan and Pam had been fighting. The boy had taken a knife from the kitchen and was holding it to his sister's throat. Pam was there when it happened, and Alan arrived home shortly thereafter. "Respondent Alan Severson, who had been drinking, reacted with rage when Petitioner informed him of the knife attack. He grabbed the child by the neck, dragged him into the garage, and proceeded to pound him on his bare buttocks with a board," Pam's affidavit read. "Fearing personal injury or worse, Petitioner physically restrained Respondent."

Photos of the child's buttocks were posted as exhibits to the affidavit. The bruises were inflamed, and the outlines of the board were clear from the bruises.

I took another look at the order. Both parties were restrained from physical contact with the other. Alan was barred from the home and the children until a full hearing the following week.

"Can you represent me again?" Alan asked. "I did what any other father would. The kid has to learn. He could've killed his sister."

It wasn't hard to imagine where his son had learned his behavior, and I had no intention of being Alan's lawyer. Technically, I could have taken the case, since I'd never represented Pam before, but the thought of going against her on Alan's behalf was anathema to me. I conjured up an excuse.

"Sorry, Alan. Since I got to know both of you so well last time, I'd have a conflict of interest, but I'll refer you to a lawyer I trust. Mickey Silver."

Off he went, but it wasn't over yet, because a few hours later I got a call from Pam.

"I heard from Alan's lawyer, Mr. Silver. He said you heard what happened with me and Alan. I wanna tell you my side of the story. Can you represent me?"

I told her that it wasn't possible because of my prior relationship with Alan. Still, I wanted to hear what Pam had to say.

"I'm sorry I hit him, but he was wailing away on our son and he would've kept doing it if I hadn't stepped in."

"Is it true that he's back to drinking?" I asked.

"Only since two weeks after he finished that program you got him in," she said. I gave Pam the names of two trusted lawyer friends and wished her luck. It was disappointing that my plan for Alan had failed, but we can't control how other people live their lives.

A few months later, I opened the *Saint Paul Pioneer Press*. A headline jumped out at me – "Double Homicide in NE Mpls." It read, "The deceased were Alan Severson, age 44, and Pam Severson, age 38." The short article concluded with the sentence, "There is no threat to the general public, police report." That was a sure indication of a murder/suicide.

I gave Mickey Silver a call to see what he knew. Mickey, who must read too many detective stories, speaks in "police talk."

"Yup, he killed her, then himself. She'd gotten the DANCO on him, but he showed up anyway, and she must have let him in, because there wasn't any sign of a struggle. He had a 9 mm. Smith & Wesson and he plugged her right in the middle of the forehead, then he stuck it in his mouth and cut loose. I saw the pictures. What a mess."

"Do you know if he'd been drinking?"

"Just a bit," he said with a snort. ".28 BAC, about three times the legal limit.

Must've been the hard stuff."

CHAPTER 36

It's Better This Way

In our district, there is an annual Judge's Day. Historically it started with a golf tournament, moved on to a cocktail hour, dinner and skits. The skits were seen as the lawyers' opportunity to "get back" at the judges for the indignities perpetrated on them throughout the year. Some, or most, of the judges were lampooned, but it was all good natured, and the judges, in turn, were given an opportunity to make a "rebuttal", most of which were well-rehearsed, ribald and as hilarious as the skits themselves. At its best, especially in the past, Judge's Day promoted a bonhomie amongst the lawyers and judges, and it fostered an environment of cooperation during the rest of the year.

In the old days, my favorite companion on Judge's Day was Judge Stanton Thorsten. When I first met him, he was a DFL (Democratic-Farmer-Labor) state senator, but was shortly thereafter appointed judge by the governor, a member of his own party. Word had it that he'd been at odds with the governor, who saw the appointment as a way to get him out of the state legislature. With his square jaw, silver hair and steel-blue eyes, Judge Thorsten looked like a judge. To me, three words captured Judge Thorsten -- justice, golf and gin.

On the bench, he was fair and principled. Unlike many of his colleagues, he never suffered from arrogance, or what we lawyers call "black robe disease." Although I knew him well, he wasn't above busting my chops when I deserved it. One day, I was before a jury, laying it on a little thick about a miscreant who insulted my police officer. Judge Thorsten interrupted me. "Get off the cross, Jeff."

One Judge's Day strikes my memory. I was paired up with Judge Thorsten for the golf tournament. He was just plain fun on the golf course. Although the events started in the morning, it wasn't too early for a gin and tonic for the judge. "It's five o'clock somewhere!" he kept saying. Even though he hailed the drinks cart every two or three holes, it didn't seem to affect his play. He was a terrific golfer.

One time, we were in a fairway that ran along the railroad tracks, and Judge Thorsten's drive went straight down the middle. Another of our group, just an ordinary hacker, sliced his shot into the rough by the tracks. He emerged without his ball, but clutching a freshly-pulled marijuana plant – a common weed in the Midwest. Although it was at the time highly illegal, we all (including the judge) broke a sprig off the plant and adorned our ears with it.

Later the same day, a cloudburst forced us under shelter for a while, and when we resumed Judge Thorsten's cart got stuck in a mud puddle. Everyone started pushing as the judge hit the gas. We got the cart loose but we all ended up caked with mud, laughing uncontrollably. Fortunately for me, I lived nearby and was able to go home and change in time for the cocktail hour.

When I returned to the banquet room, seventy or eighty people had arrived. Some of them had come from the golf course and others, mostly judges, straight from work in their suits. A blue cloud of cigarette smoke had already formed over the gathering, and there was a long line at the bar. As time went on the crowd grew, and the din from the conversation and laughter increased. It was just like a frat party, except that everyone was "grown up."

The skits were great, as were the rebuttals. Judge Thorsten, despite his copious consumption of gin, stood up and gave a flawless uncensored version of "Little Red Riding Hood," entirely in pig Latin. The room erupted in raucous guffaws.

How did all of these fun and games benefit the lawyers and the clients they served? Let me tell you of a couple of cases I had.

George Bednarek was a golfer of some renown. Not only was he the pro at a major metro club, but he'd won the state PGA tournament. I knew of him from my occasional golf outings at his club, but not on a personal basis, so I was surprised when he called me. Addressing me by my first name, he asked for a meeting.

At my office, I could see that he was nervous, and I soon learned why. It was a Gross Misdemeanor DWI – in other words, a DWI enhanced by the existence of a previous conviction, resulting in exposure to a maximum sentence of one year in jail. "You had some bad luck," I said. I often said this to clients to put them at ease, even though it usually wasn't a matter of luck.

"Yup, that's what it was," George said.

When I read the arrest report, however, it was clear that it wasn't a fluke. He registered a .23 percent on the breathalyzer – almost three times the legal limit, and his prior offense was only four months before. His BAC (or blood alcohol content) in the prior case was also high. As I thought about it, I recalled seeing George many times at the bar after I'd finished playing a round of golf with my friends. Certainly, part of his job was socializing with the members, but it occurred to me as I remembered it that, George didn't just sip beer – he guzzled Manhattans.

"George," I said, "this is serious. Typically, it involves jail time and sometimes an order for chemical dependency treatment. It could impact your job."

"That's ridiculous," George said. "I don't have a drinking problem. How do you think I could win all these tournaments if I did?"

After he left, I gave my friend Gina at the Assignment Office a call to schedule George's first court appearance. Unfortunately for him, his case was blocked to Judge Swokowski, a hard-nosed ex-prosecutor who was known as a tough sentencer.

"What if I filed on Swokowski?" I asked Gina.

"Oh, then you'd get Thorsten," she said.

What were we talking about? When a case is filed, it gets "blocked" to a particular judge, who owns the case from beginning to end. However, a party has a one-time right to change the judge without giving a reason by filing a Notice to Remove. It can be a risky move because there is no choice on the replacement judge, but I already knew that my old friend Judge Thorsten was backing up Swokowski on the criminal calendar that month. This seemingly distasteful process is called "Judge shopping," but I ask you -- if it would help your case, wouldn't you want me to do it for you?

Soon enough, it was time for George's day in court, and he and I were escorted back to chambers by a law clerk. Judge Thorsten liked to conduct business there. He could smoke his Pall Malls, tell a joke and talk about plea bargains without public scrutiny. I introduced George to the judge, but his arrival had been anticipated. "Oh, there's no need to tell me who Mr. Bednarek is, counsel," the judge said. "Your honor," I said, "the prosecuting attorney and I have been discussing a disposition of my client's case."

"Okay," the judge said, "we'll get to that. But first, how about next month's PGA tournament?"

George, who had meekly greeted me that morning at the office, realized that the question was directed at him. "Interlachen's a long course," George said, "so it's all gonna be about the tee shots."

Judge Thorsten was enthralled by George, and a lengthy discussion ensued about the tournament, golf techniques and equipment.

Meanwhile, several lawyers and their clients were patiently waiting out in the courtroom for their cases to be called.

"Well, George," the judge finally said, "I'll cut you a big break, but it's the last time." He scribbled a memo on George's ticket and we exited to the front desk. "Charge amended to centerline violation - $100 fine," it said.

Great for George. Bad if you're on the road with him.

The next month, I got another case involving Judge Thorsten.

This time it was for a good friend of mine. Frank was a local business owner, active in the Chamber of Commerce and well-known to everyone in town. He was an ebullient fellow, sometimes asked to emcee dinners and banquets, but when it came to legal matters, Frank was petrified. One time he'd had a dispute with one of his customers that ended up in Small Claims Court and he asked me to go with him.

"Frank," I said, "this is the people's court – they don't even let lawyers talk there."

"I don't care," Frank said, "I'll pay you just to stand next to me."

It worked for him, and Frank did fine. I wonder if he'd really needed me.

This time Frank was charged with shoplifting – golf balls.

"It was just absent mindedness," he said. "I was in Target shopping for a bunch of stuff, which I paid for, by the way. But I'd stuffed this box of Titleists in my jacket pocket and forgot about it. When they stopped me at the door, I was mortified."

It seemed pretty straightforward, and I opened a case for Frank, but, since he was so well-known in the community, I opened his file under a false name so he'd remain anonymous even in my law firm.

Before Frank left my office, I called Gina at Assignments. "You'll get Swokowski if you plead not guilty," she said.

"Is that our only choice?" I said.

"Well, if you want to come in tomorrow, Thorsten's still on the bench, but then he's on vacation and everything's going to Swokowski."

"Then put us down for tomorrow."

"We're going to court tomorrow?" Frank said as his face flushed. "I can't do it. I've gotta prepare myself mentally."

I explained the reason for my decision, and the next morning Frank and I walked over to the courtroom together. We were the first case called, and we entered the thick smoke of the judge's chambers. Frank was an anti-smoking zealot, but he was in no position to object.

Judge Thorsten was reading the report on Frank's case. "Humph," he said. "Have you read this, Jeff?"

I hadn't, and he handed it to me. As I got to the bottom of the page, I cringed, because that was the part that set out the criminal history of the defendant. It said -- Retail Theft, 2002. Walmart Coon Rapids, MN. Retail Theft, 2004. Target Minneapolis.

I glanced toward Frank but he averted my eye – he was suddenly aware that I knew that his story about absent-mindedly putting the golf balls in his pocket was a lie. Nevertheless, I launched into a lengthy introduction of Frank to the judge, laying on the BS about his good deeds and his exalted standing in the community. He was a valued friend, I said, in whom I had the greatest trust. I hoped it was sinking in.

Finally, Judge Thorsten looked at Frank. "So, these were Titleist Pro VX's?"

"Yes, they were," Frank said tentatively.

"They're top shelf, to be sure, but I like Slazengers."

Another discussion about golf ensued, and, once again, the judge scribbled a memo on the ticket. "Case continued for one year for dismissal if no same or similar offenses," it said.

In recent years, there have been many positive changes in our profession. There's a lot more transparency, so the backroom deals happen less frequently. The ribald, sometimes sexist, even racist, banter among lawyers and judges is long long-gone.

Judge's Day? We still have it, but it's a ghost of the old days. What happened? The gradual infusion of Gen X'ers and women attorneys and judges into the system has transformed the culture of legal practice. These folks won't stand for the sophomoric behavior and drunken hijinks of the old days. They still have the cocktail hour and the dinner, but the line at the bar is for club sodas. Some might sip on a Chardonnay or a craft beer -- but no one gulps down martinis anymore. The sterile smoke-free air prevails, and the few remaining die-hards are banished out to the patio. Instead of skits and rebuttals, there are self-congratulatory speeches and awards for volunteer projects.

It's better this way - isn't it?

ACKNOWLEDGEMENTS

To my wife and partner, Mary, and our children Andy, Molly, Liza and their families. To my law partners, Mike, Bob and Marna, and our wonderful staff, and the old guard, Fred, Tom and the dear, departed Dave, and all we have shared together. To my intrepid critique group – Mary, Lorre, and Tara. To my fellow lawyers, and to our clients, to whom we all indebted.

BIOGRAPHY OF JEFF HICKEN

Jeff Hicken is a native of Macomb, Illinois. He is a graduate of Cornell College and the University of Illinois College of Law. He was the President of the Minnesota Chapter of the American Academy of Matrimonial Law. He is retired and lives in Lutsen, Minnesota and Naples, Florida.

www.ingramcontent.com/pod-product-compliance
Lightning Source LLC
Chambersburg PA
CBHW071408200726
48294CB00002B/322